I0876613

MAKING FREEDOM WORK

MAKING FREEDOM WORK

FREE WOMEN of COLOR in ANTEBELLUM NEW ORLEANS

Janet Morrison

LOUISIANA STATE UNIVERSITY PRESS BATON ROUGE

Published with the assistance of the V. Ray Cardozier Fund

Published by Louisiana State University Press
lsupress.org

Copyright © 2026 by Janet Morrison
All rights reserved. Except in the case of brief quotations used in articles or reviews, no part of this publication may be reproduced or transmitted in any format or by any means without written permission of Louisiana State University Press.

Manufactured in the United States of America
First printing

Designer: Kaelin Chappell Broaddus
Typefaces: Fournier MT Std, text; Contralto, Dulcinea, display
Printer and binder: Sheridan Books, Inc.

The manufacturer's authorized representative in the EU for product safety is Mare Nostrum Group B.V., Doelen 72, 4831 GR Breda, The Netherlands. Email: gpsr@mare-nostrum.co.uk.

Jacket illustration: Detail of *Creole in a Red Headdress,* ca. 1840, by Jacques Guillaume Lucien Amans. The Historic New Orleans Collection, acquisition made possible by the Diana Helis Henry Art Fund of The Helis Foundation in Memory of Charles A. Snyder, Acc. No. 2010.0306.

Portions of chapter 4 first appeared in "'Big Businesswoman': Eulalie Mandeville and the World of Female Free Black Entrepreneurs in Antebellum New Orleans," *Louisiana History: The Journal of the Louisiana Historical Association* 62, no. 1 (Winter 2021): 61–86.

Library of Congress Cataloging-in-Publication Data

Names: Morrison, Janet M. author.
Title: Making freedom work : free women of color in antebellum New Orleans / Janet Morrison.
Description: Baton Rouge : Louisiana State University Press, [2026] | Includes bibliographical references and index.
Identifiers: LCCN 2026028836 (print) | LCCN 2026028837 (ebook) | ISBN 978-0-8071-8755-5 (cloth) | ISBN 978-0-8071-8807-1 (epub) | ISBN 978-0-8071-8808-8 (pdf)
Subjects: LCSH: African American women—Louisiana—New Orleans | African American women—Louisiana—New Orleans—Social conditions—19th century | Free Black people—Louisiana—New Orleans | African American businesspeople—Louisiana—New Orleans | LCGFT: Biographies
Classification: LCC F379.N59 B536 2026 (print) | LCC F379.N59 (ebook) | DDC 305.896/07633509034—dc23/eng/20260623
LC record available at https://lccn.loc.gov/2026028836
LC ebook record available at https://lccn.loc.gov/2026028837

Contents

Acknowledgments

I wish to express my gratitude to Dr. Rebecca Fraser and Dr. Thomas Ruys Smith, for their always constructive advice and guidance. Without such excellent help, I would never have been able to produce this work. I would also like to thank Dr. Hilary Emmett from the University of East Anglia and Professor Emily Clark from Tulane University, for their support and encouragement.

I would like to give special thanks to various people in New Orleans for their amazing southern hospitality over the years. In particular, I am especially indebted to Dr. Connie Zeanah Atkinson and Dr. Mary Niall Mitchell for letting me use the resources of the Midlo Centre for New Orleans Studies, at the University of New Orleans, which helped make this work possible. I would also like to thank Sister Doris Goudeau, Sister M. Carolyn Leslie, and Sister Sylvia Thibodeaux from the Sisters of the Holy Family Order, for allowing me to visit their archive, and for providing such excellent advice and guidance. A vote of thanks is also due to Carolyn Morrow Long, who very generously shared her research on Marie Dolores Laveaux.

Finally, I am grateful for the support of my family, especially that of my late mother, Renée Morrison, who spent endless hours looking at drafts, proofreading, and offering her advice on points of grammar.

MAKING FREEDOM WORK

FIG. 1. The house once owned by Eugène Macarty, from which Eulalie Mandeville may have dispensed her wares. This photograph of 925–929 Barracks Street was taken in the 1940s/1950s. The Collins C. Diboll Vieux Carré Survey, a project of the Historic New Orleans Collection, courtesy of Special Collections Division, Tulane University Libraries, negative no. 2-081-031.

INTRODUCTION

Eulalie Mandeville, a free Black businesswoman, stood at the door of her house in New Orleans in 1832, watching as her marchandes (street vendors) walked down the road, baskets on their heads full of assorted dry goods from her armoire, including shawls, lingerie, cloth, and various other feminine articles to sell in the street, or door-to-door. With the help of her friend, the Widow Chavenet, she had sorted out the choicest goods, recently brought back from Paris by her son Pierre Villarceaux. She had already alerted her clients from the upper classes of New Orleans society that she had new stock straight from France and planned to personally call on them that morning to show them this latest finery, while also dispensing guidance on how to style these newest fashions. This picture of a typical day in the working life of one of New Orleans's most successful free Black entrepreneurs demonstrates how a free woman of color used all the resources at her disposal to create and run a successful business in New Orleans. That Mandeville was a productive and wealthy businesswoman throughout her adult life is a testament to her achievements in an antebellum slave society.

It demonstrates her tenacity, and that of other free Black women, not only to make a place for themselves in New Orleans society but also to succeed beyond all expectations in their chosen endeavors.

Antebellum New Orleans presented a challenging social environment for women of African descent, as chattel slavery had produced a culture in which Black bodies were objectified, used, and abused. From the traditions of the slave markets, Black women were viewed as being either drudges, breeders, or the objects of sexual fantasies. Although free, the five women studied in this work suffered from the same stereotypical representations. Therefore, they were always aware of the fragility of their social status and, indeed, their freedom, as well as living under the constant fear of sexual pressure or violence. Certainly, all women in patriarchal New Orleans led restrictive lives. Married white women usually relinquished control of their finances and real estate to their husbands and were subject to their domination. During this period, there were socially prescribed rules for the behavior of women, chaining them to domesticity and denying them any visibility in public spaces. Therefore, these women were repressed by virtue of their sex as well as their race.[1] Despite all these disadvantages, the five women featured in this work provide examples of how women of African descent could overcome challenges and oppose the system that sought their repression.

Saba Mahmood's research eloquently articulates what constitutes increased empowerment in a society that is repressive toward women. It is not only that women seek to assert their autonomy when allowed to do so but also that they do it in a way that challenges social norms. She describes it as being behavior that manifests "in ways that confound our expectations."[2] This definition would easily apply to the five women discussed here. Their resistance was "the refusal of women to submit to systems that physically, emotionally and spiritually deny their humanity."[3] As described in later chapters, they used a mixture of "refusal and defense" in their practices, thereby negating the idea that "licentiousness and subservience was the sum total of their gender and race."[4]

I first came across Eulalie Mandeville while researching court cases from the Louisiana Supreme Court on a very rainy afternoon in the University of East Anglia's library. My interest in New Orleans had been sparked during my time in America as an international undergraduate student from the College of St. Mark & St. John in Plymouth, United Kingdom. In 1987, at the end of a semester at Frostburg State University in Maryland, I decided to make the long journey to New Orleans by Greyhound bus, and, like many nineteenth-century travelers, I was immediately fascinated by the city. As a historian, I was eager to avail myself of the various walking tours and trips around historic buildings, cemeteries, and streets, and it was during these excursions that I first heard the names of some notable free women of color of the nineteenth century. It seemed remarkable to me that not only had they managed to make an impact on the city's consciousness during their lifetimes, but their stories had survived through the centuries. Many years later, I remembered them and the city that had so fascinated me, and I resolved to examine the lives of some of these women.

I decided to research women whose stories not only were compelling and interesting but also served to demonstrate the main premises of this book. My research suggested that these women had contributed to the economic and cultural life of New Orleans more than had been previously thought. They were aware of how the changing times in New Orleans could benefit them. They were also outward-looking, taking advantage of the opportunities provided by increased mobility in the Atlantic World. The arrival of refugees from Saint-Domingue (now Haiti) and Cuba, as well the migration of free people of color to the Caribbean, Mexico, and France, gave their society a more fluid definition of identity and nationhood, allowing for increased networks and trade. They were also very cognizant of their rights under Louisiana law and attended law courts both as witnesses and litigants. They claimed this privilege by virtue of their status as free citizens. The women's familiarity with the law and its power was possibly handed down by their forebears, who may have learned about contracts and transactions as they participated in the market economy, or through negotiating emancipations. Free women of African descent therefore turned to the courts far more often than white women and, often with the support of white lawyers and witnesses, used its power effectively to challenge unjust treatment.[5]

They also actively cultivated networks with other Black and white men as a means of obtaining advice and guidance. But it was their networks with both Black and white women that often proved more advantageous in terms of support and a sense of community in an often-hostile world. Enterprising free women of color such as Marie Couvent and Henriette Delille realized the value of altruism in combating the difficulties both they and the Black community faced. They came to understand that by working together they could create a support system that would benefit them and their community.

All five women featured in this study provided stories of achievement and defiance in a largely hostile society. Thus, it is important that their voices are heard. Although their histories may defy easy conventionalization, they contain much of interest for those fascinated by gendered resistance. For example, Eulalie Mandeville single-handedly ran her business empire, which crossed international borders, utilizing all the advantages available to her, while planning to send her children to another country, away from the strictures and prejudices she had faced. Her unwillingness to surrender what she believed to be rightfully her and her children's inheritance, and her knowledge of Louisiana law and her prudent business practices were evidenced when she was taken to court by her deceased partner's white relatives in an effort to relieve her of her hard-earned fortune. Henriette Delille founded a charitable group of religious women who eventually became the Sisters of the Holy Family, the first order of free Black nuns in New Orleans, and successfully led them until her death. Cécille Bonille and Marie Dolores Laveaux also used the courts as a means of resistance. Laveaux took her abusive husband to court in order to separate herself from him in an era that did not look kindly on divorce, and Bonille, like Mandeville, attempted to defend her property against the claims of her partner's white relatives. Finally, Marie Couvent, who was probably the most disadvantaged of all the women, overcame her enslaved background and refugee status to forge a life for herself in New Orleans. She also actively supported the future of the free African American community that had embraced her, by her philanthropic bequests, which included the establishment of a school.

These five women lived during a period of transformation, their lives reflecting New Orleans's changing racial and sexual mores. Although the influences of the previous French and Spanish administrations remained, the advent of an American hierarchy had a profound effect in shaping their experiences. They lived in an era that was affected by the increased mobility of people and goods throughout the Atlantic World. There were influences from other parts of the globe that contributed to these women's lives. Their stories were marked by the transformation of New Orleans into a thriving port city, attracting people from many other countries and providing increased opportunities for trade. This book demonstrates how these changes had consequences for the women, both good and bad, and how they took advantage of any opportunities offered. For example, the legal right of free people of color to own property, along with access to equal protection of that property under the law, was accorded to them in New Orleans in the colonial period and maintained after the Louisiana Purchase. This right marked an important boundary between the free and enslaved people of New Orleans. Some free women of color, therefore, took advantage of these rights to become landowners, sometimes owning multiple properties in the city. It also allowed them to become the holders of enslaved people when they had the means to do so.

Slaveholding by free people of color has always presented a complex and challenging phenomenon for historians. Free Black people owning enslaved people does not fit the common narrative of slavery in the United States as white subjugation of all Black people. All five women were enslavers, and their desire to hold enslaved people may be attributed to various factors. Perhaps the most important of these was their overarching desire to protect their tenuous freedom, as the more enslaved people they held, the greater their household's perceived wealth and standing, and the further away it was itself from the specter of slavery. This research looks at the complicated relationships between enslaver and enslaved, also from the point of view of engendering networks. Relationships between enslaver and enslaved were complicated. Some of the women, like Eulalie Mandeville, seemingly had no personal connection with her enslaved women, viewing them as economic necessities. Others, like Marie Couvent, formed associations with certain of her enslaved people while viewing others from a purely business perspective. thereby demonstrating how, within a household, enslaved people could be viewed and treated differently according to skills, status, and parentage.

When describing and writing about the women, I have used several terms that have sometimes caused disagreement among scholars. For example, the use of the word "plaçage" as a blanket term for those unions between a free woman of color and a European-descended man has caused some discord. It suggests to some the idea of the concubine and thus a lack of morality, further enhancing negative portrayals of these biracial women. However, current scholarship suggests that these so-called plaçage relationships were far from being the fleeting, immoral unions previously associated with the term. They were often long-term domestic partnerships, closer to marriage than to concubinage. In this book, for clarity and brevity, I use the term "plaçage" to describe these relationships while also making clear the variety of unions that word encompasses.

This study uses the various terms utilized in legal documents to describe the racial origin and status of these women, such as "quadroon," while noting that these labels can also be problematic and uncertain. In the slave markets, sellers and buyers attempted to categorize enslaved people, mostly by perceived skin color, resulting in a multitude of adjectives such as "grif" or "mulatto" or "quadroon." In contrast, U.S. census takers were limited to a description of the person as either being Black or mulatto. The courts, too, had their own way of determining race, which involved behavior and culture as much as racial characteristics.[6] The research therefore reflects this constant shifting of perceptions concerning the characterization of race according to time, place, and subjective classification.

This conflation of mixed racial ancestry and free Black people has been further complicated by the use of terms such as "Creoles of Color" or "Afro Creoles." Throughout the book when describing African American women I have used the words "free women of color," "free Black women," and "Afro Creoles" interchangeably. I have used "free women of color" because, in legal documents of the period, they were generally designated as such, usually abbreviated to "fwc" to distinguish them from white or enslaved women. I have also often referred to them as "Creoles of African descent" because this is how some women identified themselves in public records, particularly dictated wills. However, the definition of the word "Creole" has caused dissent in Louisiana from its settlement to the present day. "Creole" was originally used to describe the descendants of French, Spanish, or Portuguese settlers living in Latin America, the West Indies, and parts of the southern United States. This term distinguished them from the Indigenous population and other immigrants. It may have derived from the Portuguese "Crioulo" and the Wolof "Kréyol," originally describing a person of European descent who was born in the "New World," and denoting a separation from their country of heritage.[7] In the nineteenth century, the word took on a variety of forms in an "attempt to name an ethic of in-between-ness—to connect multiple allegiances and to channel them into a singular identity with deep roots in a particular context." In the antebellum period, it was commonly thought among Europeans that people of African descent could only be called "creole" in the form of a lowercase adjective, which was also applied to subordinate beings or inanimate objects such as creole horses or creole cuisine. However, as Rodolphe Desdunes's later writings make clear, New Orleanians of African descent had long considered themselves as Creoles of color, reclaiming the term from white supremacists and also using it to distinguish themselves from other members of the Black community.[8] Although some free women of color clearly described themselves as such in public records, arguably all the women in this work may have identified as Creoles.

All the primary material for my research comes almost exclusively from these public archival documents including censuses, city directories, notarial records, as well as wills and successions. Unfortunately, there is little in the way of more personal documents written by hand, such as letters or diaries. This research acknowledges the ways in which use of public documents can be problematic, as all these archives were created and sustained by white authorities. I have therefore taken into consideration the restraints imposed by these archives and will reflect on issues of veracity in my examination of these public documents. I have been careful to include wide-ranging research from secondary sources when considering the primary documents. However, despite the problems, these fragmentary glimpses can offer crucial insight into the lives of these women, who lived under the domination of a patriarchal, slave society. Wills, even when recorded by a notary, were generally dictated. Therefore, by using a mixture of the testator's own words and legalese, they become the closest thing to personal papers. Testaments also disclose networks of family members, friends, business associates, and other social relationships forged during the testator's lifetime. Among the most important contacts named in any will are the beneficiaries who receive bequeathed property, and executors who manage the testator's estate. Comparison of these documents reveals noticeable variations in the personal information included. Therefore, when looking at these archives, I consider the silences and what they might mean, as well as what these documents reveal. Although my research uses some of the same records previously utilized by historians, it provides different analyses by looking at these women's lives through the lens of identity and community, as well as a broader examination of the innovative ways they circumvented their challenges and navigated their way through New Orleans's complex society.

I am aware that as all my five case studies left a public record of themselves, either personally through their own testimony or via public documents, they were all from the privileged stratum of New Orleans's free society. Thus, they assumed a place as women of note in some way. It might be argued that by using these privileged women as my case studies, I am perpetuating the marginalization of free Black women who lived and died without leaving any traces of their existence. However, the life histories that this project focuses on spotlight the challenges that all these women faced while living in a racially ordered patriarchal society. They all experienced the common factors of urban life, the powerlessness caused by their race and gender, as well as the struggle for increased economic stability for themselves and their families. This research also highlights the intersections of race, class, and gender for *all* free women of color in New Orleans during the antebellum era, while reflecting on the ways in which some women were able to find a mode of life that allowed them a degree of autonomy.

We cannot know for certain the hopes and dreams of these women. What is certain, however, is that as mothers and educators they had a huge influence, not only on their own children but in shaping the future of the Black community. Therefore, as this research demonstrates, these women's lives certainly did matter.

Chapter 1 examines the background to the history of New Orleans's free people of color. Through an exploration of New Orleans's historical evolution as a city, with its administration passing through the hands of the French, the Spanish, and finally the Americans, this chapter lays out the foundations of the antebellum society in which these women lived. The mixing of various cultures shaped the lives of its inhabitants and meant that New Orleans evolved differently from other cities in the southern states. The chapter looks at how the colonial policies of enslavement and manumission led to the formation of a distinctive free Black community. It also foregrounds the topics to be discussed throughout the book by providing the background to various important aspects of these women's lives, including religion, relationships, and employment. It was also in these areas where the women often became successful in organizing their own affairs.

Chapter 2 provides the first case study, that of a free Black nun, Henriette Delille. This chapter describes her success in founding the Sisters of the Holy Family, the first order of Black nuns in New Orleans. She also created various educational and charitable institutions for the free Black community despite much opposition from various sources. This chapter primarily focuses on Delille's trajectory as the creator of a religious community that was eventually recognized by the Catholic Church. It illustrates the many ways in which Delille was successful in negotiating with the Church hierarchy. She thereby gained leave from them to organize her order. Delille was a talented leader, partly through the force of her personality, her position as a member of the free Black community's elite, and the way in which she actively promoted the order within New Orleans society. This chapter also looks at the other important themes running throughout this book that had a profound effect on these women's lives, including class, racial origin, and self-identity. I begin the investigation of the diverse networks formed by free women of color by looking at Delille's own feminine network of support, which included white women, and which eventually evolved into an order of nuns.

Although Henriette Delille and her nuns eschewed a life of domesticity, most free women of color did not. Chapter 3 therefore looks at the case studies of two women: Cécille Bonille, who was the "plaçée"— the name given to a woman who entered into a plaçage arrangement—of a white man, and Marie Dolores Laveaux, who was married to a free man of color. Unlike the other women of this study, they were mostly reliant on their connections with men, both Black and white. The chapter examines the two women's domestic unions, exploring the complexities posed by both relationships. All women were subjugated in antebellum New Orleans and, whether free women of color or white women, were often married young to men considered suitable by their families. This chapter also demonstrates, by its exploration of Marie Dolores Laveaux's situation with her husband, that exploitative relationships were not confined to those with white partners. I will also investigate how the two women utilized their connections and the power of the judicial system to mount a resistance against the white authorities.

Chapter 4 looks at Eulalie Mandeville, who used the power of the court to protect what was rightfully hers, and she had much to protect, because she was one of the richest free women of color in New Orleans, and the protagonist of the vignette at the beginning of this introduction. It also examines the life of another successful entrepreneur, Marie Couvent. This chapter looks at how changing times in antebellum New Orleans contributed to these women's economic success. The chapter also studies the various business and personal strategies employed by both these women and speculates on how these contributed to their achievements. It investigates the personal characteristics and backgrounds of the two entrepreneurs and how these affected their lives. The chapter also examines the differences between Mandeville's and Couvent's own enslaved experiences and their subsequent relationships with their enslaved people, and the different outcomes these engendered.

Chapter 5 delves into the lives of two of the families, the Macartys and the Augustes, whose children were descended from Eulalie Mandeville and Marie Dolores Laveaux, looking at their lives after the Civil War. This chapter examines the ways in which two of the families went forward during a period of great societal upheaval in New Orleans. It studies the difficult challenges faced by Mandeville's and Laveaux's children, and the decisions they faced after the Civil War. It also analyzes how the main themes of this book, which include class, identity, kinship, and community, were continued in the next generation, notwithstanding the very different circumstances after the war. Although necessity dictated that I research men more than women in this chapter because more of them survived into older adulthood, the influences that affected the lives of their feminine forebears did indeed filter down into the succeeding generations, While one of these families ultimately disappeared into European society, some family members made their presence felt in the political arena, often to their own personal detriment.

1

FAITH, FAMILY, AND ENTERPRISE

Free Women of Color in New Orleans

The emergence of free women of color as a visible force in New Orleans is closely allied to the history of the Crescent City, and how Black people took advantage of the policies, customs, and changes in the colonial period in order to secure their manumission and gain economic security. Colonial tradition also impacted the freed people of New Orleans, as custom often favored the manumission of mixed-race women over the purely African-descended woman or man. This created an imbalance in the ratio of free women to men and resulted in a disproportionate number of mixed-race freed people.[1] It also had the effect of encouraging free women of color to form relationships with European-descended men and created a hierarchy in freed people's society that was based around lineage. Evidence indicates that the ways in which Black women escaped slavery, as well as subsequently finding jobs and acquiring property, were tied to the nature of their enslavement. After manumission, free people of color often sought to distance themselves from their enslaved pasts, striving to gain increased control over their lives and protect their always-fragile freedom. Women had to overcome prejudices relating to both race and gender, which shaped not only the terms of their labor but also their modes of dress, worship, and recreation. That they were often successful in their endeavors is a testament to their ingenuity in overcoming these challenges and their determination to secure a better life for themselves and their children.

Societal, cultural, and economic influences impacted the lives of these women during the colonial and antebellum periods. The common factors of the urban condition, race, gender, and legal status worked together in critical ways, shaping their lives through their challenges and opportunities. I analyze this in further detail in later chapters by looking at examples of how particular free women of color used legal, economic, and social systems to try to acquire a stronger position within the existing race and gender power structures. However, to understand more fully what forces influenced and fashioned their lives, it is necessary to go back to the beginning of their story, which was rooted in slavery.

ENSLAVED AND FREE BLACK PEOPLE IN FRENCH NEW ORLEANS

New Orleans was founded in 1718 by Jean-Baptiste Le Moyne de Bienville after previous settlements in Mobile and Biloxi were deemed unsuitable as commercial and governmental centers for the growing colony of French Louisiana. This coincided with a pivotal time in French thought and philosophy as the Bourbon government was flirting with new forms of social control and enlightened absolutism. Thus, France's colonies were often viewed as testing grounds for policies of social, economic, and political reform. Eventually New Orleans came to be viewed by the Crown as unsuitable because of the need for massive investment, but French thought and philosophy continued to be a significant factor in the life of all its inhabitants from the French colonial period onward.[2]

In 1719, the first large group of one thousand enslaved Africans came to Louisiana. Two-thirds of them were from the Senegambian region of West Africa, and the rest from the Bight of Benin and Angola.[3] The economy quickly became dependent on them, as they brought desperately needed knowledge of the cultivation of rice, corn, tobacco, and cotton, as well as an assortment of skills related to the cultivation of these crops, and to the production of tools and crafts.[4] Through its creation of many plantation economies in the Caribbean, France had decades of experience with the slave trade. However, the way in which enslaved people were controlled and incorporated into the social system was still very much in flux. Colonial administrators used different methods for the maintenance of the status quo in the position and condition of the enslaved within their particular society.[5]

The demographics of New Orleans were changed by the advent of enslaved people being forcibly brought to its shores. By 1721, there were more African-descended men than European-descended men in the city, with the ensuing disquiet among the authorities that this may have engendered. Indeed, until the massive European immigration of the 1830s and 1840s, nonwhite residents formed the majority of the population of New Orleans.[6] And Black men outnumbered Black women 2:1.[7]

In 1724, Bienville, who was by this time governor of New Orleans, instituted the Louisiana Code Noir, which regulated the treatment of enslaved people. A comparison to the Code Noir of Saint-Domingue (now Haiti), written forty years earlier, illustrates how French ministers increased their knowledge of their colonies and adjusted their governance accordingly. Although parts of New Orleans's Code Noir were influenced by those produced for the French Caribbean and Indian Ocean colonies, it also contained provisions to meet local needs.[8]

As with many other codes, the legal status of the enslaved was defined as the "moveable property" of the holder. Children born to the enslaved followed the legal status of the mother. Enslaved people were forbidden to bear arms and were prohibited from assembling in large crowds. They were not permitted to sell anything without the express permission of their enslaver. If they struck their enslavers or any member of their family, they were to be put to death. If they ran away and were caught, they could have their ears cut off and would be branded with a fleur-de-lis. For a second offense they would be hamstrung and branded on the other shoulder. A third offense merited a death sentence.[9]

Marriage with white people was prohibited, as was the concubinage of whites and freed people with the enslaved.[10] This was different from Saint-Domingue. Although concubinage was also forbidden there, marriage between African-descended people and European-descended people who had been baptized in the Roman Catholic religion was allowed. That Louisiana's Code Noir differed from that of Saint-Domingue in this respect shows the preoccupation in Louisiana with the perceived danger of interracial unions. The Code Noir of 1724 may therefore have been an attempt to design an "improved" slave society, strengthening the difference between Black and white by delegitimizing any form of biracial relationships. In practice, however, the Louisiana Code did very little to dissuade unsanctioned interracial relationships because of the imbalance in the number of white women and men in the colony. Thus, although the Code Noir tried to change established customs through law, in reality circumstances in the colony allowed for their continuation. Importantly, the Code allowed for manumitted enslaved people to have (in theory) the same rights, privileges, and immunities enjoyed by those who were born free: "It is our pleasure that their merit in having acquired their freedom shall produce in their favor, not only with regard to their persons, but also to their property, the same effects that our other subjects derive from the happy circumstance of their having been born free."[11]

In Saint-Domingue, manumission of the enslaved was initially encouraged by the Crown, in order to create a class of artisans and skilled workers, but by the 1720s, there was concern about the size of the rapidly growing free population on the island.[12] Eager not to make the same mistake in Louisiana, the 1724 Code made it more difficult for enslavers to free their enslaved workers by stipulating that they (the enslavers) had to be over twenty-five years old. They also had to gain the prior approval of the Superior Council.[13] Therefore, the numbers of freed people remained relatively low during this period. Of those who were freed, more than half of them were women, either alone or with their children. The census figures suggest that certain enslaved people were more likely to be freed than others. According to these documents, being a woman or a "mûlatre" significantly increased the chances of manumission.[14] One must exercise caution as to the accuracy of these numbers, as freed people were often recorded by the census takers as mixed-race because of their free status. However, it gives some indication of the characteristics of those who were freed during the French period.[15]

Between 1733 and 1742, no new shipments of enslaved people came to New Orleans, and only one shipment in 1743. The moratorium on these shipments continued until after 1776, when the Spanish reinstated the trade.[16] It was this stasis that may have eventually created a distinctive Afro Creole society that synthesized aspects of European, African, and Native American culture. None of these cultures were entirely subsumed into a European melting pot.[17] The second generation of these enslaved people began to take on the mores, culture, and religion of their French enslavers, while simultaneously maintaining their links with African traditions. This produced a syncretic blend of cultures that could be seen in many of the port cities with ties to Africa and the Caribbean throughout the Atlantic World.

FINDING FREEDOM IN SPANISH NEW ORLEANS

In 1763, the king of France ceded Louisiana to Spain. Although Spain, like France, looked upon Louisiana as an economic burden, it hoped to use it as a buffer zone against the increasingly aggressive North American colonies. However, the transition from France to Spain did not go as smoothly as the Spanish may have hoped. The French inhabitants of the colony seemed to have "a distinct aversion . . . for anything Spanish."[18] On 5 March 1766, Governor Antonio de Ulloa arrived in New Orleans with a small number of soldiers to begin the business of transferring French Louisiana to Spanish Louisiana. After his arrival, Ulloa, seemingly somewhat unwisely, made several unpopular threats to restrict popular pastimes such as gambling, drinking in taverns, and

Sunday markets. As a result, Ulloa was chased out of New Orleans, and his governorship was deemed invalid by local community leaders. According to them, his claim was illegitimate because he had not registered the transfer orders with New Orleans's Superior Council, and he had also failed to recognize local dignitaries and local economic interests. Ulloa exited New Orleans in a hurry, quickly sailing to Havana.[19]

Spain answered the reluctance on the part of New Orleans to accept Spanish administration by sending Governor Alejandro O'Reilly in 1769. He restored order by executing, imprisoning, or exiling some of the dissenters. Thus, French laws gave way to Spanish ones, and the Cabildo, or town council, was created.[20] Although O'Reilly issued no specific decree on manumission and indeed stated that the 1724 Code Noir remained the law of the land as long as it did not contravene Spanish law, the institution of slavery underwent dramatic changes during the Spanish period. First, Spanish law decreed that in line with the rest of Spain's American colonies, Indigenous people could not be enslaved. However, the Spanish Crown did modify its laws to fit in with existing practice, allowing Louisiana's enslavers to retain any enslaved Indigenous people they already held while prohibiting their sale or transfer to other enslavers. Nonetheless, this still resulted in a small number of people petitioning for their freedom by claiming that their enslavement was unlawful.[21]

Second, Spanish law was similar to Roman law in that enslavement was not seen as a permanent state and therefore provided greater opportunities for freedom than had existed under the French regime. There were several ways in which enslaved people could obtain their *carta de libertad*, or freedom. And enslavers were no longer required to obtain the governing authorities' approval for their manumissions. Also included in the Spanish law was a practice known as *coartación*, which had been developed in Cuba, giving the enslaved the right to obtain their freedom for a price agreed upon by their enslavers. If they could not pay the money immediately, they could pay in instalments over time. If the enslaver refused to grant them freedom or set the price unreasonably high, the enslaved person could petition the Governor's

Tribunal to reassess their monetary value. The same procedure could be applied to a third-party purchase by another interested person.

Bowing to local pressure, the administration reopened the slave trade in 1777, permitting Louisianians to purchase enslaved people from the French Caribbean. Five years later the trade again expanded as they were also allowed to import enslaved people from neutral or friendly countries. In 1786, however, the trade was curtailed by a ban on imports from the French or British Caribbean, followed by a total ban between 1795 and 1800. This relaxation of restrictions on the import of enslaved people for many years meant that enslavers may have felt more inclined to reward an individual with their freedom. Indeed, it took only four years of Spanish rule for the number of manumissions to surpass all of those freed during forty years of French rule. In total, almost two thousand of the enslaved were freed during the four decades of the Spanish administration.[22] The increased prosperity of Louisiana during this period meant that New Orleans became a flourishing commercial center, with many opportunities for the enslaved to hire themselves out or to sell their crafts and produce. They could then use the money to buy their freedom. Toward the end of the eighteenth century, self-purchase or third-party purchase became more common than voluntary manumission.[23]

As in the French administration, certain enslaved people had a better chance of gaining their freedom than others, and women were still more likely to be freed than men. An enslaved man was worth more than a woman, so it was rarer for enslavers to free them voluntarily, and if they wanted to buy their own freedom, it cost them more. It was also customary for French and Spanish men to free enslaved women, especially if they had a previous sexual connection with them, and they also often freed any children resulting from these unions.[24] Although African-descended people and "mulattoes" were freed in roughly equal numbers, darker-skinned individuals were one and a half times more likely to buy their own freedom.[25] Therefore, the lighter a woman's skin, the more likely she was to be freed when younger and through the actions of others, whereas those with darker complexions were more likely to be freed at an older age, and through their own endeavors.[26]

This inequality of numbers may also have been occasioned by the preponderance of mixed-race enslaved women who worked in the house. As a result of the more intimate nature of their employment, they often had a closer personal relationship with their enslavers, whether it was a sexual one or not.[27] The sacramental registers and notarial records from the Spanish period also revealed that there were more liaisons between white men and free women of color than during the French period. The increasing number of interracial relationships and their resulting offspring meant that by the end of the eighteenth century, New Orleans had a thriving population of free people.[28]

Under Spanish law, when an enslaver wanted to free an enslaved person, they merely had to appear with two witnesses in front of a priest or notary. The Code also made it legal to free the enslaved not only during the lifetime of the enslaver but also in a last will and testament. By the end of the eighteenth century, giving the enslaved their freedom through wills happened very frequently in New Orleans. Although there was no legal need to do so, enslavers often listed their reasons for granting their freedom. There were numerous cases of petitions where the enslaved person was being freed in "especial thankfulness for devoted caretaking during an illness," probably the enslaver's final illness.[29] However, these reasons given by enslavers may not have necessarily signified deep relationships between the enslaver and the enslaved person. Phrases like "for good services" and even "for the love I have" appeared frequently in these documents, even for those who were buying their own freedom, and therefore may have been stock phrases provided by the notary, with the enslaver choosing the phrase that seemed most appropriate.[30]

Although some African-descended people learned to utilize European slave codes to their own advantage, by pursuing formal manumission and improving their economic status, this is not to say that things were better for the enslaved as a whole. Indeed, in general the Spanish period was a difficult one for people of color, especially the enslaved. Far more people of African descent were enslaved in Louisiana after the Spanish reopened the slave trade. The expansion of the plantation economy and the ready availability of enslaved people meant that enslavers could afford to treat them more callously as they were easily replaceable. There were also instances of elderly enslaved people being manumitted and turned out of their household because they were no longer useful.[31]

Even if they gained their freedom, people of African descent did not by any means enjoy the same privileges as white people: "Although the government and the ruling whites protected the distinction between a free man of color and a slave, they took equal if not greater care to preserve the distinction between themselves and a free man of color."[32] Despite the fact that free people were allowed to own real estate and keep all of their earnings, they had no political rights and thus were always hostages to fortune in regard to any laws passed directly affecting their status.[33]

Even if the authorities conspired to minimize any opportunities for equality for free people of color, however, the development of New Orleans into one of the most important port cities in the United States gave free Black people the chance to strengthen their position economically. The growth of large plantations and the Mississippi River trade, which linked the South and the Midwest, brought cotton, sugar, pork, and hundreds of other commodities to the city.[34] This commercial metropolis, the third-largest in the antebellum South, needed an urban middle class to work at the skilled trades, to run the hundreds of retail shops, and to perform commercial transactions.[35] Free people of color filled this basic need. They came to be increasingly regarded as an essential part of the social order, and some of them began to enjoy a superior social and economic status. These wealthy free Black people began to emulate the lifestyle and manners of wealthy whites. The most prosperous had grand houses and carriages and sent their children to Europe to acquire education and social polish.[36]

By purchasing properties all over the city, free people began to shape their environment and society. Like white southerners, they often became enslavers. Some of them inherited enslaved people from their white or free Black family members, whereas others purchased them. Not all these enslavers were from the higher echelons of society. In South Carolina, Black people who worked as draymen, stable keepers, and even washerwomen had enough money to buy enslaved people.[37] Although people from different areas of employment held enslaved people, the statistics appear to show a distinct difference in the racial characteristics of those who were likely to hold enslaved people. According to the Charleston census of 1850, 83 percent of free Black holders of enslaved people were "mulattoes," while nearly 90 percent of the enslaved people were Black.[38]

Evidence from wills and other legal documents has shown that although free people of color sometimes viewed the holding of enslaved people as a moneymaking enterprise, there was a difference in the way that they treated enslaved relatives or friends, allowing them special privileges and often granting them manumission and a legacy in their wills. However, enslaved people who were purchased as investments and were not a relative or friend of their enslaver were more likely to be viewed as commodities to be exploited for profit.[39]

The establishment had no problem with Black holders of enslaved people. These enslavers enhanced New Orleans's economy and were therefore tolerated by the white hierarchy. It was also deemed that by their holding of enslaved people they would be more interested in preserving the status quo than in encouraging rebellion. Despite these beliefs, the holding of enslaved people by free people may have in fact weakened the structure of southern enslavement, which was based on the premise that this was a natural state for all Black people. Thus, the holding of enslaved people by free Black people contradicted these mores and may have enhanced enslaved people's desire for freedom, precipitating discontent among the community.[40] But for the economically ambitious free person of color, holding enslaved people was an important marker of their prestige in society: "Nothing was more likely to inspire whites' admiration than owning slaves. No investment promised such handsome returns—both economically and socially. No act put as much difference between a free Afro-American and slave."[41]

This is a further indication that by the end of the Spanish period, those who could afford to do so were increasingly taking on the mores of elite white people, not only by amassing wealth to purchase real estate but also by the holding of enslaved people. However, these outward trappings of success among free people of color may have also been a "mode of survival" in a gendered and racial hierarchy, as by the end of the eighteenth century, their privileges started to come under attack.[42] Free people of color had often been pushed to the fringes of society by a white elite determined not to grant them equality and full citizenship. Eager to preserve the white supremacist order of New Orleans, the authorities began to put in place more and more economic and societal structures intended to maintain and defend their control. This denigration of the position of free people of color became even more pronounced after the Louisiana Purchase in 1803.

AMERICAN RULE

The Louisiana Purchase

Louisiana was retroceded from Spain back to France on 3 November 1803. Napoleon Bonaparte received back the colony in exchange for a small kingdom in northern Italy. Thomas Jefferson then bought land from Bonaparte in 1803, which included the Louisiana Territory. The Louisiana Purchase gave the United States control of both the Mississippi River and New Orleans. It also ensured that France and other European countries would not try to retake the land.[43] It was during this period that New Orleans rose to its greatest heights of prosperity. By 1840, according to the *New Orleans City Guide*, it was second only to New York as a port.[44]

The incoming American administration was nervous about taking over a territory whose population had seen frequent changes of government, with loyalties torn between France, Spain, and the United States. The large numbers of Black people in New Orleans, both enslaved and free, were also perceived as a threat by authorities unused to dealing with cities where white people were in the minority. The first American census of New Orleans in 1805 recorded 8,212 inhabitants, of whom only 3,551 were classified as white. Whites were therefore outnumbered by 3,105 enslaved and 1,556 free Black people.[45] The situation was further exacerbated by the arrival of thousands of immigrants from Saint-Domingue (present-day Haiti). This mass exodus resulted from the revolution fought by the enslaved between 1791 and 1804 in Saint-Domingue. In 1803, as a result of the decisive defeat of Napoleon's troops, sent to restore order on the island, most remaining white people and many free people of color and their enslaved workers fled to Cuba. The Spanish authorities expelled them in 1809, forcing them to seek refuge elsewhere. Because of its cultural similarities to Saint-Domingue, New Orleans was a popular destination.[46] These refugees more than doubled the French-speaking population and added to the growing numbers of free Black and enslaved people. The authorities feared that many of them may have absorbed revolutionary ideals from Saint-Domingue, which they might use to incite the local population.[47] Uncomfortable with the racial mix of New Orleans, the administration therefore set about undermining the legal and social position of free people of color.[48]

Initially, the free Black community had hoped that the Louisiana Purchase would offer them a chance to obtain increased equality, but the actions of those in charge firmly disabused any aspirations in that direction. For example, moves were made to restrict manumission and thus curtail any further expansion of the free population. The Civil Code still maintained the right of the enslaved to sue directly for their freedom. After 1807, however, and with the imminent closure of the transatlantic slave trade, tighter restrictions were placed on enslavers wishing to manumit enslaved people, as there would no longer be fresh shipments of people from West Africa and the Caribbean. Enslavers had to prove that the enslaved person they wished to manumit was over thirty years old and had exhibited "honest conduct" for four years. The only exception allowed was if an enslaved person had saved the life of an enslaver or any of his family.[49]

Despite this, Louisiana's population of free people of color increased by 53 percent between 1820 and 1830, from approximately 10,000 to 16,000. Thus, by the 1830s, further legislation was put in place to expel those who had recently entered the state and also to enforce the removal of the newly freed from the state. All those who had come to Louisiana after 1825 were therefore required to leave within sixty days or face a prison sentence or hard labor for one year. The law also declared that those who wished to free an enslaved person had to post a one-thousand-dollar bond to guarantee their departure within one month of their manumission. The statute ordered that all free people of color who were legally allowed to remain in the state had to register with their parish judge. The 1830 law also discouraged white people from engendering any discontent or rebellion among the enslaved by threatening a sentence of six months to three years for those who disobeyed. Free Black people who flouted this law faced a sentence of hard labor of from three to five years, and afterward permanent expulsion.

This demonstrated an increasing fear on the part of the administration of an insurrection that might be aided and abetted by the free population. However, the protests and demands for exceptions were such that the following year a further law was instituted, which softened the previous one a little. Parish police juries could now permit the newly freed to remain in the state, and anyone freed for "meritorious conduct" had no restrictions: A study of parish police records from 1831 to 1846 showed that no freed people were required to leave the state as a condition of their manumission. Resident free people of color who left the state were also allowed to return "if they owned property there, exercised a useful trade and conducted themselves with the utmost respect and good order."[50] This shows how the customs of manumission and the reliance of the economy on the labor of free people of color in New Orleans were so ingrained that these increasing strictures were often vetoed by public opinion.

By the 1850s, slavery had moved to center stage of the political arena as the antislavery movement grew more vocal in the northern states. Although the free population of New Orleans had severely declined from 19,226 in 1840 to 9,905 by 1850, the laws around manumission became even stricter. A new law of 1853 compelled enslavers to send all of the newly freed to Liberia within one year of manumission. Those who returned to Louisiana or who did not go to Liberia lost their right to freedom. This resulted in enslavers besieging the authorities for exceptions, and the number of freed people with permission to remain in the state increased. Finally, in 1857, Louisiana fell in line with many other southern states by banning manumission altogether.[51] The legislature of the 1830s also meant that free people of color had to be clearly identified as such in all legal documents, thus attempting to curb the efforts of those of ambiguous racial origin to pass for white.[52]

The number of interracial unions also declined, partly due to increasing adverse public opinion. Equally important, however, was the trend for free women of color to reject interracial liaisons with white men in preference for marriage with free Black men.[53] These increasingly repressive laws also resulted in the further solidification of kinship and community ties among the free Black community in defense of their freedom.

A FEMALE SACRED SPACE
The Catholic Church in New Orleans

Catholicism played an important part in the lives of the enslaved and free people of color from the beginning of the colonial period. In the 1700s, missionaries were sent from France to Louisiana to convert the Indigenous population and the enslaved, and to administer to the spiritual needs of the colonists. Their mandate was to ensure that all those who inhabited the colony were Catholics, whether colonist, Native, or enslaved.[54] Latin Catholicism in Louisiana differed from the racial rigidity of the Anglo-American Protestants and Catholics who colonized North America's seaboard. Although the Roman Catholic Church accommodated racism and the institution of slavery, the 1724 French Code Noir required enslavers to teach the precepts of Catholicism to their enslaved people and have them baptized into the faith. The Code also prohibited them from encouraging the practice of any other religion.[55] This contrasted sharply with the Protestant English colonies to the north, whose clergy were uncertain as to whether churches or enslavers held any religious obligations to the enslaved. That some Louisiana enslavers took their religious instruction responsibilities seriously is evidenced by the frequency with which white people stood as sponsors for Black baptisms.[56] French and Spanish clergy extended the sacraments to free Black Catholics as relative equals, nurturing a loyalty among the city's free Black residents that outlived both French and Spanish colonialism.[57] Clergy also acknowledged the children of interracial relationships and sought to bring them into the faith: "They administered to their spiritual needs, conducting baptisms, confirmations, marriages, and burials, thus forming a life-time habit among the free community, in support of the Church."[58] The Roman Catholic Church of New Orleans gave free people of color privileges that were denied to the enslaved. For example, the Church allowed them to create their own religious charitable societies, thus tacitly acknowledging their superior status.

By the antebellum period, free Black people had become an important factor in the strength of New Orleans Catholicism, forming most of the congregation and providing financial support in several of the city's parishes. By 1810, Black Catholics constituted nearly two-thirds of the membership of St. Louis Cathedral, their numbers having been swelled by the influx of refugees from Saint-Domingue and Cuba. Antebellum travelers to the city often commented on the integrated nature of the cathedral's congregation. It was a popular destination for visitors as its impressive structure was clearly visible to travelers arriving by boat on the Mississippi River.[59] When architect Benjamin Latrobe went to services at the cathedral, he was struck by the diversity of the congregation, which "consisted of at least 4/5th women, of which number one half at least were colored."[60] This was unusual, as in the rest of the South, in accordance with public convention, Black worshippers occupied a prescribed space and were not allowed to mix indiscriminately with whites during services.[61]

Latrobe's comment shows that the Catholic Church played a key role in the lives of New Orleans's free Black women. The French Order of Ursuline nuns arrived in New Orleans in 1727. They were teaching nuns who were committed to the propagation of the Catholic religion through the education of women. They believed that the loyalty of women to Catholicism was significant in ensuring the continuity of faith through their influence with the next generation. The nuns were therefore committed to extending the opportunity of education to all young women, regardless of race. This feminine responsibility of passing down religious practice was also a tradition of the Wolof tribe of West Africa, from where many of Louisiana's enslaved people originated. Thus, by tradition, Black women were accustomed to being religious educators.

By 1728, the Ursuline nuns had established a girls' school in New Orleans whose pupils included free and enslaved Black and Native American girls. They also encouraged free and enslaved women to attend services at the convent, thereby forming a strong feminine connection between themselves and the women of New Orleans. For African-descended women, the "female sacred space" and activity at the convent was similar to the central sustaining features of their traditional religion; thus they were drawn to Catholicism in ever-increasing numbers during the colonial period.[62] Evidence from the number of baptisms suggests that the first generation of enslaved Black women were more enthusiastic converts to the Catholic religion than men. In succeeding generations, baptisms of boys and men increased, perhaps showing the influence of women in promoting Roman Catholicism within their society.

There is also evidence, however, that some enslaved and free Black women, such as Voodoo priestess Marie Laveau, practiced their African religious beliefs alongside those of Roman Catholicism. They created a synthesized version of religious practice that combined both beliefs. Although Alice Dunbar-Nelson's short story is a fictional account of the life of a young woman, it illustrates this point. "The Goodness of Saint Rocque" is about an Afro Creole woman who, in an effort to win over her lover, wears a Voodoo charm around her waist, as well as making a novena in Saint Rocque's Chapel. She also visits a Voodoo priestess in her house, where the room combines Catholic sacred objects such as an altar, a portrait of Saint Joseph, and a crucifix, along with tarot cards and other articles associated with Voodoo. This story, written by a Black woman who was brought up in New Orleans during the nineteenth century, demonstrates how African and European religious

FIG. 2. In the nineteenth century, the imposing presence of St. Louis Cathedral signaled the importance of the Catholicism in New Orleans. Historic New Orleans Collection, Gift of Boyd Cruise and Harold Schilke, 1959.178.2.

traditions were often blended together. Marie Laveau also observed Roman Catholic ceremony, as she married in St. Louis Cathedral and had all her children baptized there.[63] This open duality of religious practice does not appear to have been evident in the first recognized religious sisterhood for free Black women in New Orleans. Although the Sisters of the Holy Family resembled the Voodoo priestesses in their taking on religious leadership roles, they did so very much under the auspices of the Catholic Church. They became recognized as religious women, providing an alternative version of Afro Creole womanhood to the one portrayed by New Orleans travelers and the popular literature of the time. Their history is discussed in more detail in the next chapter.

For much of the eighteenth century, the term "quadroon" was merely descriptive and was generally applied by New Orleans society to light-skinned biracial people. During French rule, sacramental registers often assigned a phenotype to mixed-race individuals. However, with the advent of the Spanish administration, this became more detailed, giving far more attention to color terms and racial distinctions. Spanish civil and clerical officials applied the term "moreno" to someone whose ancestry was less than half white, and "pardo" for those who had more than half European ancestry. A "negro" was a person of pure African ancestry, and a "mulatto" was a person who was of half-European and half-African descent. "Grifo" referred to someone born from a "pardo" and a "moreno." A "cautarón" (quadroon) was the child of a European and a "pardo."[64]

Additionally, during the Spanish period, the lifestyle and appearance of the so-called lighter-skinned "quadroon" women came under scrutiny by New Orleans authorities. In his Bando de Bueno Gobierno (Proclamation of Good Government) of 1786, Governor Esteban Miró criticized the "quadroon" and "mûlatresse" women who "subsist from the product of their licentious life." He admonished them to "drop all communication with intercourse and vice and go back to work," with the understanding that he would be "suspicious of their indecent conduct, as evidenced by the luxury in their dressing." The Sumptuary laws therefore made it illegal for any free woman of color to "walk abroad in silks, jewels or plumes" and required that they had to cover their hair with a "kerchief."[65] These laws contributed to the creation of the image of the free Black woman as idle and vain, and living off of her immoral earnings. This engendered a reputation that would haunt them for centuries. The kerchief that they were obliged by law to wear, also known as a "tignon," was traditionally worn by enslaved women, thus reemphasizing their ties to an enslaved past.[66]

Society considered that these women were also born from immorality, as they were often the illegitimate offspring of a European man and a Black enslaved or free woman. Powerless enslaved women were clearly the victims of exploitation by their owners. However, the relationships between white men and free women of color were often more nuanced. Domestic unions between a free woman of color and a European eventually became known in New Orleans as plaçage. Interracial marriage was illegal, so the man pledged to monetarily provide for his domestic partner and any children who might result from the relationship. Written travelers' accounts suggested that these informal contracts were often brokered by the mother or other guardian on behalf of their daughter, although no written records exist to support this claim.[67]

These relationships may have given free women of color increased control over their lives, as they often had the chance to obtain financial independence and economic security for themselves and their children. However, it could also be argued that a slave society with unequal power relations and violence may have precluded any form of autonomy for these free women of color, making their sexual relationships merely an extension of the exploitation of enslaved women.[68] The way in which free women of color might benefit from a relationship with a white man would therefore depend on the benevolence of the man. Despite this, free Black women often demonstrated their hegemony by their willingness to go to court and fight for the "protection of their bodily freedom and the defense of their property."[69] The courts increasingly saw petitions from free women of color during the nineteenth century, often taking white men and women to court over property and monetary disputes. They separated themselves from the enslaved through their right to act not only as witnesses but also as litigants in private lawsuits. They had also often perceived the power of the legal process through their emancipation or the emancipation of others. Therefore, these African American women had no compunction about turning to the courts if they felt they had been subjected to unjust treatment, negating their portrayal as hapless victims of their race.[70]

The myths surrounding plaçage relationships, which were engendered by New Orleans travelers' tales, were often far from the truth. These stories of the beautiful young "quadroon" kept in luxury by her white protector, while emphasizing the inequality between the partners, were probably also no more than "the projection of male fantasy" rather than reality. Accounts written by male travelers to New Orleans deliberately titillated the reading public in order to sell more books.[71] The comments of some of these nineteenth-century authors often reduced these relationships to near-prostitution, their accounts serving to perpetuate the fantasy that the bodies of light-skinned biracial women existed to satisfy white men's desires. For instance, British aristocrat Edward Sullivan wrote, "A handsome quadroon could not be bought for less than $1,000 or $1,500, tho' the market is well supplied at that price."[72] This emphasis on a woman's monetary worth also relates back to their former enslaved status, in terms of putting a value on their bodies. Indeed, this reported cost of possession was comparable to the going rate for a young "fancy" enslaved woman. The slave dealer James Blakeney made the correlation between phenotype and fantasy clear when he described Mary Ellen Brooks, whom he was hoping to sell at a good price: "A very pretty girl, a bright mulatto with long curly hair and fine features. . . . Ellen Brooks was a fancy girl."[73] Solomon Northup, a free man of color who had been kidnapped and sold at New Orleans's slave market, described slave dealer Theophilus Freeman's account of the price that he was looking forward to receiving for the enslaved woman Emily in New Orleans: "There were heaps and piles of money to be made for an extra fancy piece as Emily would be. She was a beauty—a picture—a doll—one of your regular bloods—none of your thick-lipped bullet-headed cotton pickers."[74]

However, in contrast to the accounts of the complete objectification of these women, engendered by the slave trade, the records also show the devoted relationships that occurred between women of color and white men. Especially during the French and Spanish periods, free women of color often had lifetime partnerships with their European-descended companions. These "bachelor patriarchs" were unmarried men who stayed with their domestic partners and provided for them and their mixed-race children throughout their lives.[75] These relationships assumed an air of respectability to society at large and were sometimes seemingly accepted as legitimate by white relatives. White family members were often listed as godparents and guardians of the resulting children.[76] Eliza Potter, a free Black hairdresser from the North, observed how these domestic partnerships were formed: "When they are marriageable, they are courted by gentlemen the same as any other ladies, till it comes to the ceremony, then there is a large party assembled and the young girl is given away by her father or mother, or both, this is called placayed, it is the same in their eyes as marriage but no license is required."[77]

Other visitors also noticed how, within certain free Black families, the daughters were groomed to become the long-term placeés of white men. Frederick Law Olmsted, a landscape architect who visited New Orleans in the 1850s, wrote of a "quadroon family" to whom he was introduced, and who subsequently treated him as a prospective suitor for one of the daughters of the house. He waxed lyrical about the daughters' accomplishments, which prepared them to become fitting consorts for white men: "There were three pretty and accomplished young women in the family. They were intelligent, well informed, their musical taste was extremely well cultivated, they were interested in the literature of the day and their conversation was characterized by good sense and refined discrimination."[78] Eliza Potter also noted that these young women were educated in genteel manners and accomplishments in order to enhance their prospects of making a good match: "These young girls are brought up as particularly as any children in the world, they have the best education that can be given them, they are taught music, dance and every branch necessary to the accomplishment of a lady. They are never permitted to walk out to church or school or any other place, without a servant after them."[79]

British traveler Harriet Martineau, however, who was in New Orleans during the 1830s, eschewed the notion of these relationships as providing near-marriage status for the women, foreshadowing the antislavery writers in trying to engender public sympathy for the plight of the "quadroon," writing: "The connexion now and then lasts for life, usually for several years. In the latter case, when the time comes for the gentlemen to take a white wife, the dreadful news reaches his quadroon partner, either by a letter or by the newspaper which announces his marriage. Many commit suicide, more die broken hearted."[80] By describing the fate of the "quadroon" thus, she firmly defined the plaçeé as a dependent, defenseless woman, subject to the caprices of her white lover. Certainly, a lack of any legal contract meant that there was often no security for these women, some of whom were forced to take other partners after having been deserted. However, many other relationships lasted until the death of either partner. Therefore, instead of making a blanket judgment about these interracial relationships, they should perhaps be examined through the particular circumstances of each case. Chapters 3 and 4 look at two of these relationships in detail, demonstrating the difference between the accounts of plaçage and the realities.

Although some relationships may have been verbally contracted by families in the drawing rooms of New Orleans, it is also the case that some young women attended New Orleans's famed quadroon balls in order to meet wealthy white men. As with plaçage, opinions of the function and purpose of these balls have also been disputed from the nineteenth century onward. Harriet Martineau viewed them as a sort of debutante's ball for these young women to meet eligible white bachelors, whereas others saw the quadroon balls as nothing more than interracial orgies.[81] If that was so, it is hard to imagine the carefully brought-up young women described by Olmsted or Potter attending that type of entertainment. Scholars' views have also been mixed when it comes to quadroon balls, raising the question as to whether they constituted another form of the slave market, as "the gaze of the consumer projected a fantasy of white masculinity onto the bodies of light skinned women."[82]

The history of these balls began in the Spanish period. Before the formal institution of a ballroom in New Orleans, free Black and enslaved people and whites danced together in public entertainment places, such as taverns. Wealthier whites and free people of color also danced at private gatherings in their homes. Esteban Lelande, a prominent member of New Orleans's Militia for free men of color, regularly hosted these types of dances at his home.[83] In 1799, Bernard Coquet successfully petitioned Spanish officials to open a ballroom that catered specifically for free people of color. From the first, however, white men of different classes also attended these balls, causing anxiety among the authorities about the open racial mixing. Thus, there were calls to shut it down. Although the Cabildo initially rejected these requests, once the year's lease was over, they refused to renew it. Some wealthy free men of color from the Militia petitioned for its reopening, and it was finally granted, with the proviso that the enslaved were prohibited from attending. It was also tacitly accepted by the free Black community that white men would continue to attend.[84]

However, it was after the Louisiana Purchase that the first entertainments that came to be dubbed "quadroon balls" were held.[85] Probably noting the popularity of balls for white men wishing to meet free Black women, in 1804, August Tessier, an actor from Saint-Domingue, placed a notice in the press for a ball specifically for these two groups, which free men of color would not be permitted to attend.[86] The establishment of the quadroon ball during the antebellum era was probably no accident. In this period of increasing hostility by the authorities toward the free Black population, the inauguration of these quadroon balls emphasized the mastery of white men over Black women and the emasculation of the Black man.[87] But initially the balls were not the coarse entertainment described by some of the travelers. Tessier provided refinements that had not been seen at other balls, such as consommés, wines, soups, chocolates, and a carriage service. It also cost double the price of any other ballroom, discouraging the attendance of those less well-off. There was a dress code, and a door attendant kept out any perceived undesirables.[88] Those travelers who attended the balls described in detail the poise and elegance of the feminine attendees. Edward Sullivan wrote: "I made a point of going to some of the quadroon balls. I had heard a great deal about the splendid figures and graceful dancing of the New Orleans quadroons, and I was not disappointed. Their movements are the most easy and graceful that I have ever seen."[89] It was partly through these balls that the term "quadroon" began to be more frequently used to describe all free Afro Creole women. In the strictest sense of New Orleans's racial characterizations, many of the women who attended these balls would not have been classified as quadroons, but their presence defined them as such. Also, if free people of color tended to be categorized as lighter-skinned by virtue of their freedom, then it is no wonder that these women became known by the term used for the lightest-skinned.

As often happens in New Orleans, however, the balls quickly became a magnet for tourists and inauspicious places for a genteel free woman of color to seek a long-term partner. The quadroon balls therefore began to accentuate the darker reputation of the quadroon as a woman of easy virtue. It appears that they eventually became a front for forms of prostitution and vice. Indeed, as the mayor observed in 1835, business was so good that white female prostitutes sought to gain entry. He referred to them "as the sink of the most dissolute class of women."[90] Thus, the reputation of the "quadroon" woman became more sullied. This further downgrading of "quadroons" was also clear in the judge's pronouncement in the Sally Miller court case of 1845. He supported her contention that she was a white woman by contrasting her behavior and appearance with that of a "Quarteronne." In his final summation, he stated: "I contend that the moral traits of the Quarteronne, the moral features of an African are far more difficult to be erased and are far more easily traced than are the distinctions and differences of physical conformation. The Quarteronne is idle, reckless and extravagant, this woman is industrious, clever and prudent—the Quarteronne is fond of dress, of finery and display—this woman is neat in her person, simple in her array, and with no ornament upon her, not even a ring on her finger."[91]

However, also by the 1840s, the term "quadroon" had begun to serve another purpose for those dedicated to the cause of banning slavery. The antislavery novels published during this era assigned another role for her as a "tragic mulatta." Although termed as such, the heroines of these novels were more likely to be portrayed as quadroons or octoroons.[92] A pale skin and more European features allowed the white readers of these romances to identify themselves more easily with the protagonist. Antislavery writers such as William Wells Brown and Lydia Maria Child used these fictional accounts of biracial women to highlight the evils of enslavement by portraying their sufferings at the hands of lustful white men. These books were written in a formula that was instantly recognizable. The most typical situation was that of a beautiful mixed-race girl who had been brought up thinking that she was free, only to find, when her father died, that she was enslaved and must be sold at auction to settle his debts. The story illustrated the horrors of enslavement, as well as the difficult position of mixed-race people.[93] The conventions of these stories were so well known that readers would guess immediately that "because of the single drop of midnight in her veins, the mixed-race figure must go down to a tragic end."[94] Descriptions of these women were also remarkably similar. They were all described as beautiful, according to European ideals of beauty of the time, while gesturing toward the exotic. Thus, they often had flashing dark eyes and raven-colored, flowing hair. They were usually also graceful, well-educated, and innocent.[95]

It could be imagined that these portrayals of biracial women might have helped to rescue the "quadroon" from her notorious unchaste reputation. However, although most of these women were portrayed as pure and virtuous rather than licentious: "The sexually charged nature of these descriptions, which anti-slavery writers used to their advantage, derives from the invitation to readers to transgress boundaries of both race and class at once, since all the women are portrayed as exotic, sexually available and aristocratic all at once."[96] Thus, underneath the seeming innocence of the "quadroon" heroine, there was an underlying sexuality as a result of her tainted African blood, making her more vulnerable to white men's predation. Therefore, "abolitionists fed on the fictional fare of the tragic mulatto, expected New Orleans to be filled with 'white slaves' catering to the sexual appetites of immoral men."[97] Thus, in trying to arouse sympathy for their own purposes, these writers were also helping to perpetuate the myths surrounding mixed-race women, which endured from the nineteenth century onward.

LAWFUL MARRIAGE

In the nineteenth century, the "quadroon" was alternately depicted in the public imagination as a predatory exploiter of the white man's sexual weakness, or the unwitting victim of his lust. The reality, however, was that by the antebellum period, many free women of color were eschewing relationships with white men in favor of lawful marriage with free men of color. During the colonial period, the imbalance in the number of free women and men often meant that women were forced to conduct interracial relationships rather than marrying. However, after the Louisiana Purchase, the imbalance in the number of men and women became less marked, and evidence shows that free people of color began to marry in increasing numbers. Between 1810 and 1819, marriages in New Orleans between free people nearly doubled, and doubled again between 1820 and 1829.

There are several reasons why marriage may have become more popular during this period. Changes in Louisiana law that disadvantaged children born of nonmarital unions may have had an influence. The 1808 Civil Code stated: "Those who have lived together in open concubinage are respectively incapable of making to each other . . . any donation of moveables (including slaves) and if they make a donation of moveables, it cannot exceed one tenth part of the whole value of their estate."[98] However, the Code did allow that "children born out of marriage, except those who are born from incestuous or adulterous connection, may be legitimized by the subsequent marriage of their father or mother."[99] Marriage, therefore, became a more important institution when the inheritance rights of offspring were affected by legislation. The Militia for free men of color also campaigned for free people to marry, possibly in order to impress the incoming American administration of their community's respectability and thus their fitness to be citizens of the state. The increase in marriages may have also resulted from the influx of refugees from Saint-Domingue: "As free black Saint-Dominguan female refugees had a reputation for licentiousness, and men for possible subversive revolutionary ideals, New Orleans' native free people of color may have wished to distance themselves from the newcomers, both culturally and politically."[100] Embracing marriage was one of the ways in which they could differentiate themselves, especially from the free Black women refugees, who apparently appeared to favor interracial relationships over marriage.

Also, because of the increasing prejudice and harassment of their people during this period, many of New Orleans's prominent free Black families began intermarrying in order to protect their wealth and property and to keep it within their own community. They realized that the ability to form intimate ties with each other through marriage was essential to their individual and group survival.[101] Finally, the leadership of women within the Catholic Church may have also had an influence in encouraging marriage. The Sisters of the Holy Family order of nuns, headed by Henriette Delille, abhorred plaçage on moral grounds and through their school and other institutions may have influenced young women to marry within their own community.[102]

THE HISTORY OF AFRICAN AMERICAN ENTREPRENEURSHIP IN NEW ORLEANS

In addition to societal influences in New Orleans, economic factors played a key role in the lives of its various communities. Enslaved and free people were motivated to participate in the emerging capitalist order of New Orleans, transforming some of them into resourceful and innovative entrepreneurs. The rise of Black businesspeople in New Orleans began from the first importation of African enslaved people. From its foundation in 1699 up to the beginning of the eighteenth century, France's Louisiana colony regularly suffered from the threat of starvation. It was especially severe in the 1720s, after the collapse and reorganization of the Company of the Indies cut off not only food imports but virtually all capital supplies. Many enslavers could not afford to feed their enslaved people; thus, they began encouraging them to become more self-sufficient.[103] They assigned plots of land to their enslaved people so that they could grow their own food.

The enslavers also began to see the advantages of abiding by Article 5 of the Code Noir, which exempted the enslaved from working on Sundays and religious holidays, in order that they had more time to cultivate their crops, thus producing above and beyond what was needed for themselves and enabling them to set up a system of trade. Initially this trade followed West African tradition, which was characterized by the bartering of goods rather than cash payment. Later, however, the domestic enslaved economy moved away from its African roots and became cash-based.[104] Taking advantage of their free time, the enslaved also began hiring themselves out for wages or selling some of their surplus products.[105] Once the principle of wages for the enslaved had been established, some of the most highly skilled and talented Black artisans could seek to hire themselves out, negotiating contracts, making their own living arrangements, and paying their enslavers a specified amount.[106] Jean François Dumont, a Parisian who arrived in New Orleans in 1719, observed: "Most of the slaves clear grounds and cultivate them on their own account, raising cotton, & tobacco, which they sell. Some [masters] give their negroes Saturdays and Sundays to themselves and during that time the master does not give them food; they then work for other Frenchmen who have no slaves and pay them. Those who live in the capital generally turn their two hours at noon to account by making faggots to sell in the city; others sell ashes or fruits that are in season."[107]

With the difficulties around food production in the colony, the enslaved began to play an important role as part of the economic system. These trade activities were still strictly illegal under the Code Noir, which expressly forbade enslaved people to work on Sundays and Holy Days. They were also forbidden from owning any property, conducting any kind of trade on their own account, or selling goods, without written permission. By this time, however, these enslaved entrepreneurs were providing a much-needed service to a city that was frequently short of food products; thus, the authorities chose to turn a blind eye and assume that they were selling goods on behalf of, and with the permission of, their enslavers. This laissez-faire approach continued during the Spanish era, although the Real Cedula of the Spanish government in 1789 caused a problem for Louisiana's authorities. This new code prohibited the enslaved from working on Sundays, growing their own food, and purchasing their own clothes. The governor, Esteban Miró, urged on by the Cabildo and plantation owners, immediately advised his superiors of the impracticality of enforcing this regulation in Louisiana; so, for the remaining sixteen months of his term, he delayed implementation. His successor, the Baron de Carondelet, fearful that the revolutionary ideals of the uprising in Saint-Domingue would spread to Louisiana, was also reluctant to enforce a law that would be seen as increasing the repression of the enslaved. He therefore simply ignored the Real Cedula.[108]

Many of the enslaved took advantage of the Spanish system to buy their own freedom, thus helping to establish a distinct free Black business class. A city with a growing population like New Orleans needed to utilize the skills of its free Black population. Therefore, "free people of color took advantage of the continued demand for service businesses and the relatively small numbers of skilled native New Orleanians and immigrants."[109] By 1802, the visibility of the free Black working population had become such that a visitor to the city commented on the "great number of free mulattoes who had special skills as artisans."[110] He also noted that some of them had begun to accumulate property, and a few had established small businesses.[111] These Black artisans also held enslaved people and trained them, thus creating a sought-after commodity. It was not unusual for these skilled workers to sell enslaved people at a profit, thereby making it worthwhile to invest their earnings. By the 1830s, their numbers had increased substantially: "An 1836 tax list for the City included the names of eight hundred and fifty-five free persons of color who had paid taxes on property worth $2,462,470. Among them were several highly successful brokers, grocers, tailors, storekeepers, real estate speculators and landlords."[112] During the mid- to late antebellum period, those business owners who had wealth and property were better able to insulate themselves from the tumultuous political events taking place around them. Although the rapid expansion of the entrepreneurial class began to slow by the 1820s and 1830s, there was a continued growth in the 1840s and 1850s.[113] So, despite increasing harassment and the emigration of some free people to Europe or the Caribbean, large-scale business activity continued until the Civil War.

From the French era onward, many enslaved women used their knowledge, expertise, and skills, first to improve their quality of life, and then to earn money to buy their freedom.[114] Enslaved women were always aware that buyers valued certain skills, qualities. and abilities more highly, and they cultivated them in the hope of becoming more valuable, thereby gaining better prospects in the slave market. They were also conscious of their own monetary worth; thus, they chose the most opportune ways of making money in order to expedite their manumission.[115] In the eighteenth and nineteenth centuries, free and enslaved women marchandes (street vendors) began to proliferate in the streets of New Orleans. This new abundance of women marketers may have resulted from the influence of West African and Caribbean culture, where this was a role traditionally assigned to women.[116] Indeed, some enslaved women may have already possessed commercial knowledge and skill that they could use to their advantage in New Orleans. Apart from becoming market vendors, enslaved and free women also used skills learned in bondage, such as sewing or laundry, to earn money.[117]

As with manumission, racial characteristics may have been a crucial factor in the types of employment performed by these women. Both the Register of Free Persons of Color 1840–1857 and the 1860 census reveal that there were marked differences in occupations for certain groups according to their racial characterization. By 1860, parish officials had designated free people into four categories for the census: Black, mulatto, mixed-race, and quadroon. Differences in women's employment opportunities appeared to correlate to their racial designation. Women described as "mulatto" generally held the most prestigious and desirable jobs, such as seamstress, schoolmistress, vegetable dealer, and midwife, while those described as being "Black" were overrepresented in service positions such as cook, domestic servant, and washerwoman. The Register reveals that those mixed-race women held three times as many skilled and professional jobs as those who were considered to be of purely African descent.[118] Even given the difficulties with the census enumerators' subjective racial categorizations, the census reveals that although free women of color were dominant in roles demanding feminine skills learned in slavery, perceived racial characteristics were also a principal factor in determining occupation and earning power. This may have been, in part, because of the conceptions around those mixed-race individuals. Societal thought deemed them more intelligent and presentable because of their European blood. Even if they were enslaved, they were more often employed in people's houses, whereas those of pure African descent often held more menial jobs or worked as field hands. Mixed-race women therefore learned more transferable skills such as sewing and, in general, were taught the manners and refinement of high society by their enslavers, so that they could serve in the house.[119]

There were other lucrative occupations that became the province of free women of color due to their perceived wisdom or talent, engendered by their African roots. Nursing was one such occupation that came to be dominated by free Black women. In enslaved society, women sometimes practiced as herb doctors, and the community often preferred and trusted their medicine over ministrations by their enslavers.[120] White people in New Orleans also acknowledged these women's nursing skills, as demonstrated by novelist George Washington Cable in his book *The Grandissimes:* "The blue turbaned black nurse was tucking the covering around his feet. . . . Dr. Keene told him, 'Do as your nurse tells you and next week you may raise your head and shoulders a little; but if you don't mind her you'll have backset and the devil himself wouldn't engage to cure you.'"[121] Hairdressing was another occupation associated with free women of color. Oral tradition suggests that New Orleans's most famous free Black woman, Voodoo priestess Marie Laveau, may have practiced this occupation, gaining much of her information and power over the wealthy white population through dressing women's hair and listening to their gossip. Unfortunately, historians have never been able to find any historical documents to prove this assertion.[122] However, as Eliza Potter's experiences show in her memoir, *A Hairdresser's Experience in High Life*, free Black women could make a good living from hairdressing.

Once a woman had established a business and begun to amass wealth, she often consolidated her position further by buying real estate and by the purchase of the enslaved. It was customary practice in antebellum New Orleans, and it may have been simple expediency that necessitated utilization of the services of others. As they were frequently single heads of households, free women of color had to prioritize the economic needs of their family over those of the enslaved. Thus, they may not have wanted to consider that they were doing to other people what had been done to them or their forebears. Also, the fragile nature of their free status was such that many of them who could afford it participated in these white southern practices as a form of protection.[123] The purchasing of enslaved people was seen as an economic necessity upon which their livelihood and thus their freedom depended.

By the antebellum period, free Black women had become an increasingly important part of the labor market. By pursuing certain occupations, they also began to make themselves indispensable to New Orleans society. In doing so, they achieved an opportunity for economic security that had been denied to their enslaved forebears. They deliberately amassed wealth, real estate, and enslaved people to shield themselves and their families from discrimination and racism. Thus, they moved further away from their enslaved heritage, clearly separating themselves from the enslaved people of the city. Although this could be seen as a capitulation to the dominant culture, it has also been viewed as a type of resistance, as according to white ideology, their African heritage should have precluded these women from any of these privileges. Thus, they conducted their businesses and bought property as a challenge to white supremacist and patriarchal beliefs.[124] They also defied ideals of femininity that dictated that a woman's place was in the domestic sphere. The women's challenges to the prevailing beliefs and mores of the white population of New Orleans will become a thread of continuity throughout the succeeding chapters.

2

“WELL-EDUCATED AND REFINED WOMEN”

Henriette Delille and the Sisters of the Holy Family

Henriette Delille is one of New Orleans’s most well-known free women of color from the antebellum period. A twenty-first-century visitor to the city would be unlikely not to hear or see her name or to see her image as they explored the environs of the city (see fig. 3). If they took a tour of St. Louis Cemetery No. 1, the tour guide might direct them to view her tomb, which is incorporated into the general tomb of the Sisters of the Holy Family order of nuns, and which features the names of all the cofounders. There are also portraits of her in St. Augustine Church and the Ursuline Convent. In the Roman Catholic world, her fame has spread far beyond New Orleans, and she is being considered for sainthood.

Delille’s remarkable achievements, however, have taken a long time to be recognized. Indeed, for much of the twentieth century, her own order did not include any mention of her in their publicity material, even for their school. It was not until the 1970s, when interest in gender and race history proliferated, that her unique story came to the fore again.

This interest and research into Delille's life culminated in Sister Rose de Lima Hazeur, superior general of the Sisters of the Holy Family, petitioning Archbishop Philip Hannan to begin the process of canonization for Henriette. In 2010, Delille was declared venerable, the second step in the canonization, and the process is continuing. If it succeeds, she will be the first African American woman to achieve sainthood.[1]

As part of this process, Henriette Delille's life history has been examined by several ecclesiastical biographers and historians. Accounts of her life have therefore dwelt on her piety and charity. While acknowledging that these characteristics were an important part of her determination to found an order of nuns, this chapter also provides an exploration of her remarkable skills as a leader and astute businesswoman. It was a combination of these distinctive attributes and talents that allowed her story to be rediscovered in the late twentieth century. Her life history continues to interest both the religious and scholarly communities, as well as tourists to New Orleans.

Delille was unique in the way she achieved her goals and ensured the success of her organization at a time when African American women had few choices and little autonomy in their lives. Her creation of the first order of Black nuns in New Orleans came at a time when laws were passed that began to restrict the freedom and privileges of free Black society, meaning that she had to overcome further obstacles in order to attain her ambition. By her formation of what was initially a charitable society run by free women of color, Delille acknowledged the potential of supportive women's networks to achieve more than one person could accomplish alone. Although the women who belonged to her charity initially were concerned with assisting each other in times of need, by the time they had become an order of nuns, their sphere of influence had spread to include charitable work and foundations within the city's Black population. Although criticized in some quarters, even including the free Black community, for not following a woman's traditional function in life, Delille provided an educational establishment for Black girls and created the charitable institutions desperately needed for the poor Black people of New Orleans.

Unfortunately, Delille died young so perhaps did not achieve as much as she might have, but it is clear that her leadership was the glue that held the order together. Thus, her early death and the chaos of the Civil War meant that in the mid-nineteenth century the order struggled to recruit and keep its sisters. The Catholic Church also withdrew much of its support and lost interest in the order. Nevertheless, the community was never entirely extinguished, and it continued its efforts to help a war-weary population. Eventually, other strong women arose to take Delille's place and to revive the fortunes of the sisterhood. This is a testament to the way in which Delille laid down a solid foundation for others to follow. The order continued and eventually thrived, surviving to the present day. It is also a fine measure of her legacy that her ethos of educating young Black women and helping the sick and elderly in the community continues.

The determination and, indeed, the ability to found the Sisters of the Holy Family was very much intertwined in Delille's family background as her forebears progressed from enslavement to becoming women with wealth and property. Thus, this biographical account of her life will begin with her formative years, which had a profound effect in shaping her character and outlook on life.

EARLY YEARS

Born around 1812–13, Henriette Delille began her life during one war, the conflict between the United States and Britain, and ended her life with another war, that between the northern and southern states.[2] Although she would probably not have remembered the Battle of New Orleans in 1815, the city's victory gave the United States its greatest land victory over the British and thwarted their efforts to gain control of a critical American port. The *Times-Democrat* reported in 1891 that the infant Delille may have had family members who fought in the war in what it described as "Major Plauche's Colored Battalion." The newspaper article stated that the "foundress and her companions" of the Sisters of the Holy Family had fathers, uncles, and brothers who served with Plauche.[3] On her deathbed in 1862, Delille would have been very aware of the Civil War, as this time New Orleans's soldiers had failed to fight off the invaders, and the city was occupied by the Union forces from the North. Thus, she began and ended her life during a period of great change and turmoil.

Delille lived in the Vieux Carré, or French Quarter, of New Orleans. She was born in a modest cottage on Burgundy Street.[4] She was the offspring of Maria Josefa Diaz, a free woman of color, and her white father was probably Jean Baptiste Lille Sarpy, a Frenchman of means. According to the *Times-Picayune*, Sarpy was one of the founders of the Freemasons in New Orleans. He donated some of his land to have a Freemasons' lodge built and owned several other properties in the city. He did not appear to have played any role in Delille's life, unlike some of the "bachelor patriarchs" who lived with and provided for their families throughout their lives. Because Jean Baptiste was married and had children, he was less likely to have ever set up house with Diaz. Indeed, although Maria Josefa may have had at least two relationships with white men, all the censuses list her as the head of the household, implying that she never cohabited with any of her domestic partners. Henriette was the youngest of three children. Her two other siblings were an elder sister, Cécille, who was probably the child of a different father, as she bore the surname Bonille, and her brother, Jean Delille, who was possibly also fathered by Sarpy. It appears to have been a close-knit family, with relationships extending into adulthood as they bequeathed money and property to each other in their wills.

Although Henriette's family home was not a grand mansion, she was related to some of New Orleans's most prominent Black and white families. Her own family was also reasonably prosperous, thanks in part to her enslaved great-great-grandmother Nanette, who after gaining her freedom invested in land and property to leave to her heirs.[5] That Nanette's daughters also continued to amass wealth from their partners is evidenced by the records of her daughter, Fanchonetta Decoudreaux, the partner of Frenchman Charles Decoudreaux. In 1786, Decoudreaux sold some land to her brother, Etienne Debreuil, which was acquired by the vendress by a clause in the last testament given by Charles Decoudreaux, Captain of the Regiment of the Plaza."[6] Thus, Delille was brought up in a household with a tradition of strong women, who had not only managed to accumulate material wealth but also to carve out a position for themselves and their families in New Orleans society. Indeed, Delille's two uncles, Narcisse Lebeau and Raphael Roig, owned large plantations and were friendly with some of New Orleans's most notable white citizens. These included John McDonogh, founder of most of the pre–Civil War public schools of New Orleans, whom Raphael Roig appointed executor of his will.[7]

Aside from the family home, Delille's mother also owned several other properties, which she probably rented out to make a living. These properties often included business premises, either attached to a main dwelling or within the grounds. For example, one of them on Barrack Street was described as a lot with two houses, "one of lumber and the other built of bricks between posts with a bakery."[8] Maria Josefa may also have been running some sort of business at her main residence, as her name appears in Louisiana's business and city directories of 1822 and 1823, under the Burgundy Street address. It is also in the 1830 census that the family is first enumerated as being "free white" rather than" free black," as they are the 1820 census. Studies have shown how racial designations frequently changed by reputation, economic status, and associations. Therefore, it was perfectly possible that within a free person of color's lifetime they could be classified as Black, mulatto, and white.[9] While it was acknowledged that the extent of African ancestry was a key factor in determining race, as well as a person's physical appearance, nuances and contradictions of racial categorizations abounded in nineteenth-century New Orleans. Although there is no evidence to suggest that at this time Henriette and her family were actively trying to pass for white, it shows the subjectiveness in determining race. While white authorities acknowledged that the extent of African ancestry and physical appearance mattered, there was a set of other considerations, including a person's mode of life, their companions, reputation, and manner of self-representation.[10] Thus, the Delille family may have become more racially ambiguous as they prospered.

When she was of school age, Henriette may have been educated at Saint-Claude Street School, run by French nun Sister Saint Marthe Frontiere, a religious sister of the Dames Hospitalières near Lyon, France. Although there are no official school records remaining, a journal written by Sister Mary Bernard Deggs in the late nineteenth century, recording the history of the order, states that the women who founded the order were pupils at the Saint-Claude Street School.[11] Thus, Delille may have attended the school with her cofounders, Juliette Gaudin and Josephine Charles. Certainly, her half sister Cécille also sent her children there, further suggesting that the two sisters were educated at the school. Sister Saint Marthe came to Louisiana at the request of Louis William Duborg, apostolic administrator of the Diocese of Louisiana and the Floridas, to open a school for "young girls of color." The curriculum was quite comprehensive for a girls' school. It included "reading, writing and geography and most especially religion." It was also a center of Catholic missionary activities for Black people, both enslaved and free; and the students were motivated to evangelize others of their community. According to oral tradition, Sister Saint Marthe encouraged her students to teach religion to those enslaved girls who were allowed to attend the school.[12]

Delille may have observed the precariousness of her mother's existence compared to that of Sister Saint Marthe. She may have also noted the autonomy that religion offered a woman, as they were not under the direct control of a partner or husband. She saw Sister Saint Marthe single-handedly running the school without too much interference from the patriarchal Catholic authorities. The sister was highly successful in attracting and recruiting students, as evidenced by a letter from Bishop Duberg to Father Antoine Blanc, a priest from New Orleans who was in France to recruit missionaries for Louisiana. Duberg wrote that Blanc should "try to bring back two good Sisters of Saint Charles to cooperate with good Sister Ste. Martha. . . . [H]er school is doing much good. She has some eighty pupils and the number would increase quickly if she had helpers."[13]

Not only did Henriette's education probably form part of Catholic missionary practice, but she also came from a family with a tradition of devout Catholic women, as demonstrated by the number of times her feminine forebears stood as godparents at baptisms. Her mother was named in the sacramental registers as a godparent to a free Black girl in November 1826 and for a boy in 1827. Later in the year, she became the godmother to an enslaved man and in 1828 for an enslaved woman.[14] Thus, the importance of expanding the influence of the Catholic religion in the free Black and enslaved population would have been instilled in Delille by her relatives as well as her teachers.

Along with this religious devoutness, another feminine family tradition was to become the partner of a white man. Although this had worked well for the previous generations, who had used their opportunities to amass wealth and property, Henriette's mother appeared not to have had the business acumen of her forebears. Although she inherited real estate, she may have often been in financial difficulties during her lifetime, as she died in debt. Maria Josefa's houses also descended into disrepair, indicating that she did not have the funds to keep them in good order. These financial problems must have impacted the family and added to the pressure on the two daughters to make an advantageous match with someone of wealth. In pursuit of this goal, Maria Josefa had certain priorities for her family, including her children's education. Although this was expensive, Maria Josefa may have viewed it as an investment in their future. She was aware that education and manners would make her daughters more desirable to gentlemen of means, which would help to enhance the family coffers.

While Henriette's sister, Cécille, may have realized their mother's ambitions by allying herself to a wealthy merchant, oral tradition suggested that the devout Delille defied her family by rejecting plaçage and refusing to attend quadroon balls. A twentieth-century biographer from the order, Sister Audrey Marie Detiege, wrote that she exclaimed, "One hour with God in church is sweeter than the vanities found in the ballroom."[15] If Henriette uttered these words, she was obviously alluding to the quadroon balls, which she and her sister may have been encouraged to attend in search of a suitable partner. Despite Delille's supposed denunciation of these entertainments in her later life, the teenage Henriette may have had firsthand knowledge of those "vanities."

It would have perhaps been very hard for an impressionable young woman to resist the requests of her mother and her sister to find a wealthy partner, especially if the family finances depended upon it. Archival discoveries suggest that indeed Delille may have succumbed to family pressure. Baptismal documents discovered by the Archdiocesan archivist of New Orleans in 2004 suggest that in the 1820s, Delille gave birth to two sons, both named Henri Bocno, who died as babies.[16] Although this was tragic, the death of babies and children was an unfortunate but unavoidable fact of life in the nineteenth century. Whole families could be wiped out by the various diseases that beset New Orleans. Nearly all the women of this study had children who predeceased them, in many cases, more than one. However, the frequency of infant deaths did not make it any easier for the parents or siblings. Henriette was only about fourteen or fifteen when she had these children. Thus, by modern standards, she was barely out of childhood herself, and the grief that she felt at their death may have also contributed to her desire to enter religious life. Perhaps the Sisters of the Holy Family and the bonds of friendship between the nuns replaced the biological family that Delille never had. Although the ecclesiastical accounts of Delille's life make it appear as though her evolution into a religious woman was inevitable because of her pious inclinations, if either of the two little boys had lived, it may have been a different story.

Little has been discovered about the father of the children. However, it is likely that he was called Henri Bocno, as it was the custom to name boys after their father. He was also probably white, as there is no record of any marriage. The surname, however, may provide a clue to the father's origin. Cécille's partner, although called by the anglicized surname of Hart, was a Jewish man, originally from Galicia in Austria, which then became part of Poland.[17] Thus, Bocno was probably Bochno, a surname originating from Poland, suggesting that the two sisters could have been with men of similar ancestry, maybe even friends or colleagues. Indeed, although only part of oral tradition, Sister Detiege wrote that "Cecilia presided over [her husband's] dinner parties where she met such outstanding men of New Orleans as William Bell and John Slidell and it was through her sister that Henriette met so many wealthy whites who later on would support her in her works of charity."[18] If this was the case, it sounds as if Cécille may have been commissioned to find a wealthy partner for her younger sister. These men whom Detiege mentioned were middle-aged like Hart, suggesting that Delille's partner may also have been much older than she. It was certainly not unusual in antebellum New Orleans for young women to be married to or have a partner much older than themselves. Indeed, Delille's sister's partner was in his fifties when he formed a relationship with the teenaged Cécille.

Simple economics may explain why the sisters had relationships with these older men. Maria Josefa's declining mental health may have also made it expedient for her daughters to make financially advantageous matches rather than following their own inclinations. Maria Josefa's mental state eventually became so bad that in 1832 Cécille petitioned the court for her mother to be provided with a "curator to take charge of her person and property," as she had been "certified insane." A family meeting was convened and held at the notary's office, which included Cécille's partner, Hart, and a curator was duly appointed, Anthony Batistessa.[19] Their mother's mental health appears to have gradually worsened throughout her lifetime. This may have affected her children greatly as they grew up in her household. Her mental illness could also have been triggered by her precarious life as a plaçée. As the head of the household, she was the sole provider for her family. The failure of her relationships and the resulting financial difficulties may have contributed to her eventual breakdown. Henriette may have found solace from her mother's difficulties in the calm atmosphere of school and church and therefore perhaps came to rely more and more on the support and the stability of religion. She saw how religious white women could also exercise their autonomy brought about by their association with the Catholic Church, not only to set up schools but to look after the sick and needy. Henriette may have also noted how they had the freedom to travel to other places as teachers and nurses. Therefore, although Delille may have initially followed her mother's and sister's lead, the death of her children and increasing problems with her mother's mental health may have further inclined her to seek the sanctuary of a religious life.

FROM CONFRATERNITY TO HOLY ORDER

Although there are few public records detailing her religious activities for about ten years after the death of her two children, it seems that Delille continued with her evangelistic interests and that she began to build up a network of like-minded women. Indeed, the sacramental records of St. Louis Cathedral revealed that Henriette Delille, Juliette Gaudin, Josephine Charles, and Anne Navarre all served as godmothers to the children of enslaved and free people from 1829 onward.[20] Gaudin and Charles were cofounders of the Sisters of the Holy Family, and Navarre was one of its first nuns. On 26 May 1836, Delille also reaffirmed her strong devotion to religion by inscribing in the opening pages of a spiritual book by Comtesse de Cardo: "I believe in God. I hope in God. I love. I wish to live and die for God." This religious work, *The Soul United to Jesus Christ in the Most Holy Sacrament of the Altar*, was first published in 1830 and presented a series of meditations and conversations with Christ to be read while attending Mass. Henriette was therefore making clear that she wished to devote herself to the religious life above all else. It was also in 1836 that Delille became the leader of a lay religious sisterhood, the first one of its kind for free women of color in New Orleans.

Delille's observations of those religious women who were teachers or leaders within their institutions may have engendered her ambition to become a force within the church. The problems with her mother and the death of her two children may have also demonstrated how support for people in the free Black community was often lacking, particularly for those without families. This awareness was demonstrated by the aims of her religious and charitable organization, which pledged to care for the sick, assist the poor, and instruct the "ignorant black population."[21] Delille's rules for the society written in a document called *The Rules and Regulations for the Congregation of the Sisters of the Presentation of the Blessed Virgin Mary* emphasize support and care for each other. They had to look after any member who became ill, attend the funeral of a deceased member, and undertake to look after any of their children, funds permitting. To assist with this, each member was also to make an annual offering of at least one dollar, as well as a monthly contribution of fifty cents.[22] Thus, Delille's organization would offer to supply the help and support for its members that, in the past, she and her mother were unable to obtain.

That it was still very much a lay religious society at this time is evidenced by the way in which its members lived apart in different households. There were also no restrictions on married women with children becoming members. Following on from the popularity of the society, Delille wanted to start a school for free Black and enslaved girls. Perhaps acknowledging the importance of education in her own life, Delille may have deplored the lack of educational opportunity, especially for Black girls. Boys could be privately educated at schools run by other free people of color, but girls, if they were educated at all, like Delille herself, received their schooling from white orders of nuns. It was a radical idea that Black girls could be educated by religious members of their own community, and the Church authorities were nervous about sanctioning it. Although they eventually allowed the society to provide education for free Black girls, they refused to officially recognize them if they also intended to educate enslaved girls. The 1830 law against incitement of any rebellion or discontent among the enslaved also included prohibitions on education for enslaved children, which was seen by the authorities as posing a threat to the status quo.[23] To ensure the continuation of the society, Delille and her followers had to accede to the Church and the law by undertaking to teach only religion to enslaved girls.

From then on, Henriette Delille's personal life history became subsumed into that of her society. The evolution of the confraternity into its final form as the Sisters of the Holy Family order was a slow process. According to Father Cyprien Davis, it was not until 1840 that Bishop Blanc sought approbation from Rome for a group of religious women known as the Sisters of the Presentation. He received confirmation from the Vatican that the group was affiliated to the Congregation Prima Primariae of the Annunciation of the Blessed Virgin Mary in the Roman Catholic Church. As a result of this, the three women founders began a "more concentrated and focused ministry with the aid of [Père] Étienne Rousselon—the spiritual adviser and co-founder of the community."[24] According to oral tradition, in 1842, Henriette Delille, Josephine Charles, and Juliette Gaudin moved into a house on Saint-Bernard Street, leased for them by Father Rousselon. In 1847, the women, under the leadership of Henriette Delille, became incorporated as the Society of the Holy Family, eventually becoming the Sisters of the Holy Family.[25]

MÉRE HENRIETTE, SUPERIOR GENERAL OF THE SISTERS OF THE HOLY FAMILY

In 1848, Henriette's mother died. She left a will in which her main heirs were named as Jean Delille, Henriette Delille, and the four children of the now-deceased Cécille: Antoinette, Amelia, Samuel, and John Hart. Maria Josefa left only a small legacy. By this time, she had only one property left, the house in which she lived on Burgundy Street, which was sold to her grandson-in-law, Joseph Emile Darsse, husband of Antoinette, for $2,325.[26] Once Maria Josefa's debts had been settled, Henriette received a very modest amount of money, which she used to partially finance the buying of a house for the sisters on Bayou Street. In this house, the women catechized the enslaved and free people of color, taught basic literacy, sheltered orphans, and nursed the sick and the elderly. By 1851, they were considered by the Catholic authorities to have demonstrated sufficient understanding of, and readiness for, religious life. Thus, they had satisfied the archdiocese that they might make religious vows.[27]

Although the sisters were now supposedly recognized by the Church as a Holy Order, their lives were by no means easy. Supporters sometimes sent them food, candles, and wood or coal, but daily life was often hard for the sisters. Sister Deggs wrote about the early years: "Many ladies knowing how poor we were, often sent old shoes or boots to wear in the yard when it rained."[28] She also recounted that after the children in the boarding school became sick with measles and scarlet fever and left, the sisters were near to starving. They were apparently saved by a "kind person" who donated a barrel of the best flour and rice. These privations show that the nuns were discriminated against by the Catholic authorities, as they never received the same funds as white orders. They were also never accorded the same recognition and status. They were not even recognized as a Holy Order in the documents of the Church until the late nineteenth century. Even after having taken their vows, the sisters were still generally referred to as "a group of pious, colored females" by the Catholic press.[29] They were also listed as a Catholic Benevolent Association in New Orleans's diocesan directories until the 1870s. When they were finally listed in these directories with the other nuns of the diocese, they were last in rank and categorized by their race.[30] The order's always-dire financial situation meant that the sisters were forced to take in washing and perform other menial tasks for money. This was in contrast to white orders, whose members did not have to beg for money from their ministry or provide a laundry service. If Delille had hoped for more financial stability in her life than that of her mother, she may have been disappointed.

Apart from the disapproval of white society, some people from the free Black community also condemned the women for becoming nuns. Evidence from the interviews of the Louisiana Works Progress Administration in the 1930s shows that: "From many of their own race, particularly the glamorous women of color who yearned for the tinsel and velvet of the quadroon festivals, their work received only jeers."[31] Sister Deggs also wrote of the "malice of persecutors" from their own neighbors, which forced the sisters to rent out their first house and rent one somewhere else where "they might live in peace." Their new neighbors then constantly complained that their schoolchildren made too much noise.[32]

These hardships and persecutions made it more difficult to attract people to join the sisters. Those who did, often could not stay the course. As Deggs asserted, "Many joined them, but the work was too hard and the sacrifice so great that they did not stay more than a few months, some only stayed a few weeks."[33] Certainly, until the late nineteenth century their numbers were always low. Censuses from 1850 and 1860 record no more than twelve women in their motherhouse. However, despite their lack of numbers, they had a leader who was determined to raise the public profile of the sisters, thereby obtaining enough support to build a ministry. Despite all the challenges, Delille and the cofounders managed to ensure the continuation of the order by diversifying their roles and through the provision of necessary services. They did what they had to do in order to safeguard its survival. Importantly, Delille also publicized the altruistic initiatives of the order through her fund-raising efforts and by engaging the interest and participation of the wealthy members of free Black society. The *Daily Picayune* newspaper records a number of charitable fairs being organized by the Sisters of the Holy Family in order to fund their various enterprises in aid of the poor. There was little or no provision for helping Black people in need, so the sisters' ministrations were sorely needed.

There is evidence from Deggs's journal that Henriette also used her connections in both Black and white society to encourage support for her charitable ambitions. She may have enlisted the aid of her well-off planter relatives in encouraging others to make donations. Eventually she was successful in obtaining contributions not only from the wealthy free Black donors but also from well-to-do white people who were aware of the order's charitable aims. Delille was also a good leader in other ways, managing her sisters in the motherhouse as well as those who had superiority over her in the Catholic Church. They all had faith in her abilities, as her position as leader was never challenged during her lifetime. This was important in providing continuity of leadership for many years.

Nevertheless, Delille always had to be careful about how she approached the Church authorities. This was a challenge for the leaders of white orders as well as for the Sisters of the Holy Family. Although nuns had a measure of autonomy, they still had to heed the orders of the male clerics who were placed in dominion over them. Henriette therefore trod a very fine line in acceding to some of the decisions that were made without consultation while resisting others. It seems that she was effective in her collaboration with the Church's authorities, often obtaining what she wanted and even escaping retribution when she did not obey some of the edicts.[34] Delille challenged the hierarchy and imposed her authority if she thought that the situation demanded it. For example, she consulted with Father Rousselon when she wanted to rent out the sisters' house. He did not want to give his consent to this, as he wished the nuns to remain where they were. Deggs wrote that Henriette ignored his wishes and went ahead "of her own accord," moving the sisters to another house.[35] Also, although Delille's views toward the Civil War were not known, it is significant that mention of their order was conspicuously absent from the public records that lauded the efforts of white orders such as the Ursulines, Carmelites, or the Sisters of St. Joseph for their contributions as nurses to the Confederate army.[36] It may simply have been that as a Black order, the Sisters of the Holy Family's nursing efforts were not deemed worthy of mention, or Delille may have resisted efforts to recruit them, thereby showing open rejection of the Confederate cause. That these acts of rebellion did not result in any repercussions from Rousselon or any other higher authorities of the Church show that they respected her leadership skills enough not to challenge her if she disobeyed any orders.

Like any modern CEO of a charity, Delille was very good at promoting the Sisters of the Holy Family by creating an image of the order that appealed to the sensibilities of New Orleans society. This may have included the use of her own image as a representation of the nuns. Ironically, although after her death little use was made of this image until the late twentieth century, it may now be providing as good a marketing tool for the sisters as it did in the nineteenth century. This now-well-known portrait came from a carte de visite that she may have used in her promotional and business activities on behalf of the order. Small, relatively inexpensive portraits, cartes de visite became all the rage in the mid-nineteenth century as all classes could now afford to have their portrait taken. Their convenient size meant that women could use them to replace the engraved visiting cards that were left after social calls, hence the name. The image provided a more personal reminder of the individual who had left it. They were also used by businesspeople, actors, and other celebrities who wished to dissemi-

FIG. 3. A ca. 1850s carte de visite of Henriette Delille that demonstrates her quiet yet commanding presence, as befits the leader of a successful organization. Photo courtesy of LA Catholics.

nate their image more widely than just among family and friends. The celebrated African American abolitionist and women's rights activist Sojourner Truth widely circulated her image through her carte de visite, showing how another woman of color also recognized its value in creating a certain image.

Like many other women at this time, Delille would have regularly called upon her friends and neighbors, probably using her image as a visiting card. She may have also utilized it when visiting potential donors for her charitable institutions. Therefore, the carte de visite would have provided a representation of her organization as well as herself. This is reflected in the photograph, which shows an attractive, well-dressed woman in the peak of life. With straight hair and European features, Delille may have provided an acceptable image of Black religious womanhood in New Orleans. Her image certainly represented a big change from the way in which wealthy free women of color were portrayed. Eighteenth-century portraits of these women show them covered with jewels in high-fashion, expensive garments. In contrast, Delille's only adornments were her crucifix and a belt, thus providing a visual demonstration of how Afro Creole women were capable of eschewing showiness in favor of piety.

Although the carte de visite portrait was probably taken in the 1840s or 1850s, after the order was established, Delille was not photographed wearing a nun's habit or veil. Indeed, even after the order's inauguration, there was much resistance among Catholic clergy and white orders of nuns to Black women wearing habits. Sister Hart recorded: "The women wore a blue percale dress and a black bonnet during their early years of life together, or between 1842–1852. On October 15, 1852, when the women took their vows, Rousselon allowed them to change their blue dresses for black ones. So as not to threaten the white nuns or alarm their fellow New Orleanians, who would have seen them as having pretensions, they wore dresses, instead of habits."[37] The white sisters may also have worried that were they to don traditional nuns' habits, Delille's European appearance could have caused her order to have been mistaken for a white one. Thus, although sisters wanted to wear the habits that marked them out as religious women, this was denied them during Delille's leadership. It wasn't until 1872 that they were allowed to wear the habit.

The carte de visite served a dual purpose as it represented Delille's status as the leader of the Sisters of the Holy Family. People often used cartes de visite to promote businesses or to clearly signal their career ambitions or status; thus, the portraits were often carefully staged by photographers to gratify this desire of the sitter. This can be clearly seen in Delille's portrait. The full-length, standing position gives her a more commanding stance. Her gaze is steady, strong, and compelling, looking into the distance, as befits a leader who was responsible for planning the organization's future. She looks determined and serious. Her carte de visite was therefore very much like those of other women who were leaders of secular organizations in the nineteenth century, such as the headmistress of a school. Like these women, Delille's portrait conveys a crucial message of responsibility, reliability, and authority.

Indeed, researchers into photographic history have emphasized how these cartes de visite became a vehicle through which the sitters performed the selves they wanted to portray. Mostly this presentation was around class, as the working class often wanted to present a visual code of bourgeoise respectability. Photographers supported the performance of identity by supplying props, backdrops, and in some cases, even clothing that allowed for acts of self-fashioning. Therefore, these images reflected "a mode of performance, rather than an inherent quality."[38] In Delille's case, it could be argued, the self-fashioning was as much about race as it was about class. She may have wanted to market herself and, by association, the other sisters as pious, genteel women of color. By doing so she could engage those prosperous and influential free people of color whose financial support she desperately needed while also presenting a nonthreatening appearance to the Church and other authorities.

The image Delille wished to create may have also influenced her choice of women deemed suitable to be admitted to the order. Initially, Henriette only allowed women who came from a similar background to her and the other cofounders. This meant that the sisters, who like

Delille came from several generations of interracial relationships, also often had a European appearance. Indeed, throughout the earlier years of the order, the census enumerators were often confused about the race of the sisters, mostly marking them down as white. The rules of admittance to the order also required that applicants bring a dowry with them to pay for their upkeep and clothing during their postulancy and novitiate, thus further limiting those who could afford to enter the community. Indeed, when one of the sisters from the other Black order of nuns in Baltimore wished to leave the order, it was suggested that she should join the Sisters of the Holy Family. Her response was that she was too dark and too poor to join the sisters, suggesting that the order's preferences were well known.[39] Sister Hart's history of the order reiterates the elitist attitude on the part of Delille and the cofounders: "From the early Foundation in 1842 until the death of Père Rousselon, only the members of the privileged classes sought and obtained admission in the ranks of the sisters."[40]

Delille's restrictive admittance policies may have been her strategy to ensure that through their ancestry with links to the elite white population, and through their appearance and presentation, the nuns were viewed as pious gentlewomen. However, she would have been aware that despite their prosperity and upper-class connections, women of her origins were still viewed negatively in many quarters of New Orleans. That a Black woman could possess honor and dignity was considered impossible by many, especially in the South. Therefore, to ensure the least criticism and the ultimate survival of the Sisters of the Holy Family, Delille may have deliberately admitted only educated women from the Black middle or upper classes who she believed would make the best impression on white society. By doing so, she also proved that women of color were clearly capable of living a life of piety and forbearance. It seems on the surface that if she was trying to achieve both of these aims, she was successful in some ways. Afro Creole author Rodolphe Desdunes used the life of Delille, in his book published in the early twentieth century about Black people of note, as an example of how "most Creole women were exemplars of piety and charity."[41] The image of the Black nuns that was engendered by Delille and the founders, as devout, refined women of color therefore proved to be very powerful and enduring for the whole of the nineteenth century, even after the Civil War, when the strict rules of admittance were relaxed. However, this may also have had the effect of making the women appear as exceptional rather than the rule. Even Desdunes's approval applied only to Creole women of color, suggesting that Black women of different origins were excluded. Indeed, newspaper articles in New Orleans often damned them with faint praise, reporting on their cultured and gracious manners with a distinct air of surprise and always referring to them as "quadroon nuns" (with all the connotations the term implied) until the twentieth century.

The restrictions on admittance also caused a problem for the order, as many of the prospective novitiates had been used to a life of privilege and were not prepared for the rough work and deprivation the nuns endured. They may have thought that the order operated the same way as the white orders in New Orleans and had a rude awakening when they found out what life was like for the Sisters of the Holy Family. Sister Detiege also suggests that parents were often dubious about their daughters joining the sisters. If their children presented with a more European appearance, they often preferred that they should try to join a white order of nuns in New Orleans or France. This shows how the Church authorities would turn a blind eye to certain Afro Creole women joining a white order. Indeed, Detiege states that Delille's mother encouraged her to do the same.[42]

The parents' worries about the futures of their children and their wish for them to pass as white, if they could do so, reflected the concerns of free people of color when faced with increasing problems of prejudice during the antebellum period. The ability to successfully pass as white could have been viewed as rebellion against the racial regime, while on other occasions it was a challenge to African Americans' struggle to "shape and nurture group identities and communications."[43] The latter was obviously of importance to Delille, who eschewed the easier road of becoming a white nun and instead dedicated her life to the Black community.

Despite a decidedly rocky beginning, the order eventually became more established, and Delille achieved many of her goals through her institution of a school and charitable outreach to the poor. However, it is likely that the responsibility and the hardships took their toll, especially on her health. Neither of the two sisters was particularly robust. Cécille had died at the young age of thirty-four, possibly of the same complaint that eventually took Henriette's life, tuberculosis. Apparently Delille was also always sickly, suffering from various complaints, including pleurisy. In 1851, Henriette became so ill that she feared her death was close. She called the notary Octave de Armas to dictate her will.[44] Despite her fears, she survived. In December 1852, when she made another will, she was well enough this time to go to Armas's office. By 1860 Henriette was obviously ailing again and called the notary to rewrite her will once more. Her goddaughter Ella Bell had written her a letter earlier that year, noting that she was "rejoicing in her convalescence and wishing for her restoration to good health." In a further letter written in 1861, she bemoaned the fact that "mother has let me know that your health is still delicate."[45] By November 1862, Henriette Delille had passed away. She was fifty years old, and the cause of her death was attributed to phthisis (tuberculosis).[46] Sister Hart also ascribes Delille's death to the emotional toll and stress caused by the bombardment and capture of New Orleans by the Union army in April 1862, which, according to Hart, "told heavily on the enfeebled health of Mother Henriette."[47] Obituary notices appeared in *L'Abeille* (The Bee) newspaper. Her funeral was a modest one: The cost for the coffin and hearse was twenty dollars, and the rental of three carriages cost three dollars each.[48] This was in line with the precepts of her former lay community, which stipulated that a funeral should be simple.

Events after her death show that it was Delille's leadership abilities and her reputation within the free Black community that had held the order together. Deggs wrote that after she had passed, "several parents came to take their children from the school and another group of the sisters left the order to go to France." By 1865, seven of the twelve sisters had gone, leaving only five to carry on the work.[49] The Church also became indifferent to the future of the order, and it very nearly did not survive. However, Delille had built a strong foundation, so the remaining nuns continued with their work, despite the difficulties, and the order refused to be extinguished. It was through the efforts of the two cofounders, Juliette Gaudin and Josephine Charles, that the order endured, but this could not have happened except for the skill and dedication of Delille's leadership.

HOW THREE WEAK WOMEN TRIUMPHED

From the foundation of the lay society to the inauguration of the Sisters of the Holy Family, Henriette relied on her strong alliances with other women. Her mother's experiences had taught her that Black women, even those who were deemed as free, were vulnerable in a racist and patriarchal society. The support and cooperation of other Black women was therefore an important part of Delille's life, and she relied upon these relationships from the very beginning of her journey. Indeed, the experiences of women in this study demonstrated that they were stronger when they cooperated together rather than solely relying on the sometimes dubious support of their partners or husbands. These feminine networks also gave women increased opportunities for empowerment through economic security as well as having roles of responsibility. They were therefore able to take more control of their lives.

Like other women in this study, Delille showed that these feminine alliances could transcend racial sensibilities. Before the successful foundation of her lay religious society, Henriette had wanted to create a community of religious women with Marie Jean Aliquot, a Frenchwoman who was described by Sister Detiege as being one of Delille's "dearest and closest friends." However, the friends were thwarted in their ambitions because of the 1830 act that made it illegal for anyone to destroy "the line of distinction which the law established between the several classes in this community."[50] Thus, as with the education of enslaved children, the Church authorities were not willing to overstep the mark by allowing a Black and white woman to collaborate together in the foundation of a religious society. Even though Aliquot could not join Delille, she still supported her throughout the years. When

Delille took Holy Orders, Aliquot campaigned for monetary support from the white community. Also, after Delille's mother died and left her some money, Aliquot lent her more money so she could buy the house on Bayou Road for the sisters. Despite the racial restrictions and the prejudice she may have encountered, she was often with the sisters in their house, showing her support for them.[51] Aliquot was even at the convent when she passed away. The sisters were upset as they had appreciated her support throughout the years. Deggs wrote, "We regretted her death very much for we have not found a friend as dear as she was nor as holy a religious."[52]

This shows how these feminine networks could cross racial lines, resulting in friendships that would have been deemed impossible by the mores of the time. However, this was not so unusual, especially for those Black women with close ties to the white community. Delille was educated by white religious women, and her relatives had friends among the high echelons of white society. Sister Deggs's journal also reiterated the order's links with the white community when she wrote, "We have always been like one and the same family, going to the same church, sitting in the same pews, and many of them sleeping in the same bed. If we had any entertainment, the whites would come by."[53] These connections illustrate the often-intertwined relationships between the Black and white people of the city, both familial and through other institutions. All women would have acknowledged their inferior position within New Orleans society and therefore could also recognize the benefits of working together and supporting each other.

Apart from Aliquot, one of Delille's closest allies was cofounder Juliette Gaudin, who stood by her from the very beginning. Their close relationship meant that Henriette nominated her as a beneficiary in all her three wills, leaving her the household furnishings, the linens, and other household goods.[54] Juliette Gaudin was slightly older than Delille, born in 1808 either in Saint-Domingue or in Cuba, according to different public records that show both places as her country of birth.[55] Very likely her family was among the refugee Saint-Dominguans who were expelled from Cuba in 1809, giving rise to the confusion. Therefore, although Gaudin was the only cofounder to have been foreign-born, it is unlikely that she would have remembered living anywhere but New Orleans. Gaudin's parents were married, and her father, Pierre Gaudin, who was a teacher, opened his own school in New Orleans.[56] This was not unusual, as the refugees from Saint-Domingue and Cuba who came to New Orleans included many white and mixed-race teachers as they were generally well-educated, in many instances more so than their counterparts in New Orleans. However, the family may not have been particularly prosperous, as the influx of refugees resulted in a glut of teachers trying to make a living by teaching French.[57] Deggs suggests that Gaudin was the most intelligent of the cofounders: "She was a great reader and kept the accounts for the order until five years before her death."[58]

Gaudin succeeded Delille and presided over the most tumultuous times for the order, which led to a split in the community after the Civil War. This was engendered by the proposed admittance of Chloé Joachim Preval, a formerly enslaved woman and housekeeper at the seminary. Archbishop Odin and Father Gilbert Raymond, who had succeeded Rousselon as the father superior, were in favor of her entry, but Gaudin was not. In many ways Gaudin was still following the precepts of Delille, who had been strict about who was eligible to join the order. Gaudin may also have thought that the admittance of a formerly enslaved woman who had acted as a housekeeper to church clerics would create a precedent for the nuns to become servants for the priests, thus further undermining their status. Losing patience with the situation, Raymond requested that the nuns vote on the matter. The vote was fairly evenly split, with four sisters voting in favor, including the other cofounder, Josephine Charles. Raymond was determined that Preval should enter the order and sent Charles and the other sisters to a house in Chartres Street. He appointed Charles the mother superior, hoping to undermine Gaudin's position and force her to join the others. However, Gaudin stood her ground and remained at Bayou Road with a small number of nuns. She ran a very successful school there, which, according to Deggs, eventually helped to reunite the sisters. When old age finally caught up with her, she moved into the house on Orleans Street in 1883, dying there in 1888.[59]

Like Delille, Gaudin defied the authorities if she felt that the situation warranted it. She confounded their expectations that she would capitulate and join the other sisters by setting up and running a thriving school, which was supported by many in the free Black community. Perhaps Delille would have been better at negotiating with Odin and Raymond in order to come to a compromise and prevent the division into two factions.

The second cofounder, Josephine Charles, was, according to Deggs, the daughter of a free woman of color and a German man, Joseph Charles. The family was probably also wealthier than Delille's, as is made clear by her brother François's succession in 1841, which lists his numerous real estate holdings.[60] Like Delille, their family appears to have had a close-knit relationship, but unlike Delille's father, Charles's father had a strong bond with his children. Deggs asserted that Josephine's father could not bear to send any of his children to Europe for their education as was the custom because "he never wanted any of his dear little children to go as far away as that from home, for fear of some accident."[61] Perhaps Joseph's anxiety for his children was engendered by the early demise of Charles's mother, Philomene, which meant that Josephine was mostly brought up by her elder sister. Oral tradition suggests that Charles's family was very much against her joining with Delille, but she was a strong character and defied them.

It appears that during Delille's lifetime, the three cofounders lived amiably with no recorded difficulties. Again, this was probably a testament to Delille's leadership skills as it seems that all three women were strong personalities. It was only after Delille's demise that the sisters clashed. Probably trading on the reputation of her schoolmaster father and her own superior education, Gaudin established her own school, providing an income for the sisters choosing to remain with her. Charles, however, had no revenue after the split. Times were therefore initially very hard for her sisters. Deggs wrote that they did not have a nickel and that Josephine had to go to the market and beg for food. However, her willingness to "accept all those who came with a letter from their confessor and were well-disposed to work for Christ" meant that more nuns joined the convent. They were also helped in their endeavors with donations from wealthy benefactors. Thus, eventually the sisters' fortunes began to improve, and the work of the community began to expand outward. As they began to grow as a community, the house in Chartres Street became too small, and they eventually bought a larger property on Orleans Street. This became the main motherhouse of the order, and eventually Gaudin and her remaining nuns joined them. Charles also took their mission outside of the city, opening another convent school in Opelousas, Louisiana.

Like Delille, Charles was a successful leader and was adept at negotiating with the authorities, overcoming the resistance that had prohibited the nuns from wearing a habit. She also resisted the objections of the Sisters of St. Joseph, who thought that the veil of the Sisters of the Holy Family was too similar to their own and thus likely to cause embarrassing misrecognition. Recently many orders have been abandoning the wearing of habits, whereas the Sisters of the Holy Family have eschewed this trend, probably in recognition of the struggles they had to endure in order to be able to wear it. For them, the habit conferred dignity and a recognition of their status. Even if they still had to perform menial tasks in order to survive, they would no longer be mistaken for washerwomen when they delivered freshly laundered clothes to their clients.[62]

During her tenure, Charles had overcome past challenges and expanded the influence of the order. However, by the 1880s her health began to fail, and she eventually lost her sight. In 1882 she handed over the reins to her assistant Marie Magdalene Alpaugh and died in 1885. Despite her reputation as an excellent leader and her expansion of the convent, the *Times-Picayune* obituary mentioned none of this. Instead, it referred back to the image of the nuns as beautiful Afro Creole women. The obituary opened: "Thirty-years ago a modest, beautiful quadroon woman took up the cross and set about performing the noble task of the improvement of her people. . . . She grew up a beautiful girl, bright in complexion, tall and stately in figure and was much courted."[63] It is debatable whether the obituary of a white mother superior would have made such references to her beauty and openly hint at her attractiveness to the opposite sex. The obituary also suggested that rather than helping the Black community, the nuns were bettering them, thus again, as in Delille's time, covertly suggesting the nuns' exceptionalism.

Although this obituary could be seen as problematic in its portrayal of Charles, this was the first lengthy obituary to be printed about one of the leaders in the *Times-Picayune,* suggesting that by this time, the sisters had become well-known, respected members of the religious and lay community. Their success also showed what Black women could achieve if they worked together in pursuit of a common goal. Previously, free Black women of a certain class were often expected to marry well or to have a prosperous white partner in order to ensure the wealth and security of the next generation. Delille, Gaudin, and Charles demonstrated that there could be another path for free women of color to live a fulfilled life by serving the community. However, they could not have achieved what they did without the support of various women. Delille and Charles were talented leaders, but they needed the networks they had created in order to succeed. They could not have done it on their own.

Delille's creation of various charitable organizations during the antebellum period formed part of a growing movement in the free Black community to encourage cohesion and group identity, as a challenge to the racial regime. Free Black philanthropists such as Thomy Lafon became so impressed with the endeavors of the order that they left money in their wills to the sisters, enabling them to expand their charitable institutions. Thus, the Black community benefited from a change of attitude within free Black society, causing people to become more outward-looking and concerned with the future of their community as a whole. Delille also headed a successful organization, giving her a sense of increased control over her life and her destiny, things that appeared to be lacking in her mother's life. So, her life history shows a positive trajectory for free women of color, echoed by the lives of other Black women in the antebellum period. The other sisters also often defied family and societal objections to join the order. The harsh conditions of the nuns' lives meant that those who were not committed left very quickly, ensuring that only the most strong and dedicated women remained, further enhancing the nuns' reputation.

Although one could argue that by creating strict admittance rules, the order may have been discriminatory and restrictive, there were many good reasons at the time why this was initiated. And in many ways Delille's order was only following the practices of white orders, which also often placed restrictions on the admittance of novitiates. As the community of sisters evolved during the upheavals in society, so did its recruitment practices. And notwithstanding any criticisms of elitism, the Sisters of the Holy Family certainly served all the Black community throughout Delille's life, without any prejudices and often in the face of opposition from critics. Thus, they engendered their own tradition of determination in the face of racial discrimination and a patriarchal Church. Despite the difficult times of the Reconstruction era and beyond, the order flourished in the late nineteenth century, expanding its influence in Louisiana, Texas, Oklahoma, California, and even into Belize, Central America. Thus, what had begun as a small group of religious women in New Orleans led by Henriette Delille eventually evolved into a well-respected institution that continues its charitable work in the twenty-first century.

3

THE PLAÇÉE AND THE WIFE

Cécille Bonille and Marie Dolores Laveaux

THE PLAÇÉE
Cécille Bonille

Cécille Bonille was born to Maria Josefa Diaz and Juan Bonille or Bonilla, a European man of unknown origin who eventually resided in Havana, Cuba, but who may have been originally from New Orleans.[1] Her baptism was registered in the archdiocesan records in 1807, in a volume designated for "Slaves and Free People of Color." She was described as Bonille's "natural daughter," showing that he had recognized her as his child, but it is doubtful that she had much contact with him.[2] As with Henriette Delille's father, there is no record of his playing any role in Cécille's life. Her maternal background was one of interracial relationships, as her enslaved and free ancestors all had children with white men, going back to her enslaved great-great-grandmother Nanette, who had five children with her enslaver, Claude Joseph Dubreuil. The relationship between Claude Dubreuil and Nanette was at best likely to have been an exploitative one and at worst violent, because rape was an all-too-common and horrific reality for many enslaved women.[3] Although not manumitted by Dubreuil, Nanette was eventually freed in 1763 by his son.[4] After this, she disappeared from legal records until 1770, when she bought, and subsequently freed, her daughter Cécile, the youngest of her four daughters, and Cécile's two children. She paid a total of 2,800 livres for their release.[5] Thus, in seven years, she had amassed a considerable sum of money to free her daughter and grandchildren, indicating that she was a resourceful and hard worker with a talent for making money. However, she may also have benefited financially because of her kinship with the Dubreuils. Her daughter Cécile had two children while she was enslaved, one of whom was Henriette Laveau, Cécille Bonille's grandmother. After Henriette was freed by her grandmother, she conducted a relationship with a man named Miguel Roig (or Roche) and had two children with him.[6] Cécile had obviously inherited her mother's business acumen and began to invest in property. Very soon she was "counted among the most well-to-do property-holders in New Orleans."[7] Presumably Cécile inherited properties from her mother, but she may have also profited financially by her association with her partners. Her daughter, Henriette, had relationships with three other white men apart from Roche, Chevalier (Charles) Morant, Pedro Foucher, and Antonio Diaz. This last relationship produced Maria Josefa Diaz, Cécille's mother.[8] Their relationships with white men had proved very advantageous in an economic sense. Apart from monetary benefits, the family's European appearance and kinship with elite Spanish and French families gave them a certain amount of status in New Orleans society.

The records from the Vieux Carré Survey at the Historical New Orleans Collection, and acts from the Notarial Archives show that when she was young, Maria Josefa also bought and sold property for financial gain.[9] Thus, she carried on the family tradition of putting her wealth into property in order to continue improving her economic position. It is difficult to ascertain whether Maria Josefa was also financially or emotionally dependent on her white partners. The fact that she had more than one seems to suggest that she needed to have a domestic partner, possibly for financial reasons, as her economic situation began to worsen during her lifetime. A later problem with her mental health also suggests that she may have endured hardship, despite or possibly because of her relationships.

There are no descriptions of Cécille, and no known portraits of her, either as a girl or in adulthood, but it is likely that like her half sister, Henriette Delille, she looked more European- than African-descended. The census enumerators were always confused about the racial classification of Cécille's family, sometimes recording them as Black or "mulatto" and sometimes as white. By 1822, her grandmother, Henriette Laveau, was described as a "quarteroon," and the subsequent interracial relationships may have resulted in an even more European appearance for the family.[10] It could certainly be argued that by exclusively choosing high-status white partners, Cécille's relatives had actively pursued certain benefits throughout the generations in an effort to achieve increased financial security and status within society, and even perhaps to allow their descendants to eventually pass for white.

As with Henriette Delille, there are no records of Cécille's early life in her mother's house on Burgundy Street (see fig. 4). It was situated in the Faubourg Marigny, an area of New Orleans founded by Bernard Marigny, who sold off areas of his plantation land, often to free people of color. According to contemporary reports, it was a reasonably pleasant area to live. Henry Castellanos described it as having "small flower gardens with clusters of creeping Spanish jessamines, which relieved the monotonous aspect of the quarter."[11] It was also home to many of the Saint-Dominguan refugees. Castellanos observed that it was a cohesive community where people looked after their neighbors, especially in times of sickness.[12] When Cécille was of school age, she probably went to the same Saint-Claude Street School, where she would eventually send her two daughters. It was described as a Maison D'Education (House of Education) pour les jeunes personnes de couleur (for young people of color) run by the Carmelite nuns at St. Augustine Church.[13] She may have been tutored in other skills, like music lessons, which were deemed essential for a young *demoiselle*. During her spare time, she and her siblings probably engaged in the same type of activities described by Eliza Ripley in her childhood recollections of midcentury

New Orleans. Like Ripley, they may have played in the street, gone crawfishing in the ditches bounding some of the streets, or sneaked off to the French Market, where they could buy a cup of coffee for one picayune.[14]

As Cécille became older, she may have attended the soirees described by the hairdresser Eliza Potter, and it was possibly then that she acquired her love of fashion, which would become evident in later documents. Potter noted the sumptuous dress of the women who attended these social events: "On entering I was met by the hostess, who was a tall fine-looking woman, who looked as though she might be white but a little sunburnt. She was dressed in white silk with a headdress of crimson, a full set of coral. Her mother, a brown skinned woman was dressed in black silk, with a full set of white lawn. At half past eleven, in walked a most beautiful brown skinned woman, elegantly dressed in pink brocade, and a full set of diamonds."[15] Cécille's desire for fashionable and expensive clothing may have been influenced by the style and richness of dress adopted by some free women of color. Indeed, Frederick Law Olmsted noted that "quadroons seem to have inherited or acquired much of the taste and skill, in the selection and arrangement, and the way of wearing dresses and ornaments, that is the especial distinction of the women of Paris."[16] In adulthood she probably dressed very differently from the sober outfit her sister Henriette Delille was wearing in the carte de visite image shown in the previous chapter (see fig. 3).

Perhaps it was her fashionable appearance that attracted Samuel Hart, who was to be her only partner and the father of her children. She apparently met him when she was around seventeen years old. As part of her autobiography about Henriette Delille, Sister Detiege writes: "In 1824 . . . Cécile had the thrill of attending the ball where she met and gave her love to Samuel [Hart], a wealthy commissioned merchant of New Orleans, originally from Austria."[17] The date of the beginning of her relationship with Hart is supported by the birth of her first child, Antoinette, in 1825.[18] It is feasible that Cécille attended quadroon balls. But with the lack of any accompanying evidence, Sister Detiege may have only assumed that she met Hart at a ball, in keeping with the tra-

FIG. 4. This postcard shows the modest property, on the 500 block of Burgundy, where Henriette Delille and Cécille Bonille were born. *In the French Quarter, New Orleans, LA* (The Rotograph Company, 1904). The Collins C. Diboll Vieux Carré Survey, a project of the Historic New Orleans Collection, negative no. N-569.2.

ditions surrounding these relationships. The contemporary travelers' accounts suggested that this was the main method for free women of color to find a white partner. However, there were many places of entertainment in New Orleans, so quadroon balls formed only a small part of the diversions on offer. Eliza Potter's account also suggests that these women were just as likely to meet eligible men in their family parlors.

Samuel Hart was certainly not the typical suitor portrayed in the accounts of these liaisons. Indeed, the myths surrounding plaçage are still so strong that a movie filmed in 2000 about Henriette Delille's life portrayed Cécille's partner as a handsome, wealthy Creole planter in his early twenties.[19] These assumptions about the partners of Afro Creole women have been somewhat debunked by research into the recorded cohabitees of free women of color in the censuses between 1780 and 1860. Far from being mostly of the wealthy planter class, they were more likely to be from the middle ranks of society.[20] Hart was an immigrant, a Jewish man from the Austro-Hungarian Empire, who was already fifty-three years old when he met Cécille.[21] Hart may have been a member of the small Jewish community that was established after the Louisiana Purchase. The promise of economic security and increased opportunities enticed Jews to seaports like New Orleans, where they reconstructed their lives and values, adapting to the multiethnic milieu.

The alliance between Bonille and Hart also broke with the tradition of Cécille's forebears, who had always conducted associations with Catholic French or Spanish Creoles, with whom they shared a common language and culture. However, the influx of immigrants to New Orleans during the early part of the century may have brought about more diversity in these interracial relationships: "Many of them were newcomers, outsiders and economically challenged in some way, making them unpromising competitors for . . . European women."[22] Even wealthy Protestant John McDonogh from Baltimore found it difficult to marry anyone from New Orleans's staunchly Roman Catholic families. His suit was turned down by Micaela Leonarda, who eventually married Baron Pontalba and became one of the richest women in New Orleans. Even a family also originally from Baltimore declined his bid for the hand of a Miss Johnson unless he converted to Roman Catholicism.[23] Hart was also wealthy and well-established, as he was a prosperous merchant who came to New Orleans sometime before 1805.[24] Therefore, it is likely that, like McDonogh, it was his religion that alienated New Orleans's upper-class eligible women. In legal documents he was also variously described as being Polish, from the Austro-Hungarian Empire, or Austrian, the confusion unsurprising as during the nineteenth century, the borders of these countries were often changing.[25] However, his Jewish ethnicity was also evident in the names of his relatives. Although he was called Hart, his brother was named Saul Kalman Robinsohn, and his sister was Hendel Rosenberg, suggesting that he may have wished to hide his identity by the adoption of the anglicized surname.[26] It was, therefore, on the face of it an unusual choice of partner for a French-speaking Catholic Afro Creole. One wonders how her piously Catholic family may have viewed the Jewish Hart, or if they eagerly welcomed him into the family fold because of his wealth. The big age difference meant that this was probably not a romantic connection and could have also been a potentially exploitative one, as Cécille was still very young. Indeed, Sister Detiege wrote that before meeting Cécille, Hart had conducted a relationship with his enslaved woman Betsy, who was subsequently gifted to Henriette Delille. Betsy had a son, John, who may have been fathered by Hart. Betsy was no doubt defenseless in her relationship with Hart, showing how Hart's previous unions with Black women had been based on the abuse of power.[27] Even Sister Detiege did not comment on or condemn this inappropriate connection in her written account of the order's history, published in the 1970s, showing how unremarkable this was in antebellum New Orleans. Indeed, there was often an acceptance among women in the South that they might have to come to terms with the visibility of their husbands' enslaved or freed children. Some of them even had to submit to their future husbands' exhortation to "behave kindly" toward them.[28]

Betsy had no choice in her relationship with Hart, but Cécille, as a free Black woman, at least had the option of rejecting his advances. She did not reject them, though, and that she seemingly chose to be with a man old enough to be her grandfather shows that other factors, apart from physical attraction, favored an alliance with Hart. Despite his past relationship indiscretion and advancing age, for Cécille, a partnership with Hart had obvious benefits. He had wealth, which would be of value to Cécille and her family, and despite being an outsider, as a prosperous man, he also had some status and influence in the general community. She may have seen how these new immigrants were making their mark on the economic life of the city. Thus, she must have decided that an alliance with someone who was contributing to a changing New Orleans would be an opportunity to protect herself, her family, and any children she might have in the future against the increasing prejudice toward the free Black community.

In making her decision, Cécille was also no doubt influenced by economic and cultural factors. First, Hart's origins and more advanced age meant that he was less likely to marry another woman, leaving her without any financial support. Also, Hart's isolation, as he had no other close family members nearby and was far from home, meant that he was more likely to want to cohabit with Cécille, giving her increased status as Hart's recognized "near-wife." As her subsequent actions show, this was important for Cécille. And, despite the differences of age and culture, her relationship with Hart proved to be a more stable one than the previous partnerships of her mother, lasting until his untimely death in 1832. By that time, he and Cécille had four children: Antoinette, Amelia, John, and Samuel.

The year 1832 was generally a very difficult one for Cécille, as it was also the year when her mother was certified insane.[29] Cécille's desperation about the state of her mother's mental health was so acute that she applied to the courts in order to try and sort out her mother's affairs. A family meeting, which included Samuel Hart, was called at the office of the notary Felix de Armas. Hart's inclusion shows that by this time he was an accepted and trusted family member. Of course, it was always an advantage for free people of color to have a white man present at meetings involving the public authorities. However, his attendance also made clear that, unlike the absentee Creole partners of her mother, Hart was by now supportive of Cécille and involved in her family's affairs. Hart also filed a will in 1832, making clear his obligations to his children with Cécille by providing for them in the event of his death. Although he did not openly acknowledge the relationship with Cécille in his will, declaring that he was "unmarried and had no children," he clearly stated that he wanted to bequeath one-fifth of his estate, in line with Louisiana inheritance law for natural children, "to the four children of Cecilia Boni, female of color."[30] He left the rest of his estate to be divided up among his heirs in Europe. His will stated, somewhat poignantly, that he was at that time "in good health but aware of the uncertainty of human life." The fatefulness of this phrase soon became clear because, although Hart was obviously feeling well on 8 September when he wrote his will, by November of that same year he had succumbed to cholera.[31] Between October and November 1832, a terrible cholera epidemic raged in the city, claiming the lives of an estimated five thousand souls.[32] People were understandably terrified by horrific symptoms that seemed to afflict victims instantly. Someone who woke up healthy could suddenly become violently ill, have their skin take on a ghastly bluish tint, become severely dehydrated, and die within hours.[33]

Hart was not the only one in the household to be infected. His nurse recalled that she had to tend to other members of his family (probably referring to Bonille and the children), but they all survived.[34] Perhaps their relative youth made them less susceptible than Hart because there was no known treatment for the disease. He died in his house in the suburb St. Mary, his death certificate recording, "Samuel Hart aged about 60 years, native of Poland died on the 9th November at 8 o'clock and that he was unmarried."[35] He had an expensive funeral, befitting a man of his status, at a cost of $175 for "one full mounted mahogoney [*sic*] coffin, two horse herse [*sic*] and 10 carriages at 8 dollars each."[36] If he had been a Catholic of high standing, he would probably have had his funeral service at St. Louis Cathedral and been interred in St. Louis Cemetery No.1. Instead, he was buried in the now-demolished Gates of Mercy Cemetery, the first Jewish cemetery in New Orleans.[37]

After Hart's death, and with the loss of his protection, life became more difficult for Cécille. His will had given powers to the executors, William Brocke, James Ramsey, and James Hopkins, to take possession and make an inventory of his estate. Thus, after Hart's death, a notary went to his house where Cécille and the children were residing and asked her to "exhibit to me all the property and effects, rights and credits of every description appertaining to the said estate, which were in her possession or of which she lacks any knowledge."[38] It must have been traumatic for Cécille after the loss of her partner to have people going through the family's personal possessions, and to know that she would have to leave the house that she had shared with Hart. Although he had left the children provided for in his will, like many other men with long-term partners, and in the knowledge that he was about to die, he also tried to make provision for Cécille, by giving her money while he was still alive. Cécille therefore declared to the notary that she had been given several notes by Hart, as a donation to her, five or six days before his death, in the presence of witnesses. There were seventeen "billets" amounting to the very large sum of $123,451. The notary immediately took possession of these notes and deposited them in a bank subject to "the joint orders of the said executors of the one part and of the said Cécille Bonilla and John Slidell Esq., her attorney of the other part."[39]

Hart had a large number of siblings residing in Europe, and although some of these had already predeceased him, they also had large families of children and grandchildren who were no doubt all hoping to benefit from the estate of the "unmarried" Hart. The executors therefore decided that these notes given to Bonille should be included in the estate and took her to court to reclaim the money. Cécille, possibly in anticipation of trouble, had already hired a noted lawyer and friend of Samuel Hart, John Slidell.[40] Sister Detiege suggests that Cécille was well acquainted with Slidell, as she and Hart had thrown dinner parties for him.[41] As a result of his friendship with Hart, Slidell may have felt obligated to help Cécille. However, it was not altogether unusual for eminent lawyers to take on the cases of free women of color being sued for inheritance monies by the white relatives of their deceased partners. Another woman featured in this book, Eulalie Mandeville, also hired leading defense attorney Pierre Soulé to protect her money from her deceased partner's Creole heirs.[42]

Perhaps Bonille placed too much faith in the support of Hart and his friends, however. It appears that unlike her sister, who concentrated her efforts in creating links with other women, Bonille had focused on maintaining networks and negotiating with white men. Although the law also played a critical role in Bonille's ability to defend her rights, she needed the support of these connections in pleading her case. Despite still only being in her twenties at the time of Hart's passing, Cécille Bonille had the confidence of her convictions to try to protect her position and her inheritance by defending her case in court. By doing so, she demonstrated that she would take an active role in the protection of her welfare and that of her children. She may have been influenced in her actions by the plight of her own mother, who did not have much financial security in later life. But Cécille also clearly believed that she was entitled to defend her property, and she had no hesitation about defending her case in court.

At first it appeared that she might be able to keep the money as her case went to the Parish Court and was dismissed by the judge. The executors then appealed, and the case went to the Louisiana Supreme Court in 1833. By this time, the main executor, William Brocke, had also died. Cécille's defense therefore made the case that a petition to set aside a donation made by a testator could only be brought by the heirs and legatees, not by executors, and that, as Brocke had died, and his coexecutors had been appointed merely to aid him, it was not valid for them to bring this action. The plaintiffs' counterargument claimed that as the executors were authorized to recover the possession of any property at Hart's death, Article 1669 of the Louisiana Code recognized their right to bring actions on behalf of the succession. The Supreme Court judge overturned the decision of the Parish Court in favor of the plaintiffs, stating, "Although executors cannot alone maintain an action in relation to the rights of heirs, they may, if those who are interested are made party to the suit."[43] He therefore ordered that the case "be remanded to be proceeded in according to the law."[44] As it seemed that the court case would drag on, with the aid of Slidell, Cécille negotiated a monetary settlement with Hart's heirs out of court.[45] How much money she received was not recorded anywhere, and her later financial difficulties suggest that it was probably nowhere near the amount initially given to her by Hart. However, she was fortunate that as Hart's heirs lived in Europe, they were perhaps less willing to come to New Orleans for another court case, so she retained at least some of the money. After this was settled, Cécille also asked John McDonogh, the aforementioned wealthy businessman and friend to her two uncles, to purchase four lots of land belonging to Hart for the sum of $32,000, on behalf of her children.[46] This seemingly headstrong act on Bonille's part caused a problem, because she did not seek any authorization of the purchase from the executors or from the Court of Probates, or, indeed, from her own family. Although it was unauthorized, the purchase was finally approved by all those concerned. However, it would turn out to be a contentious issue after her death.[47]

It seems that Cécille had enjoyed a somewhat privileged life with Hart, possibly even passing as his lawful wife, a fiction that was strengthened by her European appearance. Other evidence also implied that Cécille was keen to validate her relationship with Hart. Despite her relative youth, she did not have any other partners until her death and always referred to herself as the Veuve (widow) Hart in various written documents.[48] By doing so, Bonille was also attempting to claim a position in society and the respectability that had been denied her by virtue of her race. The uncertainty surrounding her mother's domestic life may have also made her crave increased security through a more stable domestic partnership. Bonille's relationship marked a change from the more temporary unions of her mother and grandmother, perhaps reflecting her desire for a longer-term commitment that would better ensure a secure future for herself and her children. It was unfortunate that with Hart's untimely death, Cécille's plans did not come to fruition.

Despite her relative youth, Bonille would only outlive Hart by nine years. She was taken ill in the summer of 1841. Detiege suggests that Hart's death and the struggles with the inheritance, as well as her mother's mental illness, had taken a toll on her health. According to oral history, Bonille had suffered from consumption (tuberculosis), the same illness that finally took the life of her sister, Henriette Delille. As evidenced by Hart's demise, diseases such as cholera and tuberculosis spread rapidly through the United States and thrived in New Orleans's unhealthy environment. It was sad that after managing to survive one killer disease, she would eventually be felled by another. By the time of her death, in America and Europe, tuberculosis had reached a peak of ferocity after the Industrial Revolution and the massive urbanization that followed it, killing more people than smallpox and cholera. It was also a disease that affected the young as much as the old. Although often romanticized in contemporary art and literature, especially because of the youth of the sufferers, in reality it was a debilitating and harsh disease. Charlotte Brontë's letters describe the stark physical reality of the death of her consumptive sister Emily in 1848: "She is *very* ill. . . . A more hollow wasted, pallid aspect I have not beheld. The deep, tight cough continues; the breathing after the least exertion is a rapid pant;

and these symptoms are accompanied by pains in the chest and side. . . . [M]oments so dark as these I have never known."[49]

Detiege also claimed that Henriette Delille moved in with her sister in order to help nurse her. Although there is no record of her being in the house in the 1840 census (as the only other woman recorded as living in the house was older than Cécille, possibly her mother), Henriette probably did help to care for her sister, thus very likely contracting the disease from her. However, Delille was not there on 29 March 1841 when Bonille called the notary Louis T. Caire to her apartment on Saint-Claude Street. He found Cécille lying on a daybed with Mr. and Mrs. Jean Louis Dolliole and Paynal Auguste in attendance. She had also called them to be witnesses to her last will and testament. The severity of Cécille's illness is evidenced by the statement to the notary that she wanted to dictate her last wishes to him "while she had use of her mental faculties, to put her affairs in order."[50] She told him her name and described herself as a "Creole." It is significant that Cécille identified herself thus. By classifying herself as a Creole, Cécille was proclaiming her allegiance to a specific cultural group that was not designated by race but rather by culture and tradition. She was also distinguishing herself from outsiders, including her previous partner. Cécille had broken family tradition by her association with Hart, thereby also seemingly eschewing her links with the old Creole families of New Orleans in favor of the new people flooding into the city. Yet she still evinced pride in her culture and origins, which were as important as her race. Bonille's insistence on being named a Creole, long before political activists like Rodolphe Desdunes appropriated this cultural title, was perhaps also a further conscious effort on her part to emphasize both her origins and her status in her will.

Although Cécille had many doctors to attend her and fought a battle against the disease that was afflicting her, it was all to no avail. She died on 25 August 1841, leaving behind four children, three of whom were still minors.[51] Her will and subsequent succession revealed more details about her personality and mode of living. She should have been a wealthy woman, her succession stating that she had two properties on Saint-Claude Street and Villére Street, as well as holding two enslaved women. In reality, however, her financial situation was in disarray, as she also had many debts. She owed in excess of $3,000 in outstanding accounts, which her executors, Henry Leaumont and William Bell, had to agree to settle immediately. Indeed, the inventory of her possessions shows that Cécille was a woman who liked to spend money, and who was sometimes slow to settle her accounts. Her death expenses were also extremely costly, as she had a grand funeral and interment. Indeed, the cost of the funeral, which was held in St. Louis Cathedral, amounted to a staggering $299.75. This was much more expensive than the funeral of Samuel Hart, and certainly much more than her sister Henriette's modest affair. Her coffin cost $127.13, signifying that it was probably at the top of the range, and her tombstone cost $60.00. This suggests that even in death, Cécille wanted to put on an impressive show for friends and family. The cost of her last illness was also inordinately high. She was attended by no fewer than three doctors, their fees ranging from $20 to $50. Her medicines cost $76.24, although it all proved to be ineffective in curing her illness.[52] She had obviously not expected to die at the young age of thirty-four, leaving her children vulnerable from her debts, and though she evidently made every attempt to avert her fate, she could not stop the inevitable.

Her succession also revealed a woman with a penchant for luxury clothes and finery. She owed money to several ladies' clothing and millinery shops, including $27 to the Bellone Magasin, where she purchased, among other things, stockings, collars, and muslin. Her account from this shop ran from 1836, and although she had paid some of it off in 1839 and 1840, there was still an amount owing.[53] She used this shop to buy her more mundane garments, whereas her outer garments, such as hats, came from an altogether grander place. Madame Delouvre's store was situated on Royal Street, where, according to Eliza Ripley, there were many high-status clothing establishments. Ripley described one such shop called Barrièr's, "where could be found all the French nouveatés of the day, beautiful barège's, marcelines and chiné organdies stamped in gorgeous designs, to be made up with wreathed and bouquet flounces."[54] She also described the popularity of bright colors, as well as luxurious materials for the women of New Orleans: "Bottle green gloves were considered very comme il faut. They harmonized with the green barége."[55] Delouvre's, which was described as a "fancy store" in the New Orleans City Directory of 1842, advertised itself as a "new and fashionable store, selling a variety of lady's clothing, including articles of fantasy."

By dressing in fine French clothing, Cécille was also making a visual statement about her identity and status. Elite free people of color deployed material expressions of their Frenchness in order to uphold their social position in the face of increasing prejudice, and also as a means of showing their European origins: "Those who had the resources would therefore fill their armoires with the latest French inspired fashion."[56] Cécille Bonille also proclaimed her Creole heritage during her lifetime by means of her material possessions. She may have also been showing an outward expression of her freedom, and as a testimony to her belief that she was the equal of white women.[57] Thus, by preferring to shop at an exclusive French store that was patronized by well-to-do women of both races, Cécille was upholding her right to do so, and effectively giving a slap in the eye to those who might not approve. Unfortunately, this also resulted in more debt.

Cécille's property was auctioned in an attempt to cover her debts, including her two houses and the two enslaved women, "Fanny, a negress aged 26 years, and Pauline, a griffa aged about 35 years."[58] As with Maria Josefa's real estate, which after her death was bought by the Darsse family to clear her debts, the house and land on Saint-Claude Street was bought by Cécille's married daughter, Antoinette Darsse, for $2,610, thus clearing her mother's debts. There was, however, little money left over from Cécille's estate for the children. At her death, three of her children, Amelia, Samuel, and John, were still in school. She owed $110 for their school fees and $71 to a private tutor.[59] Antoinette was married to a free man of color, Joseph Emile Darsse, thereby being the first of the generations, apart from Henriette Delille, to break with the plaçage tradition of the family. Sister Detiege maintains that it was her aunt Henriette who persuaded Antoinette to eschew the family custom.[60] However, perhaps Cécille also encouraged her daughter to marry. She had already broken tradition in her choice of partner, as a reflection of changing times and shifting power structures in New Orleans. Therefore, like other free Black families at that time, she may have encouraged Antoinette's marriage as a further move away from the old practices. She probably did not want her daughter to experience the difficulties that she and her mother had endured as plaçées. Indeed, Antoinette married into a prosperous family, thus combining the benefits of having a wealthy partner with the increased security of legal marriage.

Although Cécille's arrears were all resolved, there were still legal problems associated with the houses that she had bought for her children with their inheritance from Hart. These houses proved not to have been a wise investment, as they had not been well maintained. Cécille's brother, Jean, was concerned about the state of the two properties, "one of which had fallen down, owing to the giving away of the foundation by which accident the other brick house, which is said to be considerably damaged, has been rendered uninhabitable." Therefore, "the revenue of the said minors is much reduced, what remains is insufficient for their support." Jean advised that a portion of their property should be sold, or money borrowed to rebuild the house.[61] There were also further difficulties with these houses in the settling of the estate, because Cécille, who had bought them for $32,000, maintained that she had only received $15,196.95 from Hart's estate on behalf of the children, and therefore they owed her $17,639.41. Although Cécille had credited the children's account with the rents of the properties, she had also debited it for expenses such as education and clothing, thus the amount was never paid off, and the interest accrued. Her accounts show that at her death her children owed her, and therefore the estate, $25,020.89, an amount that the executors wished to recover from the children. Antoinette Darsse brought a suit against the executors. She claimed that as her mother took matters into her own hands by buying these properties without consulting the family and did not disclose that the children would be in her debt by doing so, the purchase of the property in the children's name should be annulled. However, during the investigations, it was also revealed that as Hart's estate totaled $171,960.22, and the fifth part of that was $35,435, which was presumed to have been received by Bonille. Therefore, she had in fact obtained more than enough money to pay for the properties, and the children could not be indebted to her.[62] The judge ruled that the executors could not recover the claim set up against the children of the deceased by reason of the purchase. The houses were finally sold in 1844 to John McDonogh at a huge loss for $18,900, which was then divided between the children.[63]

On the face of it, the succession and subsequent court case do not give a very favorable impression of Cécille. They seem to portray her as an extravagant woman who was concerned with outward appearances and possibly not very good at managing her finances. This was perhaps behavior learned from her mother, who had financial difficulties of her own. Cécille also made an unwise investment without notifying or consulting the parties concerned. However, her haste could have been because of her difficulties with Hart's other heirs, causing her to feel that she needed to get the children's legacy safely invested as quickly as possible. Subsequently, the court case revealed that she may have, in effect, tried to cheat her children out of some of their inheritance from Hart, as part of their legacy obviously went missing. Some of this extravagance may have been due to her desire to uphold her position as Hart's widow. She must have felt cheated out of the large amount of money that Hart obviously had wished to bestow on her; thus, she might have seen it as her due to take some of her children's inheritance. Upholding her status meant that Cécille probably relied upon the money bequeathed to her children, in order to try to make ends meet. Despite this, Cécille's admittedly extravagant lifestyle meant she still ended up spiraling into debt. She also may not have realized the implications of her financial dealings for her children in the event of her death. She seems to have been a strong-minded woman who thought she had made a good decision in her choice of partner, but her hazardous legal position became all too clear, as it did for many other women in her situation, after Hart's demise. Although he tried to ensure her financial security before his death, the lack of any legal marriage contract made it impossible for him to protect his partner from the claims of his European heirs.

After Bonille died, her daughter was able to sort out her financial affairs and ensure that the other children were not left penniless. She was by this time a prosperous businesswoman, buying and selling real estate in New Orleans. Her marriage also appeared successful as she lived with her husband until her death and had at least nine children with him. Interestingly, her family had also inherited the ambiguous racial appearance of Cécille's family. The census recorders enumerated them as "mulatto" in 1850 and as "white" in 1860. Also, although Samuel Hart's heirs had tried to disinherit the family, Antoinette appears to have been proud of her half-Jewish ancestry, as she named one of her children Joseph Rosendahl Darsse, in honor of her father's origins. Like her mother, she died young at the age of thirty-six in 1861 and left her property to her surviving children. Her eldest daughter, Staella, never married, in a trend that appeared throughout all the families studied in this research in the postbellum period and that will be discussed later in the book. She lived with another unmarried sister until their deaths in the mid-1880s.

Cécille appears to have been very much a woman of contradictions. Although she adhered to the traditions of her family by becoming the plaçée of a white man, she had a partner who was very unlike those of her forebears. He represented the changes in New Orleans after the Louisiana Purchase, with new people coming into the city from various European countries and other parts of America. Yet it also seems that rather than wholly allying herself with these new immigrants, Bonille very strongly identified with her Creole background throughout her life and in death. Although her life also appeared to emulate the myth of the indulgent free woman of color who was more concerned with money and fashion than anything else, she battled her cause through the courts. Even if she ultimately lost, she proved that a Black woman was capable of fighting against unfairness engendered by her race and gender. Unlike her sister and Eulalie Mandeville, Bonille relied on her connections and networks with white men, which in the end failed her, as they had failed her mother. Her daughter Antoinette, however, was a successful businesswoman who retrieved the family fortunes through her wise investments.

THE WIFE

Marie Dolores Laveaux Auguste

Although Cécille's daughter Antoinette appeared to have been fortunate in her choice of husband, many women were not, and they often endured years of unhappiness due to societal expectations or lack of finances. Marie Dolores Laveaux Auguste, the half sister of one of New Orleans's most famous free women of color, Voodoo priestess Marie Laveau, was one of these more unfortunate women. Marie Dolores Laveaux came from a similar background to Cécille Bonille, as she was brought up in a family from the wealthier echelons of New Orleans's free Afro Creole society. However, her parents, who were both free people of color, were married. Her father, Charles Laveaux, was the son of a white man and a free Black woman. His father was possibly Charles Laveaux Trudeau, who at one time was the surveyor general of New Orleans. Charles Laveaux married Marie Dolores's mother, Marie Françoise Dupart, in St. Louis Cathedral in 1802.[64] The marriage certificate described Laveaux as "the natural son of Marie Labeau, free woman of color and an unknown father."[65] As Laveaux's father refused to recognize his son, Laveaux may not have had the kinship and connections with New Orleans's elite white society that was enjoyed by some others in the free Black community. Although Henriette Delille and Cécille Bonille seemingly did not have any contact with their fathers, they had both been recognized by them as natural daughters. Thus they had a status that Laveaux lacked, although he appears to have been well-regarded in the free Black community through his own entrepreneurial efforts.

Laveaux's wife came from a prosperous free Black family, bringing a substantial dowry of four thousand dollars to the marriage.[66] In these days of arranged marriages, Laveaux's bride must have at least had the consent of her parents in order to marry. Both husband and wife came from business backgrounds. Laveaux was in the alcohol trade, and his name appeared in the City Directory of 1830, where he was described as a victualler. Then, in 1832, he was listed as owning a tavern on New Leveé, a notorious place for riotous drinking establishments. John Williamson Carey, a brick-making machine inventor who visited New Orleans in 1835, was amazed at how much commerce and activity there was in the city, even on "the Lords day." He wrote: "As I proceeded down old Leveé Street, the gambling and the liquor stores were all open and in full blast." He thought the scene was "unique, grotesque and profane."[67]

At the time of his marriage, Laveaux had already fathered Marie Dolores's more well-known half sibling, Marie Laveau—famed for her Voodoo expertise—after a brief relationship with her mother, Marguerite D'Arcantel.[68] Although it was a short-lived affair, Charles took an interest in his daughter by Marguerite. After the death of her husband, he helped to establish her in the alcohol business, as shown by his signature on a bond for a license to sell liquor (see fig. 5). That Charles put up the security for the bond shows his concern for the welfare of his natural daughter. Laveau may have also been working in one of his buildings. She was referred to in this document by her married name as Veuve (Widow) Paris. It also revealed that, unlike her educated half sister Marie Delores, who always signed her public documents with her name, Laveau was illiterate, as she could only manage a cross rather than a written signature. Thus, as with the family of Henriette Delille and Cécille Bonille, it seems that the Laveaux family also recognized the importance of education for girls. Marie Dolores's mother owned a delicatessen, and as a businesswoman she knew that she was giving her daughter an increased advantage in business if she followed in her footsteps by becoming an entrepreneur.[69] This was obviously not always the case for all free families of color, evidenced by Marie Laveau's illiteracy and the illiteracy of other women studied in this book.

For most of their life, Charles and Marie appeared to prosper, as evidenced by an inventory of their community property after the death of Marie François Dupart. The estate was valued at $10,631, and the number of enslaved people they owned put them into a high economic bracket for free people of color. At Dupart's death, their community property comprised "ebony, cherry and mahogany furniture, silverware, china, household linens and utensils, wearing apparel, a horse, three milk cows and their calves, two houses on Dauphine Street be-

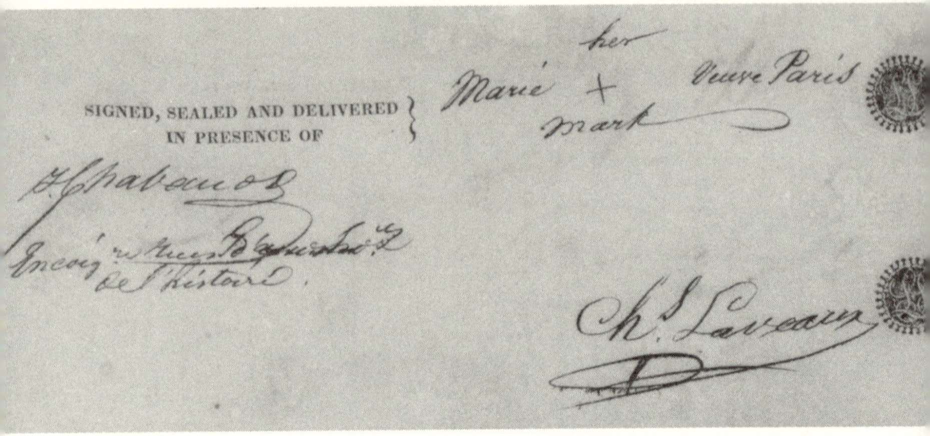
SIGNED, SEALED AND DELIVERED IN PRESENCE OF
Marie her + mark Veuve Paris
Ch. Laveaux

FIG. 5. Charles Laveaux signed a security bond for a liquor store for his natural daughter Marie Laveau, while seemingly not even giving a wedding dowry to his legitimate daughter Marie Dolores. New Orleans Office of the Mayor, Security Bonds for Having a Liquor Store Selling by the Pint and Above, Vol. 1, 1832, City Archives and Special Collections, New Orleans Public Library.

tween St Philip and Dumaine, a house at the corner of Grand Hommes (Dauphine) and Mysterious Columbus, in the Faubourg Marigny, a tract of land with buildings on Chantilly Road, and eleven adult slaves with three slave children."[70]

Charles and Marie Françoise had only two children, Laurent and Marie Dolores, who was born in 1804.[71] This was an unusually small family, as most married women of the time spent their fertile years in a near-continuous state of pregnancy, and large families were the norm. Marie Dolores was the younger of the two.[72] She may have been brought up in this house on Dauphine Street (see fig. 6), which was listed in the Vieux Carré Survey as belonging to Charles Laveaux, far away from his rowdy taverns.[73] This was a slightly grander house than the one Bonille and Delille lived in, as it had two stories and a balcony. However, the details of her childhood while living in this property remain as much a mystery as the childhoods of other women in this study. There are no more records of her life until 1818, when, at the tender age of fourteen, she married François Auguste.[74] Fourteen may seem young to be a bride by today's standards, but in nineteenth-century New Orleans, Creole girls were considered ready for marriage by their early teens. They also often died young, taken by childbirth or by New Orleans's many epidemics. Indeed, both Cécille Bonille and Marie Dolores died while only in their thirties.

Like her father, Marie Dolores's husband, François Auguste, was described as a victualler, so Marie Dolores may have known him through her father's business.[75] On 5 October 1818, Marie Dolores Laveaux, accompanied by her father, signed a marriage contract with François Auguste before the notary Narcisse Broutin. Auguste was described as a natif d'Irlanda (a native of Ireland). Their marriage contract revealed much about Louisiana's property laws, as well as about their union. In this document, Marie Dolores and Auguste agreed to "hold in common all goods, moveable or immoveable that they may acquire during marriage." It was also stipulated that "any debts that either parties may have are to be paid and acquitted by them before the celebration of the marriage and those [debts] that are unknown are to be considered null from the date thereof."[76] The document also gave details of any goods that would be brought to this union. Thus, under Louisiana law, the contract provided a measure of security for the prospective bride by enumerating her dowry, exempting her from any debts Auguste may have incurred prior to their marriage, and acknowledging that the couple would share community property.

Marie Dolores contributed "a bed, an armoire and a piano, in addition to other moveables for household use," valued at $500, which she had acquired "from the wages gained by her labor and savings and which the said François Auguste acknowledges as the dot (dowry) given to his account."[77] Husbands could not sell any property that was immoveable from their wife's dowry unless expressly stipulated in the marriage contract or ordered by a judge in extreme circumstances.[78] This was an important stipulation in the case of women who brought property to the marriage classified as immoveable such as real estate or enslaved people. However, in Laveaux's case, although she brought a substantial dowry for such a young woman, it did not include anything immoveable. Auguste brought nothing to the marriage. He was appar-

FIG. 6. A house where Marie Dolores Laveaux may have lived as a child. It shows the contrast between this more impressive property and the one in which Cécille Bonille and her half sister, Henriette Delille, were raised. *A Curious Building* (923–929 Dauphine), by J. O. Davidson, from *New Orleans—Picturesque Bits from the Older Portions of the City, Harper's Weekly* (6 December 1884), p. 811. Historic New Orleans Collection, 1974.25.3.717.

ently living in a house, probably either owned or rented by a previous wife or partner, as he declared that "the furniture in his household belonged to the three children of the late Marie Magdalen."[79] If this was the case, it appears Marie Magdalen had bequeathed her goods to her children after her death rather than to Auguste. As they were all still living in what could have been her house, she may have died shortly before Auguste and Marie Dolores were married. Also, there is no mention as to whether Auguste was the father of any of the children. He did not seem to have had any responsibility for them. He also had at least one other natural son, called François, with a woman named Fatina Detrèn, a native of Saint-Domingue. The child was born one year before he married Marie Dolores.[80]

Marie Dolores Laveaux signed the marriage contract with a clear hand, as did her father and the other witnesses. Auguste did not sign at all, not even with an *X*, declaring that he did not know how to write. The document therefore highlighted how François Auguste was an unlikely bridegroom for the daughter of a prosperous free Black family. This was a very unequal partnership from the beginning. She was a very young woman, marrying a much older man, possibly a widower with other children, and who seemed to have little or no money or goods. It did not seem, on the face of it, a very advantageous move for Marie Dolores or her family.

From the records, it was unclear exactly how much older François Auguste was when he married Marie Dolores. According to the Louisiana death records and *The Bee* newspaper, he died in 1873 at age ninety-six, which would have made him already forty-seven when he married Marie Dolores.[81] However, a census entry for 1850 recorded that he was born in 1790, putting him at twenty-eight when he married her, a more reasonable age gap but still many years older than her.[82] Although this was probably not any kind of love match, convenient strategic alliances were not unusual in New Orleans. The expectations surrounding marriage in the city were such that "for the young Creole woman, it was the pursuit of a husband not the pursuit of love, that became her chief preoccupation."[83] Marriages were often based on financial considerations rather than romantic ideals, but "with nineteenth-century expectations of men and women, and the valorization of wifehood and motherhood, they were expected to last until the death of one of the partners."[84]

There was also no record of Charles Laveaux contributing toward his legitimate daughter's dowry, as he did for his natural daughter, Marie Laveau, when she married.[85] This lack of any financial contribution or dowry from the father was unusual. However, there is a possible reason for this omission, which also suggests why Marie Dolores married Auguste. It may have been her choice, or it may have been forced on her by her father. The year before marrying Auguste, Marie Dolores gave birth to an illegitimate child named Laurent. Although this child could have been fathered by anyone and could explain why Laveaux hustled his daughter into marriage, evidence suggests that the child was possibly Auguste's. This would explain why Marie Dolores may have been willing to marry him. Her father could also have insisted upon this marriage against Marie Dolores's wishes. By this time, an illegitimate child might have created a scandal, damaging her future marriage prospects in New Orleans's upper-class free society, who were becoming more concerned with emphasizing the moral virtuousness of their community, and especially of their women. Although the child Laurent was baptized in 1824 as the legitimate son of Marie Dolores and Auguste, two years later, in 1826, Auguste and Marie Dolores filed a suit against the godparents, Laurent Charles Laveaux and Madeleine Marie Herveau, stating that the ceremony had been performed by them without the parents' consent. The Augustes then filed a petition declaring the child nonlegitimate and that the child's birth had been put forward one year to 1819 so that he appeared to have been born during the marriage of the petitioners. It is not clear why they did this, unless Auguste insisted on doing so in revenge after it was clear that the marriage was unsuccessful. Despite this, Auguste always treated Laurent as if he were his legitimate son, giving credence to the notion that he was indeed his father. Laurent and his wife lived with François and probably looked after him in his later years. He also bequeathed his house to him after his death. However, Laurent's untimely arrival may have meant that Charles forced Marie Dolores to marry François Auguste, thus solving the problem of the illegitimate child while signaling his disapproval of her behavior by not providing a dowry.[86] This is also probably why Marie Dolores married a much older man, of questionable finances and origins, rather than a man from an established New Orleans family.

Auguste's background was as obscure as his age. The marriage record described him as being from Saint-Domingue; however this place-name was crossed out at a later date and replaced by "Ireland."[87] Later census records also recorded his birthplace as Ireland. It is possible that he was of Irish birth, as there were small numbers of Black people living in Ireland in the eighteenth century. Many worked as servants of wealthy families; others were tradesmen, soldiers, traveling artists or musicians.[88] Despite his claim to Irish birth, though, there was no suggestion that he ever passed as white. He was always described as a "free man of color" in various legal documents. If he had passed, the Naturalization Act of the 1790s, which declared that "any alien being a free white person, may be admitted to become a citizen of the United States," would have given him the full citizenship denied to free Black people.[89] In 1825, Auguste traveled by ship from New Orleans to Santiago de Cuba and back again, suggesting that he may have had links there, but his country of origin on the ship's records was still named as Ireland.[90] If he was from Saint-Domingue originally, there were a number of reasons why he may have decided to obscure his origins. He may have been an enslaved person who had never obtained manumission legally, or, given the fears around Black people from Saint-Domingue spreading revolutionary ideals, he may have thought it expedient to conceal his heritage. This confusion around his identity is similar to that surrounding Hart and shows the difference between these new immigrants and the established Creole population of New Orleans. In antebellum New Orleans, opportunities for self-fashioning and refashioning abounded in a society where people and goods circulated widely. People could deliberately change their names and obscure their origins, in contrast to the old Creole families who proudly proclaimed their heritage. No doubt Charles Laveaux would have preferred an alliance for his daughter with another Afro Creole family of standing in New Orleans rather than an unknown man with ambiguous roots. For François Auguste, however, the chance to ally himself with a wealthy and established New Orleanian family probably inclined him to marry Marie Dolores rather than abandoning her with a child. It certainly appears that he may have benefited financially from the marriage, whether by association with Charles Laveaux or through the business efforts of Marie Dolores, as it was only after his marriage that he began to acquire multiple properties.[91]

That it was very much a *marriage de convenance* between Marie Dolores Laveaux and François Auguste is also evidenced by the way in which it did not take very long for trouble to occur between the ill-matched pair. The marriage began to break down after only a year. In 1819, Auguste went to the extreme measure of placing a notice in the *Louisiana Courier*, announcing, "his wife, Marie Laveaux, having left his bed and board since the sixth day of this month, he is determined to pay no debts of her contracting."[92] This was unusual because such notices were not generally published in the local newspapers until after a legal separation was sanctioned by the courts. In that case, such announcements were important, alerting creditors to the wife's changed legal status.[93] Thus, it might have been a ploy by Auguste to shame his wife in the eyes of society. However, there must have been some sort of reconciliation, because Marie Dolores and François then went on to have five children between 1819 and 1826: Marie Henriette, Eveline, Françoise, Hermogéne, and Felix.[94]

In 1824, Marie Dolores's mother died, aged around forty, after what was described as a "lingering illness."[95] The two siblings, Laurent and Marie Dolores, then filed a suit against their father to claim their inheritances. Marie Françoise Dupart had died intestate, but under Louisiana Civil Law, one-half of the estate, and their mother's separate property, should have been divided between Laurent and Marie Dolores. On 19 May 1825, Auguste, Marie Dolores, and Laurent took Charles Laveaux to court, accusing him of withholding sums of money, in particular the dowry brought to the marriage by their mother, amounting to $4,500, thereby attempting to defraud them. In retaliation, Laveaux claimed that despite the impressive inventory included in Marie Françoise's estate, after the debts had been settled, there was only $422 remaining, plus the $550 owed to Marie Françoise from the community property, making a grand total of $761.16½. Obviously, the dowry and other assets were missing, so Laurent and Marie Dolores eventually had to agree to their father taking charge of the sale of the properties and discharging all of his debts.[96] It appears that although the Laveaux family had been prosperous, by the time of Dupart's death, their fortunes had reversed. Auguste may have been disappointed that his wife did not inherit a large fortune, perhaps contributing to further disagreements.

The marriage between Auguste and Laveaux limped on for another four years, but in 1828 Marie Dolores decided to file for a separation of bed and board.[97] On the day that Marie Dolores filed her separation suit, Auguste placed another notice in the *Louisiana Courier* stating that he, "wishing to put the public on their guard, now declares that he will pay no debts contracted by his wife, Marie Laveaux." Thus, it seems that as before, Auguste did not mind letting the public know of his marital and financial problems and was also happy to broadcast the imminent breakdown of his marriage.

The cause of action for divorce entered the Louisiana Civil Code in 1827. Prior to this, spouses could only seek separation from bed and board under fault-based grounds. The sanctity of the family was a central theme in the eighteenth and nineteenth centuries. Since divorce was seen as a negation of this ideal, Spanish law did not allow absolute divorce. Thus, in the Spanish colonial era, only death could dissolve a marriage. Suits brought against husbands in the eighteenth century were virtually always based on the charge of cruelty, suggesting that this was the most legally acceptable ground for separation. Even after the Louisiana Purchase, divorce was still not an option. The 1808 Digest signed by William Claiborne also made clear that separation by bed and board did not dissolve the bonds of matrimony.[98] Even by 1827, a judgment of separation was required, followed by two years living apart without reconciliation, before divorce was granted.[99]

Marie Dolores may have been unlucky in her relationship with her husband, but she was fortunate in Louisiana law, which gave women increased power and independence from their husbands. The civil law allowed Louisianian women to keep their legal identity after marriage, a privilege denied to women in most states under common law. The common law of coverture virtually erased women's legal identity, declaring them femme couverts, or under the legal protection of their husbands. Women living under Anglo-American law lost legal ownership of the property that they had brought to the marriage as well as ownership of any income earned by them during the marriage. Women therefore became wholly dependent on their husband's economic support, making it more difficult for them to leave a marriage.[100]

In contrast, Louisianian women had the right to inherit equally with their siblings from their parent's estate. They also owned half the community property with their husband and could hold and control their own separate property. This gave them the motivation and the security to challenge a marriage that no longer served their interests. Marie Dolores Laveaux's subsequent actions proved that like many other free women of color in New Orleans, she understood her legal rights and trusted that the equity guaranteed her under the legal system would allow for the redress of her grievances against her husband.[101]

In her petition, Marie Dolores cited physical and mental abuse as the reason for wanting to separate from François Auguste, testifying:

> [She had] always lived with him and behaved like . . . a dutiful, tender and affectionate wife, and not withstanding all her efforts to preserve peace and harmony at home and to win the affections of her said husband, she has been intentionally ill-treated by him and of late been severely beaten without any provocation on her part whatever; that the excesses, cruel treatment and outrages of the said François Auguste . . . are of a dark nature to render their living together unsupportable; that he has not only ordered but actually turned her out of the matrimonial domicile and threatened to ill-use her if she should return thereto, and that in consequence thereof, your Petitioner [she] is reduced to the necessity of receiving from an acquaintance, Madame Montplaisir Thomas, that hospitality which is denied to her by the father of her children.[102]

By the nineteenth century, the sentimentalization of women and motherhood had also created an increased expectation of benevolent patriarchy, whereby traditional male misbehaviors toward their wives, such as authoritarian control, physical abuse, drinking, and unfaithfulness, were increasingly frowned upon. Husbands who continued to indulge in these vices were therefore at added risk of finding themselves in court, mostly on charges of cruelty.[103] In the case of a divorce suit, counsel often garnered increased sympathy for women by "the use of high emotive words such as 'most violent' or 'barbarously beaten.'" Lawyers then sought to prove that these vicious and uncivilized attacks served to demonstrate how these men violated societal expectations of manhood, proving that they were barbaric and undeserving of any support from the public and the courts.[104] Thus, Laveaux and her defense counsel detailed Auguste's crimes against her in order to secure her separation.

The defense also placed much emphasis on her affectionate behavior toward her husband and her attempts to win back his regard. However, witness testimony shows that Auguste was not willing to try to resolve the situation between him and his wife. A. Maurises recalled how he "went to see the husband in order to perform reconciliation between them [and] far from listening to such an offer told him that if she dared show herself he would break her bones with a big stick which he showed to him."[105] Use of weaponry against a woman was not unusual in antebellum New Orleans. Prewar court cases show that defendants often used an object to attack their wives: "The weapons and knives, trowels, slingshots, shoes, hand irons give insight into the incidents. In these cases, men grabbed whatever lay nearby and attacked their wives in the home."[106] The use of physical objects to abuse women formed an even more valuable tool for the counsel to argue in their favor, as it further emphasized the man's violent temper, lack of control, and disrespectability.[107] It was also revealed during the trial that Auguste was unfaithful to her with one of the enslaved women living in the family house. A witness stated "that he heard him say that he had one of his house as a wife and would continue to keep her as such."[108] This evidence further besmirched his reputation, but Laveaux's testimony about her ill treatment by Auguste was probably the deciding factor in the case.

Auguste's defense tried to tear down the petition of Marie Dolores by attacking her claims of wifely virtue, stating that "the testimonies contained manifold errors" and that what happened between him and Marie Dolores "was normal for a marriage." It was also alleged that Marie Dolores was a bad mother, "owing to her improvidence, carelessness, and habit of being constantly out of doors." She was also described as "unworthy by her habitual dissipation after the birth of her young children."[109] Thus, the defense countered the emotive language of the prosecutors by suggesting that Marie Dolores was an inadequate mother, a role that was considered her most important position in life, and by claiming that she was hardly ever at home to carry out her domestic duties.

The petition revealed much about Marie Dolores's marriage to Auguste. Although it seemed on the surface to be a straightforward case of husbandly abuse, petitions for separation could not always be taken at face value because there were often other underlying factors that contributed to the breakdown of a marriage.[110] This marriage was one of inequality from the start, with the big difference in status and wealth between Marie Dolores and her husband. They may also have been forced to marry through pressure exerted by Laveaux's family. Auguste may have resented that Marie Dolores could bring so much more in material goods to the marriage. Also, like her husband, Marie Dolores dealt in the buying and selling of properties. With her business and educational background, she may indeed have been more successful in her business life than he was, sparking further acrimony. Auguste was also slapping her in the face by openly conducting a relationship with one of the family's enslaved women. It is telling that Auguste was conducting an association with a woman who had no legal status or power, perhaps suggesting that he preferred this type of relationship to that with his wife, who had a measure of power over him. Therefore, although Marie Dolores's bid for separation was primarily as a result of marital abuse, under the surface other factors may have combined to precipitate a struggle over gender roles and distribution of power and property.

Many witnesses testified in favor of Marie Dolores's motherhood and domestic skills. One of them, while allowing that Auguste was "an honest man," refuted the accusations against her, noting that "his children and slaves are well kept and dutiful," the second statement seemingly contradicting the first.[111] Another also saw "the wife at home, taking care of her children and contributing to the cleaning of the house."[112] The judge therefore awarded Marie Dolores her separation of bed and board from Auguste. Importantly, he also gave her custody of the children, further negating Auguste's charges of her unfitness as a mother. It was still unusual at this time to grant full custody to the mother. As late as 1836, parental rights still conferred family authority primarily on the father: "Whereas the mother was entitled to reverence and respect, the husband still had a paramount right to custody."[113] Many women therefore stayed married to avoid losing their children. English-born actress Frances Kemble stayed with her husband, Georgia planter Pierre Butler, for many years because of this fear. Eventually she left Butler, who divorced her for desertion in 1849. The decree gave her a yearly allowance, but she could only visit her children for two months in a year. Thus, although she gained her personal, social, and economic independence, she essentially lost her children.[114] However, the idealization of motherhood also encouraged some judges to reject the traditional notion that children belonged to their fathers. By the 1820s, some judges evinced the view that children were better off with their mothers. They began to consider the matter of guilt in making child custody decisions. If the wife could prove her husband's guilt to a judge's satisfaction, he was more likely to award her custody of the children.[115] It appears therefore that this may have been the case in Marie Dolores's petition, as the judge also validated Auguste's guilt by granting her separation settlement. In accordance with the law, she was to receive the $500 she brought to the marriage. Marie Dolores was also awarded half the couple's community property, and Auguste was ordered to pay court costs, alimony, and child support. The couple's assets at the time were "mahogany and cherry furniture, china, silver ware, a looking-glass, kitchen furniture and washing tubs." The community assets totaled $7,117.50, half of which was awarded to Marie Dolores.[116]

The relationship between Marie Dolores and François Auguste was certainly a complicated one, as they did not live separately after the court case. Thus, Laveaux did not ever divorce Auguste, completely dissolving the marriage. Her settlement gave her the right to live entirely separately from Auguste. That she chose not to do so after having gone to all this trouble remains something of an enigma. However, it may have been easier for her to continue living in New Orleans as a quasi-married woman. Indeed, her daughter Lizida wrote of the scandal and judgments of other people in the community following the estrangement, which may have influenced her choices.[117] This may have been a reflection of the free community's increasing desire to be seen as respectable, responsible citizens of New Orleans.[118] Therefore, despite her will of 1820 still making clear that she was "separated from the body and goods of Auguste," Marie Dolores was still living at 159 Philip Street, which was also the address of her husband, indicating that they still shared a house together.[119] Marie Dolores and Auguste also had three more children after their legal separation.[120]

Despite still living with Auguste, Laveaux had the advantage of the independent wealth that underwrote her separation from her husband, making it much easier to completely sever ties from him should she choose to do so. She was able to control her own property and make a will in which she could leave her worldly goods to her children, without interference from Auguste. It would also perhaps not have been to her children's advantage to divorce him at this time, as he was making money in his own right, which would add value to the eventual inheritance of their children. If they had fully divorced and he had married again and had another family, their children's inheritance could have been diminished. Laveaux always had the option of leaving him at any time if she so chose, and that would have left him the poorer one. Thus, she may have had a measure of influence over him and his actions.

After Laveaux's will was written in 1829, there were no more records of her life until 1839, when she went to France. Although there is no concrete evidence to suggest that she went to France without Auguste, as there are no definite passenger records detailing her departure from New Orleans, it seems that her relationship with Auguste may have deteriorated again. She may therefore have moved to France to separate for the required two years in order to finally divorce him. This may also be indicated by her new address in New Orleans. She had moved out of the family home by this time and was residing on Dauphine Street in a house that had belonged to her mother. A more permanent move could also be inferred by her writing a new will before she left. On 25 March, before departing to France, she called notary Charles Victor Foulon to her home to make a new will. She still described herself as being separated from Auguste, and by this time she had "seven children, all minor, issue of my marriage with François Auguste: Laurent Auguste, Henriette Auguste, Lizida Auguste, Hermogéne Auguste, Mirtile Auguste, Telesfort Auguste, and Hermina Auguste."[121] She therefore must have actually given birth to around eleven children with Auguste, although many of them did not live to be named in her final will. However, despite being possibly further estranged from François Auguste by this time, she still named him as her executor and "defender of her property," thus showing that she still thought he was the best person to look after her financial affairs, and those of her children, after her death. She then departed for France, dying about three months after her arrival there, on 22 June 1839, at the young age of thirty-five. The causes of her sudden death remain a mystery. However, her succession confirmed that she "died in the city of Paris in the Kingdom of France."[122] Her body was returned to New Orleans for interment at St. Louis Cemetery No. 1.[123] It seems likely that two of her children, Henriette and Lizida, also accompanied their mother to France, while the others presumably remained with their father. New Orleans's passenger ship records of 1840 show that an H. Auguste, an eighteen-year-old woman, accompanied by someone two years younger identified only as Françoise, which was Lizida's first name, traveled from Le Havre to New Orleans shortly after Marie Dolores's death in 1839. This suggests that they either went to France after the death of their mother, or they were returning to New Orleans from France because of her passing.[124] A "negress" belonging to "Monsieur Auguste" also arrived on the same ship at a different time in 1840.[125] In her will, Marie Dolores's daughter Lizida documented the difficulties after her mother's separation and definitely suggested that it caused a split in the family, with Laurent and Hermina firmly on their father's side, whereas Henriette and Lizida supported their mother.[126]

Like Cécille Bonille, Marie Dolores's property had to be sold immediately to cover her debts, which amounted to the large sum of $7,236. However, unlike Bonille, Marie Dolores was a wealthy woman until her death. According to her succession, her properties consisted of:

> A lot of land, 344 Burgundy Street with buildings, a lot of land in Faubourg Marigny, with one brick house, 157 Champs Elysees, a lot of land in Faubourg Franklin with a brick building, two lots of ground adjoining each other in Faubourg Franklin, two other lots of land in the same Faubourg, two lots of ground in Faubourg Bouligny, parish of Jefferson, Delphine, a creole negress, aged about 30 years, a cook washer, Marchande, with her child Merantine, aged 10 years, Marie, a negresse, aged about 34 years, cook, washer and ironer, Louis, an American negro, aged about 18 years, a laborer and George, a negro aged 14 years, house servant.[127]

She also left instructions for one of her enslaved men, called Sans Souci, to be manumitted after her death and left him the quite considerable sum of 1,200 piastres.[128]

During her lifetime, Marie Dolores Laveaux obviously endured a miserable marriage, possibly forced upon her as a result of her having had an illegitimate child. She married a man of questionable background and resources, who was probably controlling and abusive. At this time, she appeared to be a powerless young woman who was controlled by men. However, Louisiana law ensured that this would not be the case for the rest of her life. She bought and sold property to improve her economic status and to provide security for her family. Indeed, according to the witnesses in the court case, she successfully combined motherhood with business interests, thus showing herself to be a resourceful and hardworking woman. The abuse from Auguste may have been a result of his reaction to her independence and business acumen, and the law, which meant that she could keep her legal identity after marriage, giving him less control over her. Her subsequent actions also demonstrated that she not only understood the law but also did not hesitate to apply it. Although she continued to live with Auguste for several years after the separation, her settlement from the court case meant she could have her independence if she so wished. Her untimely death was tragic as it appears that she may have finally cut ties with Auguste and could have been on the verge of starting again in France when her life was sadly cut short.

CÉCILLE BONILLE AND MARIE DOLORES LAVEAUX

Plaçée v. Wife

The challenges that Cécille Bonille faced during her lifetime may have further convinced her half sister Henriette Delille that she had done the right thing by eschewing any type of relationship with a man and instead building a community of women. While the sisters had their problems with the sometimes-overbearing masculine elements of the Church, they did not suffer the emotional and financial disappointments. While Bonille was seemingly happy with the wealthy Hart throughout his lifetime, she nevertheless ultimately ended up like her mother, constantly in debt. Indeed, both Bonille's and Laveaux's relationships show the possible pitfalls in trusting the judgment of men. Although Hart was presumably good to Bonille when he was alive, he failed to put in place any safeguards for her in the event of his death, even giving his executors the power to take her money, and leaving her vulnerable to the machinations of his relatives. Charles Laveaux was an indifferent father to his daughter Marie Dolores, by not providing a wedding dowry and cheating her out of her inheritance from her mother. Her husband was physically abusive and an adulterer.

Both Cécille Bonille and Marie Dolores Laveaux were therefore subject to various forms of patriarchal and social control. Both of them fought back against these restrictions with varying degrees of success. However, Laveaux's court case shows how a marriage contract benefited a woman in New Orleans, especially one who was already wealthy in her own right. Her husband tried to fight against the granting of a legal separation, knowing that he would be the financial loser. In contrast, Bonille's economic situation as a plaçée was much more precarious, as after the death of her partner she had none of her own finances. Even with legal backing and the support of some prominent white men, she still eventually lost her case as a legitimate heir and ultimately found herself in debt. This lack of any legal safety net may have also been one of the reasons why free women of color, especially those with property, were turning to marriage as a better bet than plaçage. Indeed, Cécille's own daughter evidenced how marriage could be more advantageous, as it was the actions of her husband that allowed Bonille's children to be able to inherit some money from their mother.

Despite this, the woman described in chapter 4, Eulalie Mandeville, showed what a financially astute woman could achieve, even if she had a domestic partnership with a white man. She proved that it was possible to keep her finances intact despite not having a marriage contract. Unlike Bonille, she did not put her trust in her partner. She kept her independence and ensured that her wealth was in her name only. This proved to be very beneficial when she was also taken to court by prospective heirs after the death of her partner.

4

TWO OF NEW ORLEANS'S BIG BUSINESSWOMEN

Eulalie Mandeville and Marie Couvent

A LABORIOUS AND ACTIVE PERSON
Eulalie de Marigny de Mandeville

Eulalie Mandeville was a woman who achieved remarkable economic success by cleverly navigating the oppressive forces around her. Like Cécille Bonille, she had a long-term domestic partnership with a white man. However, her extreme talent as a businesswoman and her reputation in New Orleans made her an economic entity in her own right, even if she did not have the protection of a marriage contract. Although she obviously had a loving relationship with her white partner, whom she lived with for many decades, she ensured that she alone maintained control of her monetary affairs. She was an astute businesswoman, and she carried this over into her private life. The value of this became clear after her partner's previously supportive white relatives took her to court after his sad demise. Although many previous studies of Mandeville's story have looked into the court case of *Mandeville v. Macarty* by concentrating on her relationship with her partner, this analysis will put it into context with her achievements as a talented businesswoman.

Born into enslavement on the Marigny plantation in 1771, Mandeville was to become one of the wealthiest free Black women in antebellum New Orleans. Although she was the daughter of an unknown enslaved woman, her father was Marquis Pierre Phillipe de Marigny de Mandeville, reputed to be one of the richest men in New Orleans.[1] He owned large tracts of real estate, living in luxury with his family in a mansion "surrounded by a village of slaves."[2] Marigny chose to recognize the young child as his "natural daughter," and she was placed in the care of her widowed paternal grandmother, Françoise de Mandeville. Eulalie was freed by her grandmother at age five. Thus, she never had to face the further challenges of enslavement experienced by women like Marie Couvent, who was enslaved until adulthood. Her grandmother also ensured that, unlike most enslaved people and some free girls, she was literate. She was also recognized to a certain degree by her other paternal relatives as being a member of the family. Indeed, one of her half brothers, Bernard Marigny, stated, "She passes in the family . . . as being [my] natural sister."[3] Thus, it seems that the Marquis's lawful children had known of Eulalie's existence from childhood onward. Bernard was the youngest son of Pierre Philippe Marigny de Mandeville and about ten years younger than Eulalie. He became a planter and a politician, although he is chiefly remembered as a land developer. In 1806, he subdivided the family's New Orleans plantation into an area that became known as the Faubourg Marigny.[4]

By the time Eulalie entered early adulthood, she had already shown her entrepreneurial inclinations by setting up a dry goods store on her grandmother's plantation, selling an assortment of wares, mostly cloth, accessories, lingerie, and other garments for women. Madame de Mandeville also helped her granddaughter's business aspirations by gifting her a large section of land before her death in 1779.[5] Her father also gave her land and cattle to set up a dairy. Her half brothers were equally generous. Bernard Marigny gave her two lots of land supplied with lumber so that properties could be built on them.[6] In 1803 or 1804, her other brother, Jean Baptiste Marigny, "gave defendant $350 with which she bought a lot of ground in Hospital Street." Dying in 1806, he left Eulalie an enslaved person in his will.[7] This suggests a familial regard for their "natural sister," as well as a sense of noblesse oblige engendered by their rank in society. Indeed, when testifying on his half sister's behalf in a court case that revealed much about Mandeville's personal and business life, Bernard Marigny stated that it was the custom among these high-status families to take care of their mixed-race relatives, maintaining that the gifts given to Eulalie were "generally done by fathers who had natural children."[8] That the brothers did not give Eulalie gifts until after their father's death shows that they felt a responsibility to continue their father's largesse toward their sister. Despite this, as a free Afro Creole woman, she understood that manumission and even acceptance on the part of her white family did not in any way equate to equality. She would never have the stability and security of her legitimate half sister, Marie Celeste. Thus, her desire to accumulate more wealth may have been motivated by attempts to consolidate her always-fragile freedom and that of her children, as well as further increasing her social standing. Like Cécille Bonille, the precariousness of her position would become all too clear after the death of her partner, and with the efforts of his family to drag her good name through the courts.

It was while she was still living on her grandmother's plantation that she formed a relationship with Eugène Macarty, a young man from another very illustrious family. Barthélèmy Daniel de Macarty, Eugène's father, arrived in Louisiana in 1732. He was a decorated French colonial officer. The Macarty family quickly became well established in New Orleans politics and real estate. Macarty's cousin, Augustine François de Macarty, was mayor of New Orleans. His son Barthélèmy Macarty became Governor Claiborne's secretary of state.[9] Thus, the two families were very similar in terms of their status within the New Orleans hierarchy. They were also quite interconnected. Eugène's sister Madame Miró was the godmother of Eulalie's half sister. Although Mandeville and possibly her family may have had an eye on an advantageous alliance with the powerful Macarty family, she certainly did not choose him because of his wealth. When she first encountered

Macarty, he had just come back from a long sojourn in France. He was practically penniless and had to borrow money from his sister to keep himself afloat financially.

Mandeville did not leave the plantation until the death of her grandmother. However, it is clear that she had begun a relationship with Macarty long before this, as her first child was born around 1794. In 1799, they set up house together in a large cottage on the corner of Dauphine and Barracks Streets in the French Quarter. During Eugène Macarty's lifetime, the relationship appeared to have been viewed as a near-marriage by both families. Indeed, Bernard Marigny emphasized the gravity with which this partnership was perceived. He stated: "This was a serious connexion, entered into with the consent of her family, the nearest approach to marriage, the law would permit and looked upon as morally binding." They had five children who survived to adulthood: Barthélèmy, Eugène, Pierre Villarceaux, Emerité, and Theodule. That the partnership also seemed to be approved by the Macarty family is evidenced by the baptismal records of St. Louis Cathedral, which show that they stood as godparents for Eulalie and Eugène's children, including his sister Catherine Macarty for Eulalie Macarty, born in 1799.[10] It was only after Eugène's demise that the family decided to sue Eulalie for everything she had accrued during their fifty-year relationship.

After Eulalie set up housekeeping with Macarty, she began her business in earnest. By selling goods in the streets, she was carrying on a tradition begun by enslaved people during the colonial period. During this era, there were many enslaved women vendors in New Orleans. These numerous marchandes not only added to the economics of the city but also enhanced the cultural richness and diversity of its life, an added attraction to the curious traveler. This is evidenced by the nineteenth-century *Historical Sketchbook and Guide to New Orleans*, which stated: "There are many colored marchandes selling callas and cakes, milk and coffee women, carrying their immense cans well balanced on their turbaned heads."[11] Benjamin Henry Latrobe also noted that some of these women provided a door-to-door service: "In every street, during the whole day, women, chiefly black women, are met carrying baskets upon their heads and calling at the doors of houses. These baskets contain assortments of dry goods, sometimes, to appearance, to a considerable amount."[12] He went on to say, "It was not then, nor is it now, the fashion for ladies to go shopping. The Creole families stick still to the peddlers."[13] Thus, middle- and upper-class white women were often confined to their houses by adherence to social convention, whereas the marchandes moved freely in the public sphere.

That some of these women became financially successful from the colonial era onward is evident from the actions of Don Fernando Alzar & Company, who in 1797, together with fifty other *mercadores* (merchants), petitioned the Cabildo (town council) to restrict the numbers of enslaved and free women selling merchandise in the French Market and on the streets of New Orleans.[14] They obviously saw the women as a threat to their livelihoods and also as an affront to their cultural values. In eighteenth-century Charleston, these women market vendors were also not always looked upon with approval by society. In 1786, jurymen complained of the "many idle negro wenches, selling dry goods, cakes, rice etc. in the markets." Four years later, market women were similarly described as "loose, idle, and disorderly." Some complainants characterized these women as "insolent, abusive, notorious, and impudent."[15] These comments suggest that even in the colonial period, these street vendors were already showing their increased confidence by interacting with their customers in a more equal manner. By not being submissive, which white people considered appropriate for their race and sex, this behavior was labeled as being disruptive. However, despite the unpopularity of these women vendors in some quarters of society, these African American women still came to dominate the trades of marketing, challenging the notions of white supremacy and patriarchal superiority in a slave society. Apart from becoming market vendors, enslaved women also used skills learned in bondage, such as sewing or laundry, to earn extra money for themselves and eventually to purchase their freedom.[16] Some of these women then went on to become property owners, sometimes owning multiple properties, and adding to their wealth by renting rooms or even entire houses.[17] All the women in this study used these methods to try to ensure their continued financial security and to consolidate their position within New Orleans society. Thus, they paved the way for their empowerment by virtue of their employment.

Eulalie was far more fortunate than most of them, benefiting from the largesse of her family. However, she capitalized on her advantages to build a business empire in the city. She began in a small way, initially using a room in her house to store and sell her dry goods. One of the witnesses for the Macarty family in the court case, J. Bermudez, tried to downplay her efforts by suggesting that she only made some money as "she didn't have much outlay because she owned her property and the slaves. She had a small store at her house, and her marchandes sold goods on the street."[18] Like many other entrepreneurs, she began by developing relationships with the wholesale merchants and with wealthy potential clients, modifying her products in line with current fashions. Many in the clothing retail trade had noticed a passion for all things French among the Francophone population of New Orleans. François Lacroix, an Afro Creole tailor and merchant, was renowned for supplying the latest French fashion for men. An advertisement for his store claimed that he had "the best and most extensive assortment of clothing of every description, made in Paris."[19] Mandeville started to do the same for her women clients. However, it was not only free Black women who were pursuing links with France in order to increase their profits. White businesswoman like Mrs. Durel, about whom more will be written in this chapter, also traveled to France to purchase merchandise.[20] Eulalie did not venture across the Atlantic herself, instead utilizing the services of her now-adult son, Pierre Villarceaux, who spent a good deal of his time in France. That he was very at home in the country is evidenced by the number of times he traveled there, eventually living in Paris in his old age. Indeed, he was perhaps educated there or, like his father, traveled there after completing his education, as was the custom for elite Creole families. Eulalie began commissioning him to buy an assortment of goods from Paris.[21] Pierre must have been good at picking out the feminine articles that would appeal to Eulalie's customers because she began to expand her business activities.

With the increase in her business, Mandeville also had more and more marchandes working for her. It was the Widow Chavenet, her neighbor and friend for several years, who first described Eulalie as a "gross marchande" (big businesswoman) because of the number of people she employed. It was not unusual for these entrepreneurs to purchase enslaved people to work in their businesses. In Charleston, so many businesswomen held enslaved people that they eventually dominated slaveholding within the free Black community there. The 1830 census revealed that at this time Eulalie held thirteen enslaved people, seven of them women, all of them probably adult, the youngest being aged between ten and twenty-three and the oldest, fifty-five to ninety-nine.[22] It is very clear, therefore, that Eulalie took advantage of her enslaved women's earning power in order to grow her business. Although these women would not have enjoyed any financial recompense for their services, evidence shows that Eulalie was also providing paid employment for free women of color. Chavenet described how, aside from her enslaved women, she had eight to ten other persons who sold for her on commission. These people took her goods, sold them, and "every 15 or 20 days would call and settle their accounts with Mandeville."[23] Hence, she was by this time the owner of a reasonably large business with international links, which was managed solely by her, and which catered to and was fully staffed by a large cohort of women, a remarkable feat in antebellum New Orleans.

Eulalie bought goods from other stores and wholesalers in the city but continued sending her son to France to purchase goods, which she then sold to favored customers. Casimir Lacoste, owner of a sugar plantation, and to whom Eulalie had lent three thousand dollars, stated, "When she received goods from France, she sent word to [my] family," probably to his wife and daughters. Lending money to the husbands of these elite women may have been another expedient way of ensuring that the men would then recommend her wares to their wives, thus creating informal contractual relationships. Terence Le Blanc also affirmed, "On receiving fresh goods, she would call on the ladies of the city and show them her wares, being in high favor with them."[24] Eulalie may have personally called on her wealthier clients, merely in order to offer them the chance to view her choicest products from Paris. However, like some of her contemporaries, who were skilled in the art of fashioning elegant and tasteful clothing, and coiffures, she could have also been providing a personal styling service.[25] The most famous of these was Elizabeth Keckley, a free woman of color who established a successful dressmaking business in Washington, D.C., serving as dressmaker and stylist to both Varina Davis, First Lady of the Confederacy, and Mary Todd Lincoln, First Lady of the United States.[26]

The skills of Black hairdressers were also valued among the fashion-conscious ladies of New Orleans. These abilities may have been engendered throughout the ages, as they were even noted by early travelers to the African continent, such as Cado Masto in 1456, who admired the elaborate hairstyles of African women. Expressing their femininity through their hairstyles was continued by the enslaved on their southern plantations. Jane Mickens Tombs, a former enslaved woman from Georgia, described how the women on her plantation still straightened their hair by combing it with the cards used for processing sheep's wool, and how they curled it by wrapping it overnight with rags.[27] For free women of color, these hairdressing talents could eventually translate into lucrative employment, as white women began to utilize their skills. Eliza Ripley reminisced about a free Black woman who was obviously talented in re-creating the elaborate hairstyles that were fashionable in New Orleans during the early to mid-nineteenth century: "Ladies had their hair done up with bondoline and pomatums made of beef's marrow and scented with patchouli; hair was done into marvellous plaits and puffs. A very much admired style which Henriette Blondeau, the fashionable hairdresser achieved was a wide plait surrounding a nest of stiff puffs. It was called the basket of fruit."[28]

A traveler to New Orleans, Sir Charles Lyell, referred to the "quadroon" hairdresser as "a refinement in which the richest ladies in Boston would not think of indulging."[29] Eliza Ripley also illustrated that the ministrations of both seamstresses and hairdressers were a normal part of everyday life for the wealthy of New Orleans: "Monday morning Mme Casimir or Mamzelle Victorine comes to sew all day like wild for 75 cents. . . . Later dusky Henriette Blondeau comes with her tignon stuck full of pins and the deep pockets of her apron bulging with sticks of bandoline, pots of pomade, hairpins and a bandeau comb to dress the hair of mademoiselle."[30] The titles of Madame and Mademoiselle that Eliza Ripley gives to the seamstresses but not to the hairdresser were also a significant indicator of race in New Orleans. In public documents, those of solely European descent were always identified using such titles. Sometimes married women from wealthy free Black families, or Afro Creoles with connections to high-status white families, like Eulalie Mandeville, were also given titles. However, most were referred to by their first name and surname, if they had one.[31] Henriette was also described by Ripley as "dusky" and wearing a "tignon," immediately identifying her status as a free Black woman. Those, like Henriette, who could offer a personal service, above and beyond that which could be offered by the client's own enslaved women, could make a good living. Also, Black women in New Orleans had an advantage over their peers in the North, because the southern elite were accustomed from childhood to intimate ministrations from enslaved people. Therefore, women from the South more readily accepted personal services from enslaved and free workers. Their peers in the North suffered more from the racial taboos of bodily intimacy, which meant that they mostly served a Black clientele, ultimately making their trade less competitive and less profitable.[32]

Eulalie's importation of goods from Europe also demonstrated the thriving link between Afro Creoles from New Orleans and other countries, especially those that were French- or Spanish-speaking. These links, both in Europe and the Caribbean, had become more important to free people of color as the nineteenth century progressed, and they found their privileges becoming increasingly limited. Many began to aspire to leave New Orleans in pursuit of increased political and racial freedom.[33] Indeed, two of Mandeville's children: Emerité and Barthélèmy, were sent away by the family to manage a coffee plantation in Cuba owned by Macarty.[34] They may have sent their children abroad in order to protect them from the increasing prejudice toward free people of color, as well as to provide them with a fresh start in a different country. Although the Spanish authorities had launched a general crackdown in Cuba in 1809, expelling refugees from Saint-Domingue, from 1814, the Spanish began inviting them to return to Cuba. Santiago de Cuba, where Eulalie's children settled, was a popular choice because it already had a large Francophone population of free Black people.[35] Barthélèmy married Maria Josefa Tabony and had four children: Albert Albin, Julia Josepha Hermina, Isabella Dolores, and Oscar. These children eventually left Cuba for France, probably after their father's death in the 1860s.[36] Emerité married Etienne Chére Rigaud in Cuba, and they had two children together, Eugène and Isabel Rigaud, before Emerité's untimely death. It also appears to have been common for some of these very successful entrepreneurs mentioned in the court case to retire to France once they had made enough money to live on. For example, both Lise Perrault, who was worth thirty thousand dollars when she stopped trading in New Orleans, and Aurore Matou, who was worth the same amount when she left the country in 1826 or 1827, went to live in France.[37]

The movement of goods and people as an integral part of these women's lives demonstrated the internationalization of New Orleans, first engendered by trade with other countries and then by the movement of refugees from Saint-Domingue to Cuba and then on to New Orleans. In the nineteenth century, nation-states had not yet mastered bureaucratic systems for monitoring migrants, facilitating ease of movement across countries. The idea of relocation to another country was also imagined by free Black children during the 1850s through to the end of Reconstruction in a school that was founded by the other entrepreneur to be studied in this chapter, Marie Couvent. They were asked by their teachers to write letters as if they were businessmen venturing into the world of the commercial markets of both the United States and Europe.[38] Their letters clearly show that they were aware of the benefits to be gained from the movement of goods and people to and from other countries, both in producing wealth as well as providing valuable connections.[39] Thus, many of the boys imagined themselves using these trade links and the wealth they engendered in order to start afresh in another country. However, this imagining of transatlantic markets and trade by the boys of the Couvent School in the mid-nineteenth century had already been played out by Eulalie Mandeville and other businesswomen from New Orleans.

Eulalie was also aware of the benefits of expanding her trade and business links within Louisiana. She therefore spread her business empire outside the city of New Orleans. According to witnesses, "Her operations extended into the country as far as Donaldson and even Attakapas. She had a large depot in the Parish of Plaquemines and some of her marchandes visited St. John the Baptist." This also suggests that she must have had agents working for her in these areas, as she would have been unable to monitor them all herself. The scale of her business was also remarked upon by Victor Romerage, a wholesaler, who said that "he knew people who merely made a living by selling at retail but they were not on so large a scale as defendant was." From early on in her business career, Eulalie also knew how to capitalize on events happening in the world around her. The wholesalers who did business with her stated that it was during the War of 1812 that the dry goods business became very lucrative because of the lack of merchandise. This was brought about by the blockades, which drove up prices. Therefore, as Romerage explained, those who managed to get hold of these products "sold their goods very high and realized a large profit."[40] That Eulalie was one of those who used the opportunities presented by the war to expand profits is evidenced by one of the other wholesalers stating that she "bought goods down the river during the war and realised a good profit."[41] Further merchants also attested to her business acumen. L. Sejour described Eulalie as "a person who knew how to purchase.[42] And Michel V. Durel, the executor of Eugène's will, stated, "The business was profitable then, and is so still when the persons know how to purchase and sell at retail."[43] These business professionals made it clear that Eulalie Mandeville was a talented businessperson who had earned their respect.

Indeed, Eulalie seems to have been far more successful in business than her domestic partner, who was very much the junior associate when it came to family finances. On his death, his assets amounted to little more than $6,000, from which he bequeathed $2,000 to his brother Theodore and to a nephew, and $500 to a niece. He also left $300 each to his natural children by Eulalie Mandeville.[44] His lack of wealth may have been due in part to his business mismanagement, but Macarty had other secrets, none of which were mentioned during the court case. Although Macarty lived with Mandeville until his death, he was unfaithful to her and fathered several other children with different free Black women.[45] The most famous of these was Victor Eugène Macarty. He was Eugène Macarty's son with another free woman of color, Héloise Croy, from Saint-Domingue, and became a talented musician and composer.[46] Although it seems that Macarty never acknowledged any of these other relationships or recognized any of these children because there was no mention of them in his succession, at some point he may have contributed to their upbringing. Their maintenance and that of their mothers may have also factored into his lack of funds. It was little wonder, then, that after his demise his collateral heirs cast greedy eyes on Eulalie's fortune, which at her death was close to $250,000 in assets, including eight properties in the city, six enslaved people, and over $150,000 in disposable cash.

She was taken to court by forty-five of Macarty's white collateral heirs, led by Macarty's brother in an effort to acquire the money and property held by her, which he believed should have been included as part of his brother's succession. The plaintiff's argument was that Eulalie never made much money from her business and that the real fortune was accumulated by Macarty, as a result of his investments. The plaintiff's petition also claimed that shortly before his death, Eugène had circumvented the legal requirements of the Civil Code by transferring a large amount of money to Eulalie's bank account.[47] The bulk of the defense was therefore taken up with establishing Mandeville's right to her fortune.

Several of the witnesses also highlighted the number of other free Black women who had run successful dry goods businesses in New Orleans. As one of the witnesses stated, "At that time Aurore Matou, Agate Fauchon, Mrs. Peuch, Mrs. Durel and some others sold as extensively as the defendant." L. Sejour also referred to two other women in his testimony: Agate Fauchon and Marie Louise Panis or Picou. The most well-known of these women was Agate, or Agathe, Fauchon or Fanchon. She was one of the first proprietors of what is now known as Preservation Hall.[48] Like Eulalie Mandeville, she owned multiple properties, which she bought and sold from 1804 until her death in about 1864.[49] She also branched out into other businesses. One of her properties had "several old buildings used as a charcoal and wood establishment," denoting that she either ran another business from there or rented it out.[50] Therefore, although Eulalie was much richer than any of these women, the court case demonstrated that there was a thriving community of prosperous businesswomen in New Orleans.

The court case also revealed that some of these women had established cooperative business practices for those in the same line of commerce. Male merchants had long formed associations and business groups in New Orleans, but this was the first hint that these businesswomen did the same.[51] Michel V. Durel's testimony demonstrated that both Black and white businesswomen cooperated in their commercial endeavors in order to maximize their profits. Durel declared that, while working at a dry goods' wholesaler, he was aware that Eulalie "purchased largely from that house in partnership with Mrs. Durel [possibly a relative, although Durel was unmarried] and others, which goods they divided amongst themselves and sold at retail."[52] Therefore, these women had recognized that they could get a better price if they bought together and formed a cooperative.

Durel was a fairly common surname in nineteenth-century New Orleans, and as her first name was never given, it is difficult to ascertain Mrs. Durel's connection to Mandeville. However, it is very significant that businessman Michel V. Durel was one of Mandeville's main supporters, suggesting a link with the family. One of the people who also came to court in her defense was Edmond J. Forstall, who was married to Clara Durel, the sister of Michel Durel. She could have been Mrs. Durel, as Forstall was also involved in the wholesale business and sold goods to Eulalie. It is therefore likely that Mrs. Durel was white, showing a cooperation between businesswomen that crossed racial lines. These associations were also probably as much about providing support as maximizing profitability. Whether Black or white, as women they could have been arousing public hostility through their business ventures, thus maintaining some sort of cooperation was also a protection.

Although collaboration across the races could be deemed unusual, this study has shown other evidence of cross-racial feminine cooperation, especially the attempt by Frenchwoman Marie Jean Aliquot to found a religious charitable organization with her friend Henriette Delille.[53] These associations may also have been more common for white women who were not born in New Orleans, like Aliquot and Mandeville's best friend, the Widow Chavanet, who came from cultures with different mores. In France, for example, the population was often more liberal in their views on equality for Black people, as evidenced by those who escaped to its more hospitable shores. Free people of color also had more status in Saint-Domingue, so white women may have had less concern about making interracial alliances.

For free women of color, the foundation of any association reflected the way in which cultural networks, religious institutions, and neighborhood affiliations became more important for an increasingly beleaguered free population, as a means of protecting their own interests. Their sense of feminine solidarity was also engendered by an enslaved past: "The terrible realities of slavery meant that women formed close-knit cooperatives in which female interdependencies were a fact of life."[54] This trend was also evident in social capital networks and in the formation of benevolent societies and women's clubs. Thus, their alliances not only gave free Black women an edge over their rivals but was also essential for increased support in a very hostile world. These women had to deal with discrimination because of their race as well as gender. Thus, as a consequence of their economic success, they faced even more criticism, and downright hostility, than did their white counterparts. A feminine business cooperative made sense.

The defense called several free women of color to testify on Eulalie's behalf, and their contribution to her case has been little noted and discussed, overshadowed as it was by the who's who of New Orleans's elite white males who also appeared for the defense. The first was Marie Louise Panis.[55] She was named as a successful businesswoman by the witness L. Sejour. Although she stated that she was not a personal friend, she obviously knew Mandeville through her business activities. Like many of the other witnesses, she emphasized the unusual size of Mandeville's business and the number of people she had working for her, thus also making clear that Mandeville's business was a very lucrative one.[56]

Besides Marie Louise, there were two other free women of color who testified. The first was Sophie Macarty, alias Sophie Mousante.[57] She had known Eulalie for forty years and also had a long-term relationship with Eugène's brother Louis Macarty, which lasted until his death.[58] The other was Modeste Foucher, probably the same Modeste Foucher who had been the partner of Casimir Lacoste, one of the other witnesses for the defense.[59] Both Macarty and Foucher stated that they had regularly visited the house that Eulalie shared with Eugène.[60] These social calls with other women who were in a relationship with men of a similar high social status signify another feminine network. These testimonies suggest that there was an active alternative social life, apart from so-called polite society, taking place in these drawing rooms. Despite this, like Panis, Sophie claimed that "she had always been on good terms with the defendant without being an intimate friend."[61] She also reiterated how Mandeville had enslaved and free women selling for her. Although these women would have received a court summons to appear or had a court appointed clerk come and take a deposition, it is very likely that they took more than a passing interest in the case. Like Mandeville, Panis, Foucher, and Macarty had white partners. Indeed, many of the businesswomen mentioned in the court case had relationships with white men. Witness L. Sejour recalled that "Aurore Matou lived with a white man named Pierre, since dead. Agathe Fauchon also lived with Mr. Heno."[62] Although some of them may have benefited from their partner's wealth or connections, their futures would also be uncertain if their partners were to die before them. They could therefore learn from Mandeville's defense should they find themselves in a similar position. Their appearance in court was also a reiteration of the rights of free Black women. Their free status meant they could testify, even against a rich and powerful white family like the Macartys.

Testimony from other witnesses for the defense also made clear that the creation of Mandeville's successful business was not due to any financial assistance from Eugène, who openly stated to a friend that he had returned penniless from France before he became her partner.[63]

He also made it very plain to his friends and colleagues that it was Eulalie's money that he used to set up his own money-lending business. A friend of Macarty's, Martin Duralde, described that "the defendant had received funds from her father, Pierre de Marigny. He [Eugène] told witnesses at all times that he was doing business with Eulalie Mandeville's money."[64] Apparently this was not so unusual in the business community of New Orleans's free Black women. Agathe Fauchon's partner, Pierre Heno, was a butcher who had such severe financial difficulties that he had to surrender his house to his creditors, and he lived with Fauchon in one of her houses.[65] These two women directly contradicted the image of the predatory penniless free woman of color or the tragic quadroon who sought a wealthy white man in order to gain from the relationship. These were independent, economically successful women who seem to have chosen partners for motives other than gain or financial stability. They were part of a set of women who would not be glorified in New Orleans travelers' tales, nor would they appear in any antislavery fictional accounts of biracial women. However, they were a force to be reckoned with in the courts. The plaintiffs tried to portray Eulalie Mandeville as a gold digger, but Eugène's openness to his friends and family about the state of his finances rendered that argument useless. Indeed, in southern society, there were men who entered marriage (or, in this case, a domestic partnership) "with little or no wealth and their unions with propertied women became their primary avenue to financial independence."[66] Therefore, the actuality could be very different from the accepted tradition of white male dominance within the domestic sphere, especially when it was the woman who held the purse strings. In Eulalie's case, it was she who was the higher earner of the partnership and the owner of more property, even in a relationship where she would be considered the subordinate by virtue of both her sex and race. The acceptance of her financial supremacy by the judge would be a significant factor in the outcome of the court case.

Eulalie's superior financial situation was also emphasized by the testimony of Mrs. Chavenet. It is probable that the Widow Chavenet was Eulalie's closest friend. She described herself as "a good friend of Eulalie Mandeville's" and said that "she had a good deal of regard for her."[67] She was the only one of the women to portray herself thus. Indeed, the other women emphasized the distance of their personal relationships with Mandeville. Chavenet was also originally from Saint-Domingue, thus again supporting the idea that such relationships may have been more common between Afro Creole women and white women from other cultures. Justine Pajaud was born in Saint-Domingue in 1769. She married René Lamothe Curtois in Jeremie in 1787. He died very soon after the marriage, and in 1790 she married Pierre Chavenet. They only had one daughter, Marie Bonne Melanie Chavenet, in 1792. In 1809, they came to New Orleans, most likely as part of the huge contingent of Saint-Dominguan refugees from Cuba. Perhaps feeling somewhat outcast by New Orleans society and alone in a strange land, Chavenet welcomed the friendship with Mandeville. Her husband, who was several years older than she, died in 1825, possibly leaving her feeling even more alone. Also, as free people of color were awarded more status in the Caribbean than in New Orleans, it may have been more usual for such close interracial friendships to flourish.

In New Orleans, animosity from white women was supposed to stem from the way in which free Black women, through their partnerships with white men, posed a threat to the sanctity of marriage and the family.[68] Despite her appropriation of a marriageable bachelor, however, according to the court witnesses, Eulalie seems generally to have maintained good relationships with her white family and clients, as well as her business colleagues. Therefore, it may be no surprise that her closest friendship was with a white woman. Her associations also emphasized the business and personal links between white Creoles and the free women of color. They lived in close proximity, did business together, and patronized each other's businesses.

The Widow Chavenet showed even greater intimacy with Eulalie, often helping her in her business, measuring out the goods, and she was also frequently present when the marchandes came to Eulalie for their payment. Chavenet was also regularly in attendance when Eulalie and Eugène were settling their finances.[69] Thus, her statement to the court was important in establishing that Mandeville and Macarty kept their finances separate and that Eulalie made her own financial decisions. Chavanet reported: "Macarty would say to Eulalie Mandeville that such and such a transaction was offered to him and asked if she wished to make an investment. She would then say yes, and either give him a check or money which she had in her armoire."[70] Her evidence made clear that Macarty did not consider that he had control over Mandeville's finances. Mandeville would probably have been grateful for Chavanet's robust defense of her in court, and they continued as friends until Eulalie's death.

All the court testimonies of these women were important in further emphasizing that Eulalie was an independent, successful businessperson in her own right, and helped her to win her case. They also delivered a further challenge to the establishment by exercising their rights as free people of color, testifying against the politically powerful Macarty family. Their declarations on Mandeville's behalf also ultimately contributed to her winning the case and keeping her fortune.

Historians have often speculated on the reasons why Mandeville was so successful in defeating the claims of such an influential family. It has sometimes been suggested that it was Eulalie's "performance of whiteness" that swayed the judgment in her favor.[71] Indeed, the masculine white witnesses often referred to her character and behavior, emphasizing traits that were considered inherently to be only displayed by those of solely European descent. Thus, Eulalie was described by her half brother as being "very steady, enterprising, industrious and economical."[72] However, this argument also implies that it was the magnanimity of the patriarchal establishment that rewarded Eulalie for her acceptable behavior. In contrast to this, other analysis puts Eulalie firmly back in control by suggesting that it was her prudence in being careful from the very beginning to separate her finances from those of the often-impecunious Eugène that resulted in the Macartys losing their claim. This meant that the judge could not "penetrate Mandeville's careful decades-long preparation of her claim to her property."[73] She always signed her own checks, and had her son Eugène Macarty Jr. deposit them in the bank for her.[74] Therefore, it could also be argued that it was Mandeville's business skills, which ironically the establishment may have also viewed as demonstrating inherently white traits, that allowed her to keep her wealth.

That Cécille Bonille did not also manage to retain her legacy from her white partner may have been attributable to a lack of planning on both their parts. However, from the beginning of her young adulthood until her court case, the less self-reliant Cécille had depended solely on her white masculine contacts for money, support, and advice, eventually with disastrous results. Mandeville safeguarded her future through her independence, ensuring that she would not have to rely on her white partner. She was also part of the New Orleans business community and may have received advice and guidance from her associates on all matters financial. Also, although like Bonille she had illustrious white male defenders, the testimony from her peers was equally important in enhancing her defense, which further ensured that it was impossible for the judge to award the disputed money and property to the Macarty family.

When she won the court case, Eulalie Mandeville was, by the standards of the nineteenth century, an old lady who had by then retired from the business world. She therefore did not live long to enjoy her fortune, dying in 1848 in her early seventies. During her long lifetime, Eulalie's acute understanding of how to operate within a racist and paternalistic antebellum New Orleans enabled her to achieve the maximum economic success. She used local events or trends to her advantage, obtaining goods during the war and accommodating the increasing desire on the part of Creole women to dress in the French style, by extending her business to France. She and Macarty were no doubt influenced by educational and philanthropic institutions that encouraged a broadly Caribbean and Atlantic perspective, inclining them to a more cosmopolitan view of the world.

Like many wealthy white fathers, Macarty may have ensured that one of his sons was educated in France, thereby inadvertently helping Mandeville's business to spread beyond the confines of New Orleans. During increasingly difficult times for free people of color, Mandeville and Macarty sent two of their other children out of the country, perhaps hoping that they would have more opportunities to become rich, or simply start a new life. All of their choices would have a far-reaching effect on their children, as will be discussed in chapter 5.

MARIE COUVENT

Refugee, Entrepreneur, and Philanthropist

Another businesswoman who became a well-known philanthropist through her deathbed legacy was Marie Couvent, or Marie Justine Cirmaire or Sirnir, as she also often called herself. She had none of the advantages of birth that Eulalie had enjoyed.[75] Indeed, her life history aptly illustrates the many abuses endured by enslaved women. According to her will, she was born around 1756 in Guinea, where, at about the age of seven (she was never sure of her true age), she was taken to Saint-Domingue by traders to be sold into enslavement.[76] This was unusual because young children were rarely taken to other countries. The Trans-Atlantic Slave Trade Database shows that children made up only 19 percent of the enslaved people taken from Africa to the Caribbean between 1751 and 1775.

Without parents or any other adult guardians, the trip must have been a traumatic one for the young girl. Although women and children were usually left unshackled during the journey, this did not stop them from experiencing other violations at the hands of the crew. Even girls of Couvent's age could potentially be abused. In 1779, the captain of the French ship the *Amiable Françoise* reported one of his crew for the rape of a girl who was aged between eight and ten. He described in graphic detail how the man forcibly closed her mouth to stop her screaming, and how the violations took place on three nights and "put her in a deadly state." According to the captain, this abuse did so much damage to the child that it decreased her value in the Saint-Dominguan slave market by one thousand livres. The captain was therefore reporting the man not so much in defense of the child but because of a loss of income.[77]

The trip also took its toll on the unwilling passengers in various ways, as disease was rife and rations often inadequate. Therefore, as the ship neared the port of Cap Français, the crew would try to enhance the appearance of their captives in order to get a better price for them. They were bathed and their skin rubbed with palm oil. Many of the sales took place on the ship, with buyers coming aboard to inspect the captives before they disembarked.[78] We cannot know what horrors Marie experienced on the ship or where she was sent after her arrival in Saint-Domingue. However, as she was so young, it was unlikely that she went to a plantation; more probably she remained in the city, perhaps to be trained as a domestic servant. As the main port for the whole of Saint-Domingue, Cap Français was a bustling city, described as the "Paris of the Antilles" for its urban amenities and cosmopolitan air. Nevertheless, for a seven-year-old girl from Africa, it would have been a frightening and strange place.

Marie was eventually held by a man called François Moreau, an inhabitant of Cap Français who worked as a merchant tailor and owned many enslaved people. She was still enslaved at the age of twenty-five in 1782, when she had a son called Celestin. Described as being of mixed race and a "natural child," he was born out of wedlock and thus was held by Moreau, who may have been his father.[79] It is conceivable that Marie was freed by Moreau, as manumissions favored those who had relationships with white men, or she may have had the means to purchase her own freedom. Despite eventually gaining her free status, as a "bossale," or African-born person, she would have been considered to be at the bottom of the racial hierarchy of the colony.

Couvent lived in Saint-Domingue for about forty years, possibly remaining enslaved for at least eighteen of them, maybe more. The bloody conflicts of the revolution forced her to leave and seek sanctuary elsewhere. Tragically, she did not depart from Saint-Domingue with her son, as she had lost contact with the child when he was only ten, well before her arrival in New Orleans.[80] It is not clear exactly when she arrived in the city, although it is probable that she was one of the refugees who came to New Orleans from Saint-Domingue in the early nineteenth century. She may have traveled with Jean Moreau, François Moreau's brother. His family left Cap Français around 1804, and Couvent's first will made clear her close connections with him and his family.[81]

Marie Couvent owned property in New Orleans from 1806 onward, so it is probable that she brought some wealth with her from Saint-Domingue. Even if this was the case, many free Black refugees still faced more challenges than their white counterparts after they relocated to New Orleans.[82] That free Black refugees from Saint-Domingue were often looked upon with more disfavor by New Orleanians is evidenced by the remarks of George Washington Cable, who wrote, "They were an unaspiring, corrupted, and feeble class, of which little was feared, and nothing hoped."[83] Contemporary writers also vilified free Black women from Saint-Domingue for their lack of morals.[84]

Couvent's position was worse than that of a mixed-race individual. Her purely African origin made her more vulnerable to losing her free status once she arrived in the city. In 1810, "the territorial courts of Louisiana decided there was a significant difference between quadroons and other *sang-mélé,* (half-bloods) on the one hand, and blacks, on the other, as the former should be presumed free. Negroes who claimed to be free would be required to establish their right to freedom by such evidence as would destroy the force of presumption arising from color."[85] Thus, Couvent could have attracted increased suspicion on the part of the authorities as to whether she was indeed legally free. Free Black refugees often sought increased protection by creating a trail of documentation attesting to their free status, and also by the testimony of fellow refugees, especially that of wealthy white families like the Moreaus.[86] Couvent may have had to call on the testimony of her previous enslavers in order to attest to her free status; thus it was important for her continued freedom to maintain her links with the family. Many refugees from Saint-Domingue also banded together in New Orleans for support and protection and to aid settlement in this new society. Couvent was a middle-aged to elderly woman when she arrived in New Orleans, and the upheaval may have been harder on her than on younger immigrants. The Catholic Church would also have played an important role in providing stability for Couvent, as it did for many of the refugees. That Couvent was a lifelong supporter of the Church is evidenced by the bequests in her will.

Although Marie's free status may have initially been verified by the Moreau family when she arrived, her purchase of two lots of land in 1806 further strengthened her claim, as only free people of color were allowed this legal right.[87] After buying her first real estate, Marie lived in New Orleans without incident, conducting her business and adding to her wealth. However, in 1812, when she was about fifty-five years old, she became ill enough to think that she might die and called a notary, Narcisse Broutin, to her house. She dictated her first will to him, which reveals much about her networks in New Orleans. It makes clear her continuing relationship with the Moreau family, as she appointed Jean Moreau as her heir. It seems paradoxical that Marie would bequeath all her worldly goods to someone from a family who had perhaps physically abused her and possibly parted her from her still-enslaved child. However, Marie may have believed that the only way to ensure her son's freedom, at least after her death, was by the appointment of Jean Moreau as her heir. His inheritance was on condition that he "locate the heirs of Francis Moreau, and free her son."[88] In addition to naming Jean Moreau as her universal legatee, Couvent also chose him as her executor.[89] Therefore, like Cécille Bonille, she appointed a white man to carry out her legal transactions. It was also the custom for free Black women from Saint-Domingue to engage a white man from the island to assist and advise them on any legal matters, not only for protection but also as a way of maintaining the old ties.[90]

She also left one of her two houses to "Demoiselle Leonice natural daughter of Emilite Moreau, the widow Monet." Leonice was the granddaughter of François Moreau.[91] Again, although this also seems generous on the part of Couvent, as already observed in discussion of the life history of Eulalie Mandeville, relationships between the enslaved and their enslavers were often complicated. There was often a two-way process where paradoxically, despite their cruel treatment, some of the enslaved came to have affection toward these families, especially those who worked in closer proximity.[92] Also, her continued connection with the Moreau family sustained her hope that she might be reunited with her son, while providing some continuity in a strange environment.

The other bequests in Marie's will also further demonstrate these often-complex relationships between enslaver and enslaved person, as she also left her other house to one of her enslaved women, Séraphine. Although the house would only be Séraphine's during her lifetime, reverting to Jean Moreau after her death, this bequest clearly shows a hierarchy in the Couvent household. It demonstrated the different ways in which she viewed her various enslaved people. She appeared to have emotional attachments to some, whereas others were merely investments. At the time she wrote her 1812 will, she had five enslaved people in her household: Séraphine and her ten-month-old son, Nöel; Sophie and her young daughter, Simonette; and a fifty-six-year-old man named Bernard. She also wanted Séraphine, Nöel, and Bernard to be freed after her death, for their "good and loyal service."[93] However, she made no mention of Sophie and Simonette, who presumably would have been sold to cover her debts or were part of Jean Moreau's legacy. On the day after she made her will, and probably while still feeling that she was going to die, as she also received the last rites, she married a free man of color called Bernard Couvent.[94]

Previous life histories of Marie Couvent have implied that Bernard Couvent may have freed her, and that she gained wealth through her marriage with him, in a more patriarchal reading of her life history.[95] However, recent research suggests that it was in fact the other way around, as it was Marie's enslaved man, Bernard, whom she married on that day.[96] Thus, it was unlikely that he was the source of the couple's wealth. The marriage was recorded in St. Louis Cathedral by Antonio de Sedella, stating, "Bernado, legitimate son of Simon and Maria a negro libro married Ester negra libre who had bought his freedom." The named witnesses of the marriage also suggested that it was Marie Couvent who married Bernard, as they all came from the Moreau family. One of them was Maria Antonia Moreau, Jean Moreau's daughter, and the other was his niece, the widow Moné (mother of one of Marie's estate beneficiaries).[97] Although the woman was named Ester in the document, in the 1812 will, Marie called herself Marie Justine Sirnir, "dite Esther," suggesting that this was also another name she used, and making it even more likely that this was her marriage record.[98] It is not known where the surname of Couvent came from, but it may have been derived from "convent" because Bernard and some of his relatives had been held by the Ursuline nuns.[99] But as Marie well knew, having a second name was important in that it made a free person indistinguishable from those of second- or third-generation free families.[100] Marie had bought her enslaved man, also called Bernard, from Mrs. Mary Wheaton in 1811, "with all the diseases by which he can be attacked and his good and bad qualities, as [she] has known him for a long time."[101] This description suggested that Bernard may not have been the best investment, thus the mention of some sort of prior relationship between Marie and Bernard may have been her motive in purchasing him. There was no record that her enslaved man Bernard was ever officially manumitted, and as on the day before the marriage he was still listed in her will as being enslaved, it is unlikely that she ever officially freed him. Therefore, if it was him that she married, he was falsely declared to be a free man.

It was often the custom among Saint-Domingue's free people of color for enslavers to marry their enslaved people; thus, Couvent may have been continuing a recognized Saint-Dominguan practice. This method of claiming freedom was well known in New Orleans. Enslaved mothers sometimes gained free status for their children by having them baptized as such, by the Catholic Church. Sympathetic Roman Catholic officials such as Père Sedella, who married the couple, were also often complicit in these deceptions.[102] However, after they were married, the Couvents set about creating a document trail that validated Bernard's status, both as a husband and thus a free man. As a former enslaved woman and immigrant, Marie would have been very aware of the crucial role of documents in sustaining claims of free status, so they created papers to validate this.[103] After 1818, all notary records in which Couvent bought and sold enslaved people acknowledged that she was authorized to do so by her husband. Bernard was also listed as the head of the household in numerous city directories from 1822 onward.[104]

Marie may have married Bernard as an altruistic gesture to ensure his freedom. However, as a refugee from Saint-Domingue who was now living alone in New Orleans, apart from her enslaved people, she may also have wished to create a new "American" family for herself.

This would be beneficial in terms of providing extra support and companionship. Indeed, the marriage proved to be a long-lasting and advantageous one for her in terms of building stronger familial bonds and forging local networks in the Crescent City.

None of Couvent's public documents make clear exactly how she managed to amass all her wealth. However, by her death in 1837, she was worth $19,145.87.[105] Although she could not be counted as one of the wealthiest free Black women in New Orleans, this was a respectable fortune for a former enslaved woman and refugee from Saint-Domingue who could neither read nor write. The notarial records suggest that she made money through the purchase and subsequent sale of enslaved people. She bought and sold at least twenty-five slaves while living in New Orleans. Like many others, she benefited financially through their unpaid domestic work, and she could also rent out their services. The inventory taken from her estate recorded the occupations of two of her enslaved young men, Pierre and Sylvain, who were described as "day laborers." Thus, their services were very marketable. She also often sold enslaved people for more than she paid for them, and some of the women had children while in her service, considerably adding to her investment.

Evidence also suggests that like Mandeville, she sold dry goods. Her estate inventory contained large quantities of items commonly sold as dry goods, such as "185 handkerchiefs" and "25 schawls."[106] Jean Moreau's occupation was described as "marchand," both in Saint-Domingue and New Orleans, and his entry in the 1805 New Orleans City Directory described him as a storekeeper. Therefore, it is conceivable that Marie might have worked for him as a street vendor in Saint-Domingue, gaining firsthand experience of the skills needed to run a dry goods business.[107] She may have joined the ranks of the marchandes, who paid their enslavers a monthly sum and were left to find their own lodgings in the Little Africa district of Cap Français. She also speculated in real estate, taking advantage of the credit offered by Eulalie Mandeville's half brother Bernard Marigny. She bought her first property from him in 1806 for five hundred piastres, promising to pay the total amount in eighteen months.[108] It was clear that by this time she felt financially secure enough in her business ventures to take on the debt. When she first bought the lot in 1806, it consisted of one house. However, by the time of her first will there were two houses on the lot, suggesting that she may have had the second one built in order to rent it out. Archival records indicate that "she lived in the original property at the rear of the courtyard for thirty-two years."[109]

Somewhat strangely, given the change in her circumstances and fortunes, Marie did not alter her will until 1832. This suggests that she had a continuing connection with the Moreau family and still had hope of her son being located. Indeed, Jean Moreau continued to vouch for her financially, endorsing the notes Couvent used to pay for the purchase of enslaved people in 1810, and again in 1823.[110] She only changed her will when, once again, she felt close to death. This will, however, would be radically different from the one she wrote in 1812, and it denotes the changed circumstances of her life. By this time, Marie Couvent had also petitioned for, and was granted, the emancipation of two of her enslaved women, Séraphine and Fillette, in 1831, for "assisting in long and grievous spells of sickness," suggesting that she and her husband had not been in the best of health.[111] Indeed, Bernard had begun the process of freeing these two enslaved women but died before completing the manumission in 1829.[112]

The household was also badly affected by the cholera epidemic of 1832. It took the lives of two people, Séraphine and an enslaved man named Joshué.[113] As Couvent wrote her new will eight days after the death of Séraphine, and with cholera already in her household, she could have been suffering from the disease or thought that she had it. In this will, Marie states that she had no children; thus it appears that she either had given up hope of locating her son or that he had already died. Marie Couvent changed not only her heirs but also her executor, by appointing a free man of color, Henry Fletcher, to take over the task. Henry also called the notary to the house when Marie was feeling so ill. In this new testament, she also left the house in which she lived, and its land, to Nöel, Sanon, and Ezaline, "natural children of Séraphine, already deceased." The 1832 will also makes clear that at least one of Séraphine's children was also Bernard's, because she left "two hundred piastres to Sanon Bernard Couvent, natural son of my husband." However, another son of Séraphine, Jules, who was still enslaved, did not receive anything and was in fact bequeathed to his half brother Nöel. This further suggests that Nöel and Ezaline may also have been Bernard's children. Marie had four other very young enslaved people in her household, namely "Pierre, around fourteen years: Radisse, around thirteen years, Sylvain, around thirteen years, and Silvana, eight years." She bequeathed Sylvain to Henry Fletcher, on the condition that he was to be freed after Fletcher's death. The other enslaved people were to be sold to pay off any debts.[114] In fact, Pierre absconded after Marie's passing, and a large reward of one hundred dollars was offered for his return. This was not unusual after the death of an enslaver, as enslaved people sometimes took advantage of the turmoil to flee. The notice in the newspaper, which was placed by Henry Fletcher, also specifically cautions English captains of steamboats and others against harboring him under the penalty of the law, as this was a very popular method for runaway enslaved people to flee New Orleans.[115] Pierre's bid for freedom may have been successful as there was no record of any recapture.

Couvent's second will demonstrates the continuing levels of demarcation in her household. She even differentiated between the children of her favored formerly enslaved woman Séraphine, preferring those who were probably also the offspring of her husband. She also left legacies to two other free people of color: Phrosine Ballon and Louis Chesneau, and also acknowledged Bernard Couvent's granddaughter, who was married to Chesneau, by leaving one hundred piastres to her infant son, also called Louis. These bequests further show how far Couvent had moved away from her ties with the Moreau family and that she had assimilated into New Orleans's free community.[116] This may have also been due in part to the influence of her marriage, as her husband was part of a large network of enslaved and formerly enslaved people who had been held by the Ursuline nuns.[117] Bernard also had a large extended family, of which Marie became a part. She stood as godparent to Bernard Couvent's grandchild, also called Bernard after his father and grandfather. Bernard's son also had a daughter, who was given the first name of her adopted grandmother.[118] Finally, Bernard and Marie's extensive business connections with New Orleans's free community may have caused her to distance herself from her old refugee ties. For example, Henry Fletcher was a carpenter like her husband and possibly a business colleague.[119]

Although Marie Couvent thought she was near death in 1832, she lived for another five years, dying in 1837. Her succession also reiterates how her circle of family, friends, and acquaintances were now from New Orleans's free Black community. For example, family meetings to appoint a guardian for Séraphine's minor child, Ezaline, included names from some of New Orleans's most well-known free Black families, such as Joseph Dolliole.[120] By the time Marie had passed, Séraphine's eldest child, Nöel, had predeceased her, dying earlier in the year. His expensive funeral, which took place in St. Louis Cathedral, shows the depth of Couvent's affection for him and provides further evidence of her by-now large circle of contacts within the free community. Fifty-one people were invited to his funeral at a cost of thirty-four dollars.[121] On the undertaker's receipt, he is referred to as her "petit-fils" (grandson), showing the bond of kinship that Marie now felt with her adopted New Orleans family.

The family that Couvent created resembled the social organization of many West African societies. Although enslaved people were defined as outsiders in these West African communities, they could change their status by forging bonds with their enslaver's family, eventually being incorporated into the family group.[122] Although Marie was perhaps too young when she was taken to have absorbed her society's culture, this more African ethos of enslavement existed in Saint-Domingue among free society, whose attitude toward the enslaved differed from that of white people.[123] Thus, Marie may have been continuing Saint-Dominguan practice in her creation of kinship bonds with certain members of her household.

Marie's will of 1832 also shows that she had forged a strong connection to New Orleans's free Black society, by her wish to bequeath something meaningful to her adopted community. She therefore directed in her will, "my land at the corner of Grands Hommes and Union Street will be forever dedicated and employed for the establishment of a free school for the orphans of color of the Faubourg Marigny."[124] In her previous will, all her accumulated wealth would have gone to white people; now it would directly benefit New Orleans's free Black population. According to Rodolphe Desdunes, the notion of bequeathing land or money for charitable purposes was not common among free people of color at this time. Henriette Delille was founding her lay society, and they had only just begun their charitable work. Desdunes acknowledged Couvent's contribution to the Black community, writing, "She was the first amongst us to give the example of enlightened charity, and for a long time she was the only one who held this distinction."[125] Certainly it would seem that some of her contemporaries were more preoccupied with the accumulation of property in order to benefit their heirs than with thinking about the future of their community.[126]

Scholars have speculated about the reasons why Couvent chose the foundation of a school as her philanthropic bequest. The location of Marie's house may have influenced her choice. The front part of the property faced the Ursuline Convent, which offered education for all races.[127] Indeed, Bernard Couvent and his family had been held by the nuns, perhaps imbuing them with a sense of the importance of education. However, her preoccupation with schooling may have also been as a result of her Saint-Dominguan background. This study has already noted that education was perceived as important in Saint-Domingue and that many of the refugees were better-educated than New Orleanians. Couvent would also have seen the importance of the written word when she was first brought to Saint-Domingue. She may have seen the documents that were exchanged between the captain of the ship and the trader who held her in captivity. Thus, the knowledge that writing confers power may have stayed with her from the beginning of her journey, especially as she was illiterate.[128]

Couvent may have also noticed that there were few or no educational opportunities for free Black children in New Orleans whose parents could not afford to pay for private education. As early as 1813, there had been private schools in New Orleans for boys, but there was no provision for the education of the poorer members of the community, except what was offered by the Catholic Church. Therefore, Couvent's bequest could perhaps also be counted as a political one because the restriction of Black people's education was a way of ensuring white hegemony. However, although Couvent was aware of the potential liberating effects of knowledge for these children, her bequest could have been motivated more by a genuine desire to help the most unfortunate in her society, those who were orphans. She may have identified strongly with the plight of these children since she had been an orphan from seven years old. They were also the least likely to receive any care, as there were no specific institutions for them at this time.[129]

Marie directed that the school, which was to be called L'Institution Catholique des Orphelins Indigents, be founded under the auspices of Father Constantine Maenhaut or his successors, for the education of free Black orphans.[130] Her appointment of a Roman Catholic official to oversee the building of the school demonstrated her continuing links to the Roman Catholic Church, which had initially probably been important in providing further support and continuity for the displaced Couvent. She acknowledged her allegiance to the Church throughout her lifetime. Many of the important events of her life were conducted in St. Louis Cathedral, including her marriage, baptisms, and various funerals, even her own. She may have also been acknowledging the power of the Church, recognizing, like Delille, that the patronage of a Catholic priest for her project meant that it was more likely to succeed. In addition to Father Maenhaut, she placed much confidence in Henry Fletcher, trusting that as executor of the will, he would see that her wishes were carried out.

Marie died in 1837. Her by-now extensive networks in New Orleans and her reputation within the community are evidenced by her large and expensive funeral, which was held at St. Louis Cathedral. One hundred invitations were sent out to mourners at a cost of $81.62. She was buried with her husband in St. Louis Cemetery No. 2, where her tomb still stands.

It would not be until long after Couvent's death that the school came into existence. According to Rodolphe Desdunes, this was because Couvent's trust in Fletcher was misplaced. Apparently he kept her legacy secret and misappropriated some of the funds. Instead of ensuring that the work to establish the school was carried out, he seems to have disposed of some of the property and used the money for himself.[131] Another source claims that it was New Orleans's public officials who deliberately delayed the opening of the school, which wasn't built until eleven years after Couvent's death.[132] There have also been suggestions that it was Maenhaut who delayed the project, in order to protect it from the management of lay wardens who controlled the finances of the Catholic Church in New Orleans. By 1844, the Louisiana Supreme Court had ruled to diminish the power of these wardens, making it safe for Maenhaut to proceed.[133] The difficult economic situation of the late 1830s and early 1840s may have also contributed to the delay in implementing Couvent's wishes. When Couvent died in 1837, there was a nationwide depression caused by a series of transatlantic financial crises. The situation did not resolve until 1843.[134]

Wealthy and influential members of the free community may have also been galvanized into further action. In 1841, the city's three municipalities each created their own public-school systems after receiving authorization from the state legislature. Although free Black people were obliged to pay the taxes that supported these schools, their children were excluded from them. The eventual establishment of Couvent's school may have been a response on the part of an aggrieved population when it was made clear that their children would be denied access to public schooling.[135] However, according to Desdunes, it was Father Maenhaut who eventually became concerned at the delay and decided to intervene. He sought the help of François Lacroix, a wealthy free man of color, and a society was created to oversee the project, which "called for an account from the executor of the will concerning the misuse of the properties involved. Restitution was duly made, and a settlement provided for the establishment of a primary school for the orphans of the Third District."[136] Through donations and fairs, the society was also able to buy other land to extend the acreage available for the school.[137]

Despite all the challenges, the school finally opened in 1848, enrolling forty-three orphans in the first year. The school also began to admit nonorphans, and by 1853 it had a total of 240 students. The orphans were taught free of charge, but children with parents could pay what they could afford. Some came from poor families, while others were the sons and daughters of skilled artisans, entrepreneurs, and property owners.[138] Maenhaut was supposedly in charge of the school, although this was probably as a sop to the authorities, who wanted to have a white man at least ostensibly in control. In fact, the society oversaw the running of the school. Only free Black men and women taught at the school, and some of these were the most eminent French-speaking intellectuals and writers in New Orleans's free society.[139]

The history of the foundation of the L'Institute Orphelins, as told by Desdunes, revealed much about the class divisions within the free community. While praising Marie Couvent, Desdunes speculated why little was known about her. He attributed it to a lack of a network of descendants and relatives, even though she had an adopted family and a vast network of her husband's relations. However, these were humble, uneducated, often enslaved or formerly enslaved people from the lower echelons of free society. As an African-origin woman from Saint-Domingue, she was not connected to any of New Orleans's prominent white families. Also, as a member of the artisan class, she was probably not known to any from the elite class of Afro Creoles like Desdunes and his associates. However, the large number of people at her funeral attests to her being well-known in certain quarters of free society.

Desdunes's reading of the history of the school has patriarchal and elitist undertones. He suggests that Couvent was guided in her choices by Father Maenhaut, thus intimating that she would not have made such a decision of her own accord. His accusations against Fletcher for not carrying out Couvent's wishes may have been spurious and also hint at elitism, as Fletcher was also an artisan, and although he was literate, he was probably not a very educated man. The running of the school by free people of color from the higher echelons of free society may have meant that it was never the sanctuary for the poor orphans that Couvent may have envisaged. Although it was one of the few institutions in Louisiana to have its finances, building works, and teaching controlled completely by African Americans, there has been some division of thought as to whether it catered to the poorer Black children of the city.

Some scholars are of the opinion that it became an academic refuge for wealthier Afro Creoles in the Marigny neighborhood, whereas others argue that evidence about charitable donations and testimony from some of the students suggest that it was indeed considered as a public school by the community.[140] However, that the school's board was not completely free of class prejudice is illustrated by an exchange between several of the board members concerning the building of a branch of the school in Faubourg Tremé, where some of the poorest free Black people resided. One of the committee members responded with disfavor, suggesting that poor children should walk if they wanted a free education. Although the members finally decided in favor of sourcing a suitable property in Tremé, this never happened. Thus, it could be argued that Couvent's wish to provide a school that catered exclusively to the poorer members of her community was never fulfilled.[141]

The story of Marie Couvent illustrates how a formerly enslaved "outsider" could transcend all expectations to become a successful property-owning businesswoman. When she first arrived in New Orleans, she still felt bound to her enslavers through family ties and a sense of uncertainty. But she soon gained the confidence to start her own business, speculating with her money and property to achieve her wealth. In the process she became an active member of New Orleans's free society and eventually wished to contribute in some way to help people like herself, the poorest and least educated of her community.

Like all the other women in this study, her life demonstrates the complicated interrelated relationships between whites and Blacks, enslaved and free, and how these lines could become blurred over time. Couvent built various networks of support in New Orleans, first with her white enslavers and then with certain of her enslaved people. Her marriage enabled her to become part of a much larger network of enslaved and free people in New Orleans, which ultimately contributed to her well-being and probably her financial success. Without this, she may not have contemplated leaving money for the founding of a charitable institution. Although Marie Couvent might have been disappointed that it did not always appear to cater to the children whose lives she had hoped to improve by education, it was the first school of its kind and paved the way for other schools and charitable institutions.

EULALIE MANDEVILLE AND MARIE COUVENT

Conclusions

Although both Mandeville and Couvent became wealthy during their lifetimes, Couvent's attainments could perhaps be counted as the more notable because of her inauspicious childhood and young adulthood, as opposed to the much more privileged Mandeville. Although Couvent did not attain her greatest achievements until middle age (or even old age by the standards of the time), her transition during her lifetime from enslaved to wealthy propertied woman is remarkable. The two case studies show the diversity of the businesswomen who managed to attain wealth in antebellum New Orleans. While some of them were from the higher echelons of New Orleans's free society, others, like Marie Louise Panis and Marie Couvent, came from a background of poverty and enslavement and were often illiterate.

Despite this, there were some commonalities of experience for both Mandeville and Couvent. Both were formerly enslaved by wealthy white families with whom they had a connection. Although Eulalie's former enslavers were also bound by kinship, nonetheless Couvent sometimes also relied on her former enslavers when she arrived in New Orleans. However, Eulalie maintained close ties with her white relatives until late in her life, whereas Marie's connections with the Moreau family weakened as she assimilated into New Orleans's free Black community. It is telling that these ties diminished when she became a successful woman in her own right and after she engendered supportive relationships with the free and enslaved Black community in New Orleans.

Both of these women created networks of support. Couvent initially engendered relationships with some of her enslaved people, which eventually resulted in her becoming part of a vast network of relatives, friends, and colleagues in the free Black community. Mandeville established successful commercial relationships with both men and women, and with the plaçées of wealthy white men. However, her closest friend and the one on whom she appeared to rely most on for support was a white woman. This may have been due to Mandeville's upbringing, as in her early years she mainly associated with her white relatives.

Both women were also enslavers, having power over the lives of their enslaved people. Mandeville's background may have accustomed her to utilizing the services of enslaved people without much thought, so she had a distant relationship with those she enslaved, putting them to work in her business. There is no record of her ever having manumitted any of them or of making provision for them after her death. Although Marie Couvent had endured enslavement for many years, she, too, had no reservations about making her money from the buying and selling of enslaved people. However, unlike Mandeville, her background may have disposed her to form relationships with certain of her enslaved people. Indeed, it appears that she eventually married one of them. Couvent also differentiated in her treatment of her enslaved people. While she manumitted some of the favored ones, and even formed familial bonds with them, she treated others as solely economic investments.

The two women probably differed in the way they viewed the free Black community. Mandeville was perhaps more focused on ensuring that her children would benefit from her hard work. She and Macarty seemed to have thought that it was better to remove certain of her children from the free Black community rather than investing in it. Perhaps because of her background, Mandeville did not feel much allegiance to free Black society as a whole, whereas Couvent, as a person with no family and a stranger in New Orleans, would have been grateful for the support given to her by people in the free Black community. Although initially she may have relied on the advice and guidance of white people from Saint-Domingue, she achieved her greatest financial success in New Orleans after she had engendered networks within the Black community. Her background in Saint-Domingue may have inclined her to form these relationships with certain of her enslaved people, which led to her forming closer bonds within the free Black community. The Saint-Dominguan preoccupation with education may have also predisposed her to found an educational establishment. Her own personal tragedies of being taken away from her parents and then losing her son may have also led her to leave a legacy benefiting orphans, the most disadvantaged of New Orleans's Black society.

Thus, although Eulalie Mandeville was the wealthier of the two women, Couvent is the one more remembered, and her name features in tours of New Orleans. Although in the 1990s her name was removed from a school in the city because of her slaveholding, her contributions to the Black community are still acknowledged. Like Delille and the sisters, her gravestone has been restored and a new plaque put on it, whereas Eulalie Mandeville's tomb now lies in ruins in St. Louis Cemetery No. 2.

5

RESILIENCE AND TRANSITION

The Macartys and the Augustes

Previous chapters have looked at the lived experiences of a cohort of free women of color during the antebellum period, focusing on those aspects that had an influence not only on their own lives but also on their city. By establishing businesses and various other institutions, and by buying land and real estate, these women helped shape the environment around them. Economic and personal stability was helped by their supportive networks, which consisted of colleagues, friends, and relatives. Initially, the women's drive to accumulate wealth and property was an effort to provide a better future for themselves and their children. As the position and privileges of free people of color eroded during the antebellum period, however, some in the free Black community began to recognize that the success of the next generation also rested on the continuation of a cohesive community, while others advocated escaping the strictures of New Orleans. These conflicting views impacted the life decisions of three of the five women studied here. Delille and Couvent chose to support the community with donations and the creation of charitable institutions, while Mandeville sent three of her children abroad, hoping to give them a better life away from New Orleans.

The changes in antebellum New Orleans, with its increased prosperity, and the influx of people from other lands would have an impact on their lives. Their choices in life would, in turn, influence the lives of their children. Therefore, as a continuation of their stories, this final chapter looks at the children of two of the families, the Macartys and the Augustes, in the late antebellum and Reconstruction eras. The life trajectories of the children of Marie Dolores Laveaux and Eulalie Mandeville may have surprised the two women, but they mirrored the ultimate life paths of many other families of free women of color in New Orleans.

None of the five women could have foreseen the societal consequences of the Civil War, which would completely transform the world of their descendants. No one in New Orleans was exempt from the sweeping changes brought about by the war, and perhaps none were more affected than the wealthier members of its free population. During the postwar era there was a decline in the value of property holdings among the formerly free in skilled occupations: "Between 1860 and 1870, the mean value of real-estate owning black bricklayers dropped from \$2,888 to \$1,022; among carpenters from \$1,406 to \$948; among merchants from \$10,925 to \$6,925; among grocers from \$10,480 to \$3,067; among shoemakers from \$1,972 to \$804; among cigar makers from \$1,780 to \$1,403; and among boarding house keepers from \$2,794 to \$2,243."[1] There was also a drop in the proportion of former free women of color who owned real estate, from 28.4 percent in 1860 to 13.5 percent a decade later.[2] Many of New Orleans's white residents suffered from the same problems of increased poverty, but some free people, especially those from the upper tier of free society, were also concerned about the potential loss of their social status, which had been below that of the white population but above that of the formerly enslaved.

In a new order that increasingly classified people as purely Black or white, they were afraid of losing their standing. Thus, the culmination of the Civil War may have led to an identity crisis for former free people of color. There was a strong belief in certain quarters that because of the changes in attitudes toward their status, there were only two main options available to them: either becoming part of the political leadership or crossing the color line.[3] There was also the third option of leaving the South in the hope of obtaining increased equality and political rights elsewhere. Some feared that those who did nothing would inevitably lose their position as Afro Creoles, becoming part of a generic Black community. Many of the decisions taken by wealthy former free people after the war therefore may have often been more aligned with their individual needs than with wishing to change political or racial ideology.[4] Despite a professed avowal of a "common cause" among all of the Black community, some of that group viewed the aftermath of the war as a disaster for property-owning free people and sought to rectify the situation.[5] Some who entered the political arena may have been more concerned with maintaining the privileges of—or obtaining further privileges for—the former free community rather than representing all of New Orleans's Black citizens.

While this may have been the case for some, as this chapter demonstrates, there were also those who genuinely saw the Reconstruction period as an opportunity to gain more equality for the Black inhabitants of New Orleans. Some of these were elite members of the former free community and were therefore not only well-educated and wealthy but also often closely linked to the city's leading white Creole families through business, friendship, or kinship. These political activists may have imagined that through their connections they could form a diplomatic bridge between themselves, the white population, and the newly freed, for the benefit of all. Thus, enterprising men such as Louis Charles Roudanez and Paul Trèvigne advocated that, apart from emancipation, African Americans should have the right to hold office, operate their own school system, and determine their collective and economic future.[6] The political and ideological aspirations of these former free men of color were also clearly outlined in two short-lived newspapers, *L'Union* and *Le Tribune*, that were published from 1862 to 1869 and circulated to the Black community.[7] The children of the women studied in this research also held their own views about what was good for them and their society. They took their own different paths, both during and after the Civil War, often reflecting society at large and the attitudes engendered by their own family backgrounds. Two of their descendants became political activists, often featuring in these newspapers' articles, whereas others took the path of least resistance.

THE IMPACT OF THE CIVIL WAR

The Civil War could be counted as a catalyst for major societal and cultural change because it forced free people of color to consider their allegiances. Were they loyal to the free population, divided itself by class and status? Or to a wider Black community, including the formerly enslaved? Or did their commitments remain with their white Confederate kin, fighting to retain racial slavery and ensuring states' rights? Or, indeed, was their devotion to their home city of New Orleans and the state of Louisiana? Certainly, when Louisiana first seceded in 1861, it appeared that many free people of color rallied around the Confederacy. About 1,500 free men formed a militia called the Native Guard in order to assist the other Confederate militias in its defense of the city and the state against the expected invasion from the North.[8] The *Gazette and Sentinel* recorded the meeting that voted for this support: "The free colored population made resolutions to offer their services to the Municipal authorities in case of invasion by the enemy; and if they are allowed to form themselves into military companies, they take the engagement to take arms at a moment's notice for the defense of their native soil and fight shoulder to shoulder as their fathers did in 1814."[9] Armand Lanusse, a leading free citizen, and teacher at the Marie Couvent School, had addressed the meeting in favor of joining the Confederate cause. The resolution to form a militia was adopted by the committee, which included one Villarceaux Macarty, Eulalie Mandeville's son. By this time Pierre Villarceaux would have been in his mid-fifties, the large fortune left to him by his mother further consolidating his status as a member of the highest elite in the free community. Some Black women also supported the war effort. Shortly after it began, the city established a Free Market to help feed the wives and children of soldiers whose companies fought far away from Louisiana. Women organized "Colored Ladies' Fairs" at the Free Market, which opened each night, as well as elaborate dances to raise money for the cause. In November 1861, the free community also organized a "fancy colored ball" to benefit the Free Market. It provided another propaganda opportunity for the *Daily Picayune* to report about the support for the war by the free Black population. An article entitled "Darkies Dancing for the Benefit of the Free Market" went on to say, "It is quite refreshing to see colored people dancing for the benefit of the sisters, mothers, daughters and wives left at home by our heroes. What would Lincoln say to this?" These balls were also successful in raising money for the cause; this one procured six hundred dollars for the Free Market.[10]

Historians have debated why many of New Orleans's free Black people reacted to the call to arms by joining the Confederacy. Indeed, after the war was over, many of them expediently defended their position by claiming that they had felt pressured to do so. They insisted that they would have been vulnerable if they had refused. This was a valid point in a city where free people of color felt increasingly beleaguered.[11] The violence toward them after the war, which will be discussed below, is also an indication of what might have happened if they had declined to support the Confederacy. It could be argued that it was mostly the wealthy, high-status free people of color who joined the Confederates, because they often had close family ties with white Creole society. As prosperous slave and real estate holders, they also had more to lose in the event of a Union victory. As a result of their background and upbringing, these wealthy Afro Creoles may have identified more closely with whites than the enslaved, so they felt little compunction about siding with them.[12] Indeed, previous chapters have discussed the sometimes-strong sense of kinship between these families, despite the lesser standing of free Black relatives. For example, although Pierre Villarceaux Macarty had seen firsthand the way in which his mother's name was dragged through the courts by his Macarty relatives in an effort to relieve him of his inheritance, he supported the Confederacy, and at his death, he remembered some of his white relatives in his will.[13] However, awareness of their subordinate status could have also precluded free people of color from having such a strong identification with their oppressors. They may have aspired to the lifestyle of the dominant group without necessarily wanting to associate themselves with it.[14] Thus, it seems that free Black people's support for the Confederacy may have been as complicated as the tangled relationships between these interracial families.

Also, the free elite comprised only a small percentage of the community, not enough to have accounted for the numbers of recruits. Those poorer free people of color who did not hold enslaved people or land had, on the face of it, much less reason to support the Confederacy. Nevertheless, the numbers of free conscripts imply that many of them also supported the cause, at least in the early days of the war. Free people of color may have hoped that by joining with the other troops, they could at least maintain their position during the war and possibly also achieve a measure of increased equality with their participation. If this was their aim, however, they were soon to be disappointed. They found out that equality with the other troops was not forthcoming, as the Confederate officials did not supply them with arms or uniforms or, indeed, assign them to any duties of importance.[15] However, the aforementioned article in the *Gazette and Sentinel* suggests another possible reason for their support. By evoking a shared experience of a war in which inhabitants regardless of race fought to protect New Orleans from the British, the article may have appealed to their sense of loyalty to their home city.[16] Indeed, following the occupation of New Orleans, Armand Lanusse attempted to defend his actions by stating that his support of the Confederacy was a reflection of his loyalty to the State of Louisiana and his fellow Creoles. He also reiterated his connection to the white families of New Orleans by asserting that although he endorsed the decision of free men of color to join the Union army, for his own part, he had to decline to fight against the Confederates whom he saw as childhood friends.[17]

After the vote to join the Confederate army, two battalions were formed that were modeled after the French Chasseurs d'Afrique. The line officers were all Afro Creole, although Governor Thomas O. Moore appointed a white officer in overall command. This militia was very short-lived and did not see any action in battle. It was disbanded after the occupation of New Orleans by Union forces in 1862.[18] After the occupation of New Orleans, some free Black people may have pragmatically switched sides, with the dawning realization that the Confederates were unlikely to win the war.[19] One of those who famously changed his loyalties was André Cailloux, one of the first Black officers to be killed in combat for the Union side. Cailloux was born into slavery but was manumitted by his enslaver when he was twenty-one. By the time of the war in 1861, he was part of the prosperous free elite of New Orleans. He was also active in the free community as a philanthropist, providing funds to the Marie Couvent School. At the outbreak of war, Cailloux was commissioned as a lieutenant in the Confederate Native Guard, but he subsequently changed his allegiance to join the Union side.[20] Telesphore, the son of Marie Dolores Laveaux, was also one of those soldiers who switched sides. He and his brother Mirtile initially volunteered for the Confederate Native Guard as private soldiers.[21] However, after 1861, Telesphore changed sides and served with the Union army in the Seventy-Fourth Regiment, United States Colored Infantry, and then in the Ninety-First Regiment, United States Colored Infantry.[22] The defections of Cailloux and Auguste may have been influenced by the stance of two influential Afro Creole newspapers, *L'Union* and *Le Tribune*. Realizing that a Union victory was inevitable, they began suggesting to their readers that the in-between position of free people of color, rather than being a disadvantage, would enable them to have an active role after the war. According to the newspapers, by providing cultural mediation between Black and white people, they could influence the founding of a future environment of social and political equality.[23] With the defeat of the Confederates on the horizon, the free Black community was perhaps striving to do what it had always done, which was to protect its future. Some of its number may have concluded that the best way to do this was to join the winning side, subsequently working on the inside toward a favorable outcome for their community. However, the reality of the aftermath of the war and Reconstruction would provide many challenges for the free community, and also for the Macarty and Auguste families, whose lives will be examined more closely in this chapter.

MANDEVILLE AND MACARTY'S "MULATTO" SONS

At Eulalie Mandeville's death in 1848, the petition for her succession stated that she had four surviving children: Barthélèmy, Eugène, Pierre Villarceaux, and Theodule.[24] At this time, Barthélèmy was still living in Cuba. His sister, Emerité, Eulalie's only daughter to have survived to adulthood, had died in Cuba before Eulalie. However, Emerité's children, Eulalie's grandchildren Isabel Rigaud and Eugène Rigaud, received their mother's portion from the succession.[25] During her lifetime, Eulalie's considerable fortune had given her children prosperity and financial security. Her succession now established them as one of the wealthiest free families of New Orleans.

Mandeville's court case revealed that the three sons who lived in New Orleans— Eugène, Pierre Villarceaux, and Theodule Macarty— were openly acknowledged by white people in the city as being the offspring of Eugène Macarty. This open public acknowledgment of their paternal origins during Eulalie's lifetime demonstrates the acceptance of the mixed-race natural children of prominent white Creole citizens in New Orleans society. This was to change after the Civil War. With the advent of increasingly binary attitudes toward race after the emancipation of the previously enslaved people, New Orleans's white families started to distance themselves from their Afro Creole relatives.[26] In addition to increasing nervousness on the part of white Creoles about compromising their own racial identity, the diminished status of the free community was in part to blame for making white relatives more nervous about admitting family ties.[27] Grace King's written work about the "illustrious" families of New Orleans exemplifies this mounting desire on the part of the white population to deny any suggestion of procreation across the color line in their families. In the chapter dedicated entirely to the Macarty family, King wrote, "The good old Creole name of Macarty has become only a memory in New Orleans. The male members of the family are extinct."[28] At the time she was writing, at the end of the nineteenth century, she would have known that there were still direct descendants from the family who bore the Macarty name in New Orleans. However, due to the Macartys' predilection for setting up house and having children with free women of color, they were mixed-race and as such, by then, would not have been acknowledged by King. King's comment may have been an implied criticism of the Macarty men for having "reneged on their social responsibility to pass off their genes and perpetuate a white Creole aristocracy."[29]

Of Mandeville's three sons in New Orleans, only Eugène Jr. carried on their father's business of moneylending. Pierre Villarceaux speculated on the property market, and Theodule lived off his mother's endowments.[30] This was not uncommon among second- or third-generation free people of color with relatives from the highest echelons of New Orleans society. They were often educated in France like their wholly European-descended kin and lavished with money, allowing them to assume the leisured life of a person of means. An example of this is provided by George Washington Cable in his novel *The Grandissimes.* One of the protagonists, Honoré Grandissime, is depicted by Cable as living off his assets, provided by his high-status white father.[31] Honoré, like the Macarty brothers, has close white relatives, in his case a half brother who has been well educated in France, with a fortune left to him by his father. Honoré could be characterized as an "economically successful person yet emotionally and spiritually neutered." He exemplifies "a still born, dead end life for those characters of color who subscribe to white models of achievement."[32] On the other hand, he could also be an "effete introvert" as a result of the "stifling contempt and hatred directed to him all his life."[33] Thus, Cable's novel was effectively highlighting the difficulties of mixed-race people in New Orleans. Honoré comes to a tragic end after killing a white man and fleeing to France with a "quadroon" woman, Palmyre. He eventually commits suicide by diving into the harbor in Bordeaux. Perhaps Cable was foreshadowing the demise of the free population in New Orleans with this allegory. Ironically, like Honoré, some members of the Macarty family escaped their problems by eventually settling in France and, indeed, in Bordeaux. We cannot know of Theodule Macarty's disposition, or indeed how his existence may have been stifled by increasing oppression. However, despite the problems he may have faced, at least the legacy left by his mother had made him a rich man. Analysis of the richest free Black families from the 1850 census reveals that, at this time, Macarty had a considerable personal fortune of $28,000, so he probably felt no need to enter the world of work.[34] Apart from this census entry, there is little or no record of Theodule's life in New Orleans. He was unmarried and had no children. And in 1854, at age forty-nine, he became the first of the brothers to die.[35] He left everything to his brother Pierre Villarceaux.[36]

Barthélèmy died shortly after his brother Theodule in 1855 in Santiago de Cuba.[37] His father may have deliberately purchased the plantation in Cuba with a view of helping at least two of his children to have a fresh start in another country. Cuba's coffee economy largely developed from the efforts of French exiles escaping from the Saint-Domingue revolution, so the Macarty children would have felt at home in this society.[38] Emigration had become a popular option for free people wishing to escape increasing discrimination in New Orleans. The Caribbean, France, and Mexico were fashionable destinations because of the similar culture and language. For wealthy free Black people there was also an added incentive to emigrate to the Caribbean Islands, as free people of color enjoyed a higher status there than in the southern states of America: "In the U.S. a person designated as mulatto stood closer to blackness, but in the West Indies a person designated as colored stood closer to whiteness."[39]

The coffee plantation purchased by Eugène Macarty had initially not proved to be a financial success for the two Cuban-based Macarty children. Coffee was a more problematic crop than sugar, and depending on the variety, it took four to seven years for the coffee plants to mature. Because of the lag time between the initial investment in land and labor and the generation of income, coffee was also economically more complex, and the trade tended to be more erratic than sugar.[40] At one point, the financial situation was so bad that Emerité's husband, Chére Rigaud, had to abandon the plantation and open a school in the town. Their two children, Isabel and Eugène Rigaud, eventually left Cuba in 1843 to return to New Orleans.[41] By this time the United States had raised its tariff on the importation of coffee from Cuba in retaliation for Spain's high tariff on flour entering Cuba from the United States. Brazilian coffee also became a major competitor.[42] Therefore, notwithstanding the increased prejudice against free people of color at this time, New Orleans may have seemed economically a better bet for two young people. They also had a wealthy grandmother and uncles living in New Orleans. Indeed, at her death in 1848, Eulalie left her grandchildren the inheritance that would have gone to their mother had she lived.[43] Unfortunately Eugène did not live long enough to enjoy his inheritance from his grandmother, dying in New Orleans at the young age of thirty-one in 1849.[44] Isabel eventually married a gentleman called Edouard de Phelps. They had no children, and at some point, possibly after his death, she moved to France.[45]

Although the coffee business was obviously not a very lucrative one, there is an intimation in Barthélèmy's will that he may well have benefited from higher status in Cuba, or he could have even been passing. The will described him as the "legitimate" son, rather than the "natural" son, of "Don" Eugenia and "Doña" Eulalia Mandeville.[46] In the will, Barthélèmy was given the title of "Don" like his parents, and the usual appellation for a free man of color in Cuba (moreno libre) was not given after his name. As in New Orleans, formal titles such as Don and Doña were generally given only to white Cubans.[47] In any event, by remaining in Cuba throughout his lifetime, Barthélèmy and his family avoided the problems that beset the free Black community in their native land. Although the difficulties with the coffee plantation and the loss of her only surviving daughter may have caused Eulalie to doubt the wisdom of sending her children away, the increased status of her son in Cuba may have been a comfort. It is also interesting to note that he and Emerité were the only members of Eulalie's family who may have felt secure enough to marry and have children. Eulalie's sons in New Orleans remained lifelong bachelors. Indeed, the lack of marriage or domestic partners and children was a common factor in the Macarty and Auguste families after the Civil War.

Eugène Macarty Jr. was the next brother to die, in 1866. He left a very brief will.[48] Although he left the bulk of his fortune to his only surviving brother, Pierre Villarceaux, he did make a significant bequest of six hundred piastres to the Marie Couvent School.[49] This bequest to one of the foremost institutions of the free Black community in New Orleans exemplifies how free people of color were drawing together in defense against an increasingly repressive environment before and after the Civil War. Although Eugène was spared sight of the further societal upheavals that would happen during Reconstruction, it would have become clear to him that, after the Union victory, and with the emancipation of the formerly enslaved people, free people of color were likely to lose their privileges and position further. For example, even by 1864, the Union administration under General Nathaniel Banks decreed that passes had to be carried by all Black people regardless of their prewar status. Before this, the Afro Creoles of New Orleans had generally been exempted from any of the constraints placed on the mobility of Black people.[50]

These increasing strictures may have caused tension and anxiety, leading the Afro Creole community to become more insular and retreat into their institutions and enclaves. Organizations such as the Catholic Church, schools, and charitable institutions therefore became increasingly important to the community because they were social markers that distinguished Afro Creoles from other non-Creole or newly freed people.[51] It is significant that Eugène became the first of the family to leave a bequest to one of these key symbols of the free Black community. His endowment also exemplified the different attitudes from those of the previous generation. His mother had been more concerned with leaving her heirs a substantial inheritance to ensure the future of her family or to encourage them to leave New Orleans. In the late antebellum period and after the war, her children became even more interested in preserving their community's future through financial support of their organizations. Thus, while childless himself, Eugène still felt an obligation to try to maintain the future of the free Black society through the education of its children. Although his brother, Pierre Villarceaux, appears to have abandoned New Orleans after the war, he, too, left bequests in his will to assist the Black community.

PIERRE VILLARCEAUX MACARTY

The Reluctant Exile

Pierre Villarceaux was the longest-lived of all the brothers, living through the Civil War and the Reconstruction era and dying in Paris in 1878. Of all the brothers, his will was the most comprehensive, its contents shedding further light on the uncertainties and divided loyalties of elite free Black society. During his lifetime he was financially more fortunate than many of his peers, and he did not face any economic deprivations because of the war. He had inherited wealth from his mother and was also the main heir in two of his brothers' successions. He had also increased his own fortune by buying and selling land. Those who invested heavily in real estate rather than enslaved people largely escaped the privations endured by plantation owners after the war. Some of these land speculators made huge increases in their personal wealth, like Thomy Lafon, who expanded his fortune from $10,000 to $55,000 by speculating in the swamplands during the Union occupation.[52] At the time of his death, Pierre Villarceaux had around $86,000 in the bank and owned numerous houses throughout the city.[53]

Despite these holdings, it appears that in later life Pierre spent less and less time in New Orleans. Although he maintained a household there, his death certificate and succession suggest that in his declining years he may have lived more in France than in Louisiana. It was not unusual for free people of color to retire in France during the colonial period, after having amassed enough money to live comfortably there. However, France's popularity as a destination for those wishing to permanently settle elsewhere grew during the nineteenth century, and by the 1820s there were already five thousand free people of color from various colonies living in France.[54] In the 1830s the French state began to dismantle some of the distinctions that had been maintained in the colonies after abolition in the metropolis. Although the new legislation did not go so far as to abolish slavery in the colonies, it stipulated that every "person born free or had legally acquired freedom" would enjoy both civil and political rights. This more liberal regime signaled a recognition that the phrase, "Frenchmen are equal before the law whatever may be their title or rank" now encompassed those deemed to be free people of color. Therefore, many now felt that racial discrimination would be less pronounced in Europe.[55] Frederick Douglass, the famed African American abolitionist who went to Europe to build an international transatlantic antislavery network, believed that, "in Europe, the black man had a right to be a man, even a gentleman."[56] Douglass felt himself to be temporarily transported from a world of discrimination into upper-class internationalism in cosmopolitan centers such as Paris and London.[57]

Pierre Villarceaux may also have felt increasingly constrained to leave his native city because of the changes happening there: "Between 1860 and 1870, the numbers of Black people in New Orleans more than doubled from 24,074 to 50,475, while the numbers of whites declined."[58] To those who remained, this influx of the newly freed appeared to pose a threat, and it also further undermined the position of the free Black community by continuing to blur the lines between the formerly free and freed people.[59] The realization that they were increasingly being categorized by the high-status white population as the same as non-native Black people or newly freed people was brought home in the riot of July 1866 at the Mechanics' Institute. It was reported that "119 black people" were wounded and "34 colored citizens" had been shot, stabbed, or bludgeoned to death. Although the media still appeared to differentiate between the formerly free Black inhabitants of New Orleans, the outcome of this riot forcibly demonstrated that they were no longer protected by their former status.[60]

This decrease in standing and the increasing dangerousness of their position may have also been instrumental in fueling a further exodus of wealthy Afro Creoles during the war and the Reconstruction period. They included Les Cenelles poet Camille Thierry, who left New Orleans for France, spending the rest of his life in Bordeaux, living off his income from his real estate in the city.[61] Like many others, however, Thierry evinced a reluctance to completely sever ties with his native city, so managing the properties and investments of these exiles became big business for their agents.[62] Tellingly, Pierre's death notice in Paris also stated that he was "temporarily residing in France," suggesting that he had planned a return to New Orleans. His last wishes also specified that he be buried in his native city.

These real estate connections, as well as the nostalgic poetry of the Les Cenelles poet exiles, could have been a way of presaging a return to New Orleans, perhaps in better times.[63] If this was Pierre's ambition, it was unfortunately only realized after his demise. His nephew, Albert Albin Macarty, who was with his uncle when he died, accompanied the body of Pierre Villarceaux back to New Orleans, at a huge cost of $785.50. His large funeral took place in St. Louis Cathedral, with one hundred mourners in attendance. The bulk of the inheritance was left to his niece, Isabel Rigaud, who by then was a widow and had lived in Paris for some time. This generous bequest intimates that she had frequently provided companionship and care for her elderly uncle in France. Indeed, by the time of Pierre's death, she was also very much on her own. She had no children, and her brother and husband had died long ago.

Pierre Villarceaux also made several other significant bequests in his will. First, he left four hundred piastres to Madame Ambrosine Chevalier, widow of Clement Lanusse. Clement was the son of Marie Celeste Macarty Lanusse, daughter of Jean Baptiste Macarty, Eugène Macarty's brother. He also left one hundred piastres to Monsieur Mandeville Marigny, Bernard Marigny's son. By this time the Marigny family was struggling financially, Bernard Marigny having gambled away his inheritance. Pierre's gifts suggest that he may have been continuing the French Romantic tradition of noblesse oblige that had also precipitated the gifts of money and property to his mother from her white relatives. His bequests also signify that he still felt some connection and responsibility to his white kin. However, he also made settlements, which are an indication of his identification with, and support for, the former free Black community.

To Aglae Robin, widow of Armand Lanusse, a prominent figure in free Black society, described by Rodolphe Desdunes as "a poet, teacher, politician and patriot of the highest order," he left four hundred piastres. He also made a bequest of one hundred piastres to "Madame Juliette Godin, presidente of the Institution of the Holy Family." Interestingly, this would have been after the split between Juliette Gaudin and Josephine Charles over the admittance of a formerly enslaved Black woman. Thus, it seems that Pierre may have supported the former rather than the latter leader of the sisters.

He also made quite a large mysterious legacy of property and the sum of two hundred piastres to a person called Omer Augustin, who was described as a "mulatto." There appears to be no direct connection to the family, but he might have been formerly enslaved or perhaps a natural son of Pierre Villarceaux or one of the other brothers. The 1880 New Orleans census lists Omer as a carpenter, and he named one of his sons Villarceaux, after his benefactor.

Pierre Villarceaux also made a series of bequests of money and land to four people who were almost certainly formerly enslaved. He described them variously as his "old domestics" or "old servants." Marie Antoinette Macarty and Marie Claire Macarty both received houses, and Marie Antoinette also received an extra two hundred piastres "because she had children." Eduard Macarty and Pierre Macarty also received one hundred piastres and houses.[64] These people, who were described in the will "as being born on the property" and who had the Macarty surname, were perhaps enslaved people who worked in the home and who had very likely remained in his household after emancipation. These bequests to them were generous and would almost certainly have set them up financially for the rest of their lives. Pierre's substantial settlements were like those of Marie Couvent, thus intimating that, like her, he may also have had a close relationship with these enslaved people. Indeed, they may have even been blood relatives. Also, before the war, favored enslaved people were often freed by their enslavers on their deathbeds as a reward for loyal service. Although there was now no need for Pierre to grant them their actual freedom, his bequests granted them freedom from financial concerns. Pierre's settlements show his support for his community, his adherence to the traditions of free people of color, and to the customs of noblesse oblige engendered by white Creole society.

After Isabel, his other nieces, great-nieces, and nephews were the main beneficiaries of Pierre's will. At the time of his passing, all of Eulalie Mandeville's grandchildren and great-grandchildren were living in France. Thus, if Eugène and Eulalie had sent some of their children away partly in order to see them removed from the racial hierarchies of New Orleans society and settled in places where there was much less discrimination toward Black people, their wishes had been fulfilled. Isabel Rigaud was in Paris. Barthélèmy's daughter Julia Josepha Hermina Macarty lived with her husband in Bordeaux, as did the daughters and husband of his other deceased daughter, Isabella Dolorita Macarty Vedey. One of his sons, Albert Albin Macarty, was also living in Bordeaux. The French city was a popular destination for New Orleans's Afro Creoles, especially for the artistic and musical members of New Orleans's free Black community. Renowned musician and composer Edmond Dédé went there and worked as a conductor of the orchestra at the old Grand Theatre. He eventually married a French woman and assimilated into French society. There is no direct evidence to suggest that the Macarty family was already passing for white in Cuba and when they first moved to France; even so, in France they did not have to endure the stigmatizing label that designated them as gens de couleur libres. They may have begun to "experience the line dividing people of color from Europeans as permeable."[65] This blurring of the racial lines in Europe is also exemplified in *The Grandissimes* novel. Palmyre, a free woman of color who practices Voodoo, flees New Orleans with Honoré Grandissime to eventually become the racially ambiguous Mme. Inconnue in Bordeaux

It is also interesting to note the story of Pierre's other nephew and son of Barthélèmy, Oscar Macarty, as he was the most truly nomadic one of the family. Pierre's succession states that Oscar's existence was unknown at the time of his death, and he had not come forward to claim his inheritance. Albert Albin declared that Oscar had not been heard from for four years and that repeated inquiries and official searches had been made, all to no avail. Albert Albin was questioned closely about his brother and stated that although Oscar was born in Santiago de Cuba, he was raised in New York. He also lived a considerable time in "Porto Rico." After that he lived a short time in St. Thomas, and a few days in Nantes, France, in 1868. He then moved back to New York for a while, and from there he went to Spain, where Albert Albin had last heard from him in 1874. Oscar was the oldest son, born around 1832, so it is possible that his father sent him to New York for his education, thus enhancing his prospects in business. Oscar appears to have then traveled from place to place, losing contact with his family. A ship's passenger record from 1867 shows that Oscar traveled from Brest and Le Havre to New York. His profession is described as a merchant and his nationality as American.[66] This again shows the fluidity of nationality and citizenship in the nineteenth century that has been a feature throughout this study. It enabled mobility and allowed disadvantaged people to escape strictures, both economic and political, for a fresh start in a new place where they were not known. It also allowed them to switch nationalities and identities. François Auguste claimed Irish nationality, possibly in order to circumvent discrimination, and Samuel Hart hid his Jewish descent through Anglicization of his surname to escape the prejudices against his people. Like them, Oscar may also have not wished to be defined by any identity or nationality.

Albert Albin maintained that he went through many processes to try to locate Oscar. He wrote to the French consul in Barcelona and Granada in Spain, asking them if they had any knowledge of his brother residing there, and if not, to make inquiries. He published the death of Pierre in the newspapers of Paris and in Madrid. After all this time had passed, the authorities eventually concluded that Oscar was no longer alive, and his portion of the inheritance probably was divided between the other heirs.[67] As an interesting postscript to all of this, another passenger ship list of 1883 shows that a J. O. Macarty crossed from Bordeaux to New York, five years after the succession of Pierre. José was Oscar's first name, so there is a good chance that this was him. This time he stated that he was of Spanish nationality, which would have been correct as he was born in Santiago de Cuba.[68] Did he eventually find out about Pierre's death and come to claim his inheritance? There is no evidence of this, but if so, it appears that he may have obtained his due from his French relatives and then continued his odyssey.

Although Pierre Villarceaux's nephew Albin Albert Macarty may also have eventually crossed the color line in Europe, like his uncle, he still retained his links with New Orleans, where his ancestry was probably well known. He would have been one of the Macartys in the city whom Grace King did not recognize. He kept the real estate in New Orleans that he had inherited from his late uncle and from his cousin Isabel Rigaud (who had also inherited her property in New Orleans from Pierre) after she passed away in 1890.[69] There is also an intimation that he returned to live in New Orleans in 1889, when he was listed as a passenger on a ship from Bordeaux. Although he may have been going there to administer to the property of his possibly ailing cousin Isabel, the ship's log describes him as a native of France and notes that he intended to become an inhabitant of the United States. His occupation is recorded as being a merchant, and as he was the only passenger traveling first class, it appears that he also had kept the Mandeville wealth intact.[70] Albert Albin certainly continued to own property in the city until 1899, when he would have been sixty. Although Isabel also kept her property in New Orleans until she died, there is no record of her ever going back to the city. She died in Paris and was buried there, leaving most of her legacy to Albert Albin.[71] Eventually Barthélèmy's two grandchildren, Marceline and Marie Vedey, born in Santiago de Cuba, both married Parisians in the 1880s and disappeared entirely into white French society.[72] Thus, the family gradually ceased to have ties with New Orleans.

It is perhaps significant that it was Eulalie Mandeville, the person who, out of all the women in this study, perhaps had the fewest links with New Orleans's free Black society, beyond that of purely business, whose children and grandchildren eventually eschewed their links with New Orleans and possibly their part-African origins. Interestingly, they made a life for themselves in the land from whence Mandeville's father had first traveled to New Orleans, thus bringing the circular movement between France and New Orleans to a close. Whereas Mandeville lived a settled life in New Orleans, her grandchildren and great-grandchildren swapped countries, perhaps in a tireless search for a better life and future. They changed nationality and identity, possibly finally eschewing any vestige of their Afro Creole heritage. Perhaps for Mandeville, with her strong sense of identity emanating from her father's side of the family, this would have signified ultimate freedom, and one that could not be obtained solely through wealth and standing in New Orleans.

VICTOR EUGÈNE MACARTY

Actor, Composer, Musician, and Political Activist

There was another Macarty child connected to Eulalie Mandeville's family, Victor Eugène, who was also well known in the city, first for his musical talents and then, during the Reconstruction period, for his political activities. Victor Eugène's mother, Héloise Croy, was probably one of the many refugees who came to New Orleans after the insurrection of the enslaved in Saint-Domingue.[73] Like Marie Couvent, there is no record of Héloise's entry to New Orleans or whether she was enslaved or free when she arrived. The first documented proof of her residence is an address in the city directory of 1822, probably around the time that her son was born. She is also listed at different addresses in the 1832 and 1843 directories. She was, however, by this time clearly a woman of some means, as the notarial records show that she bought and sold enslaved people.[74] Victor Eugène's Saint-Dominguan heritage on his mother's side may have contributed to his initial choice to become a musician. Free Black actors and musicians were one of the typical features of the Saint-Dominguan world, and the refugees brought this tradition to New Orleans.[75] Other notable musicians with Saint-Dominguan ancestry included Edmond Dédé, who, like the Macarty family, lived in Bordeaux and then Paris. Like Dédé, Victor Eugène was a talented pianist, performing at the "fashionable soirées of New Orleans." He also composed music, as evidenced by his only surviving published composition, *Fleurs de Salon: Two Favorite Polkas,* which was sold at "principal music stores."[76]

After the occupation of New Orleans by Union forces in 1862, Victor Eugène organized concerts for free people of color, raising money to assist the community. *Le Tribune* wrote admiringly of him, describing him as "one of the talented men who are an honor to our population."[77]

By the end of the Civil War he had completely eschewed his former artistic ambitions and was concentrating wholly on politics. He was elected as a member of the Central Committee of the Republican Party in 1866, and he served on the Orleans Parish Board of Police Commissioners in 1867.[78] In 1869, he was involved in an infamous incident at the French Opera House, when he was ordered out of his seat in an area traditionally reserved for white people only, while attending a performance of Rossini's *The Barber of Seville*. According to the press report, Macarty protested vehemently to the manager and "threatened him with corrections with slaps on the face and kicks posteriori."[79] After being forced out, Victor Eugène brought a suit against the French Opera House. There is no record as to whether he won his case, but other such suits followed against the Opera House several years later. He may have deliberately entered an area designated for white people as a way of testing legal privileges under the Louisiana Constitution of 1868, which granted Black people equal treatment in public accommodation. By this time, many others were doing the same by attempting to enter saloons, coffeehouses, theaters, and other public facilities designated solely for white people.[80] It may have been this very public act of defiance that brought him to the attention of the white supremacist faction, to the detriment of his later political career and, indeed, his life.

It may have been Victor Eugène's Saint-Dominguan ancestry that inclined him to campaign for the rights of the Black community after the Civil War. There was a tradition of participation in politics on the part of the Saint-Dominguan refugees. During the antebellum period, many white refugees from Saint-Domingue entered politics, occupying ranking positions of authority in the city and state. This political consciousness was also a characteristic of former free Black refugees after the Civil War. Therefore, Creoles of color from Saint-Domingue played a prominent part in the political scene until the late nineteenth century.[81] The refugees' memories of the "more fluid, less repressive racial system in Saint-Domingue" may have been a contributing factor in their political activism.[82] It was also the case that, like the children of white refugees, Afro Creoles of Saint-Dominguan descent were unusually active politically.[83] Indeed, the political leaders of America's first civil rights movement, Louis Charles Roudanez and his brother Jean-Baptist, were descended from Saint-Dominguan free Black plantation owners.[84]

Although the politics of the early postbellum period allowed biracial New Orleanians like Victor Eugène to reach positions that would have been unthinkable in the antebellum period, it was clear by the 1870s that the public mood was changing. The political prominence of these Afro Creoles alarmed those who saw them as undermining the precepts of white supremacy and the practical codification of social and political segregation. Former free people of color became much more dangerous individually to a white supremacist version of social order than the far more numerous freedmen. Consequently, they became the focus of white anger and were often attacked and vilified by the press.[85]

Victor Eugène Macarty was also targeted by newspapers. In 1875, the *New Orleans Bulletin* wrote that Macarty's role as a member of the city's school board represented "an affront to decency." In an article entitled "A Model School Board(?)," *The Bulletin* stated that all nine members of the school board were unqualified to hold office and singled out Macarty as a particularly "immoral rascal" with "vile propensities." The article went on to state that Macarty was a "lecherous, ignorant and brutal Negro" as he was also accused of having insulted a white schoolmistress.[86] *The Bulletin* then ran a front-page article entitled "V. E. Macarty," declaring that "he had made himself offensive to the white people of the city."[87] These verbal attacks eventually led to physical violence. In 1875, it was reported that he was viciously attacked by two men. The *Weekly Louisianan* described him as "miserable, beaten senseless with clubs."[88] The two white men who had assaulted him were only sentenced to "a fine of ten cents or one minute in the Parish Prison."[89] Macarty's fortunes declined further when the Republican Party's increasingly shaky rule collapsed in 1877, and Macarty lost his job at City Hall.

Not only were his political ambitions finished, but he was by this time heavily in debt. After the death of his wife in 1877, he had to sell their house in order to cover his financial arrears.[90] Victor Eugène was also living a double life, as he had a domestic partnership with Rosalie Hugon, with whom he had three other children. He was thus supporting two households and six children.[91] By 1880, he was living in a boardinghouse in Baton Rouge and working as a schoolteacher.[92] Boarding with strangers was not uncommon for elderly poor people during the nineteenth century. However, boardinghouses generally provided accommodation for those who lived outside kinship groups, and who had no children or other relatives to care for them. This suggests that at the end of his life, Macarty was estranged from both of his families.[93]

This estrangement is further implied by the actions of his legitimate daughter Corilla, who in 1877, at the age of seventeen, successfully filed for emancipation from the legal supervision of her father, giving her power "to do and perform all acts as fully as if she had attained the age of twenty-one years."[94] This was a bold move for a young woman, and indeed she went on to have an impressive career, continuing the educational and artistic legacy of her father by teaching at Southern University and directing the Ladies Symphony Orchestra in Houston.[95]

In 1881 Victor Eugène died. His obituary in the *Weekly Louisianan* praised him for his dedication in "educating our youth at Baton Rouge."[96] Thus, Victor Eugène went from being a popular and feted musician, then a respected politician, to, eventually, an impoverished schoolteacher in Baton Rouge. In contrast, his peer Edmond Dédé, who chose to leave New Orleans for Bordeaux, maintained a successful musical career throughout his life in France. Macarty's choice to sacrifice his musical career for one in politics came at a huge cost to him economically, emotionally, and physically.

Macarty represented the optimistic view in certain quarters of Afro Creole society that the Reconstruction era was a real opportunity for change. Also, unlike some in his community he was dedicated to the welfare of all, not just that of the former free Black people. He was therefore looking to the future rather than the past, as opposed to his half brother Pierre Villarceaux, whose nostalgia for the old times may have led him to self-exile in France. For a brief time, it looked as though Victor Eugène and his community could achieve their ambitions. Eventually, however, the status quo prevailed, and their hopes for more equality were dashed.

FIG. 7. Victor Eugène Macarty demonstrating his dapper appearance and gentlemanly clothing, probably similar to that of his wealthier Macarty half siblings. Louisiana Music Collection, Amistad Research Center, New Orleans, Louisiana.

Interestingly, although it does not seem that Pierre Villarceaux or any other of Eulalie Mandeville's children ever acknowledged the existence of Victor Eugène, the incident at the Opera House was first reported to have involved Pierre Villarceaux, suggesting that the two men were alike, at least in appearance.[97] However, Eulalie Mandeville's children, like her, kept their familial links with their white family, thus perhaps inclining them to political conservatism and eventual assimilation into white society, Victor Eugène's lack of any relationship with his white father and relatives may have also therefore predisposed him to espouse Saint-Dominguan political thought, imported by refugees like his mother.

THE AUGUSTE FAMILY
Activism, Acquiescence, and Rebellion

Like Eulalie Mandeville, Marie Dolores Laveaux left her children very well provided for, with both money and real estate. She made specific bequests in a thorough and detailed will, as opposed to Mandeville, who died intestate. Marie Dolores may have left a watertight will as a precaution against her estranged husband, François Auguste. It appears that he had been an unsatisfactory and possibly violent partner. Although the Auguste family did not come from the same exalted heights as the Macartys, they were also successful businesspeople. Unlike the Macarty family, they had married into their own class for several generations, attempting to create a dynasty. Marie Dolores died in 1839, leaving seven surviving children: Laurent, Lizida, Telesphore, Mirtile, Hermogéne, Henriette, and Hermina. They were all left very generous legacies by their wealthy mother.[98] Of the four brothers, Hermogéne must have died young because his name doesn't appear as part of the household in the 1850 census. Telesphore married Harriet Derchike in 1858, and he was very likely killed during the Civil War, as from the 1860s onward, his widow, Harriet, received a pension from the army.[99] Telesphore also fathered a child whose existence was not known to the rest of the family. She was legitimized by her father before his death and eventually petitioned the succession of her grandfather, François Auguste, for her inheritance after his death in 1873, much to the surprise of the only surviving children, Laurent and Hermina Auguste.[100]

After serving in the Civil War, Mirtile Auguste became a money broker, as evidenced by the 1868 Freedman's Bank Records.[101] In this document he stated that he had one brother, Laurent, and one sister, Hermina, living, as well as his father, thus also confirming that by this time Telesphore had died. However, by the time of Mirtile's death in 1872 at the age of forty-six, he had little to show for his inheritance. He died intestate, and his only collateral was his real estate, which had to be sold to cover his debts and administrative expenses. Neither his brother nor his sister dealt with his affairs, which were handled by the parish, suggesting that they were not close by this time.[102]

LAURENT AUGUSTE
From Cigar-Maker to Chief Legal Adviser and Treasurer of the State of Louisiana

The eldest son, Laurent, born around 1818, was the only member of the Auguste family to become involved in politics. He was deemed illegitimate by his parents as he was born before their marriage, but it is very possible that he was François Auguste's child. François seemed supportive of Laurent throughout his lifetime. Laurent and his wife also lived with François when he became older. Like Victor Eugène Macarty, Laurent's background was typical for a politically active Afro Creole. Profile analyses of Creoles of color who entered politics suggest that they were generally more financially secure or wealthy than many of their peers. At the beginning of the Civil War, Auguste, like Victor Eugène Macarty, was reasonably well-off, having $2,300 in 1860–61.[103] He was also in his forties at this time and thus, like three-quarters of those who pursued a political career, in the prime of life. Nearly all these political activists had also held jobs that demanded skill or schooling. Auguste was a cigar-maker and then became a money broker. Therefore, prior to the war, he channeled his energy into learning trades and making money.[104] Like Victor Eugène, he left his former business life and became treasurer to the Comité des Citoyens, a group founded by Rodolphe Desdunes and Louis Martinet. It advocated equality for all Black New Orleanians, and its members were known for being "militant, recalcitrant, and defiant."[105] The Comité's philosophy and values were spelled out in their newspaper, the *New Orleans Crusader*, which stated, "No theory of white supremacy, no method of lynching, no class legislation, no undue disqualification of citizenship, no system of enforced ignorance, no privileged classes at the expense of others can be tolerated, and, much less, openly encouraged by any citizen who loves justice."[106] The Comité eventually became renowned for organizing Homer Plessy's violation and challenging of the railroad segregation laws in 1892.[107]

In 1874, Auguste became the legal adviser to the state treasurer of Louisiana. He entered this higher office at a difficult time for the Republican Party. The White League, which had been formed by ex-Confederates, had just staged an insurrection against the Republicans and the Reconstruction government, which was by this point clearly living on borrowed time.[108] After the collapse of the Republican Party in 1877, Auguste and his colleagues were taken before a legislative committee inquiring "into the abuses in the Treasury Office."[109] Like Macarty, Laurent was castigated by the press. Singled out far more by the newspapers than any of the other accused white officials, it was evident that it was his race that caused him to be more vilified than the others. One of the articles began by describing him as a "large griffe," a racial classification from the slave markets, and one associated with those of darker skin. As they had for Victor Eugène, newspaper articles also ridiculed Auguste's qualifications for his job. They reported that Auguste, when asked why he was chosen for the position of legal adviser and "preferred to the attorneys employed by the State and to the whole bar of the State and City when he was not a practicing lawyer," replied that "he was not a lawyer, did not meddle with books, but simply gave out advice according to common sense." The article finished in an ironic tone, suggesting that "struggling young attorneys should stop reading all those law books and instead study common sense, which bore Mr. Auguste from his humble position of street broker to that of Chief Legal Adviser to the Treasurer of the State of Louisiana."[110]

Auguste was also accused of having abused his position by acting as an agent to people paying money into the Treasury, and by giving out information about money in the Treasury.[111] He denied the accusations, saying that while he was employed by the Treasury, he had lived on his salary as a solicitor, never had any commissions on warrants, nor received compensation from any other sources than the Treasurer's Office. The newspaper article again mocked his statement while also questioning its truthfulness by writing, "So lives and thrives 'solicitor' Auguste evolving an honest livelihood out of his 'common sense' and narrating cheerful anecdotes to the Legislative Committee."[112] It is significant that both he and Macarty, who were well-known Black political figures, had their reputations ruined by the newspapers in the same way. These articles show the depth of feeling by this time against these Afro Creole politicians and civic leaders and suggest that the Democratic newspapers were specifically targeting them, bringing them into disrepute.

After the collapse of his political life, Laurent Auguste went back to his former profession as a money broker.[113] Like Macarty, he may have also had financial problems because of his political career. Since 1858, Laurent, his wife, Lucie, and his sister, Hermina, had lived in François Auguste's house. Lucie and Laurent married later in life so did not have any children.[114] Upon his father's demise in 1873, Laurent rapidly sold the house that had been bequeathed to him by Auguste, suggesting an urgent need to realize some capital.[115] In 1873, he also sold the house left to him by his mother, to his sister Hermina, and by 1900 he was living with her in this property.[116] By then he was a widower, as his wife had died in 1895.[117]

As a result of increasing financial difficulties during the Reconstruction era, there was generally an increase in the number of sibling and parental coresidences in white southern families.[118] This may have also been the case for the formerly wealthy free people of color. Furthermore, Auguste appeared to have been working right up until his death, as his profession in the 1900 census, when he would have been eighty-two years old, was still described as money broker. This is unlike his father, whom the census recorded as being "retired" in 1870, just before he died. However, like his father, Laurent lived a long life, especially by the standards of the nineteenth century, passing at the age of eighty-five in 1903.[119]

FIG. 8. This image of Laurent Auguste shows a person of refinement inconsistent with the unflattering descriptions in the local press. Artist and date unknown. From *Our People and Our History*, by Rodolphe Desdunes (Arbour & Dupont, 1911).

It appears that despite the differences in their backgrounds, the lives of Victor Eugène Macarty and Laurent Auguste overlapped in various ways. Political activists Victor Eugène and Laurent would have indeed known one another, as their signatures often appear side by side in various committee meeting documents. For a brief heady moment, both men succeeded in obtaining positions of high office in New Orleans in a way that never could have been envisaged by their mothers. Unfortunately, because of these activities, they suffered attacks on their reputation and, in Victor Eugène's case, physical abuse. After the eventual downfall of the Republicans, they both faced hardship and economic difficulties. Laurent Auguste was the product of a family that had evolved from the Black business community of New Orleans. His closeness to the community may have given him the impetus to join the cause of helping to engender more civil rights and equality for Black people. Although he ultimately returned to obscurity like Victor Eugène Macarty, others would follow in their footsteps.

LIZIDA AUGUSTE
Loyal Daughter, Sister, and Aunt

Along with her sons, Marie Dolores Laveaux had three daughters who survived into adulthood: Henriette, Lizida, and Hermina. However, as a result of her separation from François Auguste, the family may have become divided, with two of Laveaux's daughters, Henriette and Lizida, possibly accompanying her to France, while presumably Telesphore, Mirtile, Hermogéne, and Hermina remained with their father. Laurent was by this time an adult and not living in the family home.

That Henriette and Lizida were very close to their mother is evidenced by Lizida's will; thus, during her lifetime they were obviously very affected by their mother's problematic marriage to Auguste. After her death, Marie Dolores divided the legacy equally between her sons and daughters, leaving them all well provided for. That Henriette and Lizida did not capitalize on these financial advantages immediately after coming of age by becoming independent from their father is a puzzle, but it could have been as a result of the changing mores in the Black community, which began in the antebellum period and continued after the Civil War. Instead of becoming self-reliant women of means, they lived most of their lives in their father's house. Ironically, it seems that after Henriette's death, Lizida did defy convention. Like her mother she moved to Paris, possibly in 1856 after selling one of her properties.[120] Unfortunately, in a cruel mirroring of her mother's life, she only lived in Paris for a short time, dying there in 1858.[121] The will she wrote herself in 1854 while she was still living in the family home revealed the unhappy dynamic that prevailed between Lizida, her father, and her siblings. She wrote this will shortly after the death of her "beloved sister Henriette."[122] The will shows that at the time Lizida was in very low spirits and may have thought that she had not long to live.

This will is the only testamentary document used in this study that was handwritten rather than being dictated to a notary; therefore, it is invaluable in giving information about Lizida's existence and thoughts rather than echoing the usual stilted legalese that came from the notary's pen. It also gave an indication of her life as a middle-class free woman of color in late antebellum New Orleans, an existence that appeared much more restricted than the life of her mother and Eulalie Mandeville.

Lizida's will paints a bleak picture of family life in the Auguste household, referring to her mother as her "poor mother" and to Henriette as her "poor sister." She also described her own life as a "sad existence."[123] Her will makes clear her animosity toward and distrust of her father and brothers. For example, she did not appoint any of them as executors of her will, something that would have been very unorthodox during this period. She flouted convention further by choosing a female relative, Estelle Auguste, as her executor. This person was someone whom she variously referred to as her "dear sister" or "second mother." Lizida knew that this will would cause problems in the family and scandalize her community, stating, "Her enemies would be happy that there was something else they could malign her for." The wording of the will also suggests a rift in the family. She wrote: "Two hearts and two martyrs were broken for Henriette and me after our return from France. We had a lot of pain and slanders in our family."[124]

This suggests that the two young women were vilified, not only by their own family but also by other people in their society for accompanying their erring mother to France. However, they had their own supporters, as Lizida went on to say, "We found consolation in our sister Estelle and Mr. Lacroix. They were brothers for us." This ironic statement also intimates how she was estranged from her real brothers who had stayed with François August. Instead, she was obviously close to Mr. Lacroix, whom she described as her "friend and second father." His inclusion in her will as a friend and adviser show a deep trust; however, deviating from the usual custom of appointing a male executor, Lizida did not instruct Mr. Lacroix to oversee her will. That she chose another free woman of color to perform this task suggests an independence, female solidarity, and a recognition by her that a woman could deal with legal matters as well as a man. This feminine esprit de corps was a feature of Lizida's will.

Lizida may have chosen Estelle Auguste as executor because she had already shown her strong character and loyalty by supporting Lizida and her sister after their return from France, in the face of adverse public opinion. She wrote that she wanted Estelle to administer her will because "she would not listen to anything her father would say." Thus, she intimated that any person in her family, or indeed even Mr. Lacroix, might defer to François Auguste's wishes, as the head of the household. She referred to Estelle as her "sister," but she was not Marie Dolores's daughter nor obviously related to the family, despite her surname. It is likely that she was the daughter of François Auguste from an earlier marriage or liaison. Auguste had at least one known natural child, and there may have been more. Before his marriage, Auguste had been living with Marie Magdalen, a woman with children. She had died before Auguste's marriage to Marie Dolores, and although these children were never again mentioned, one of them may have been Estelle. There is further evidence of this, as Estelle's son Arnold Bertonneau, who worked at the State Treasury with Laurent Auguste, was described by him, during the investigation, as his nephew.[125]

Although Lizida's will defies the conventions of her time, it also clearly shows the Romantic view of death that had taken hold of the public imagination during the mid-nineteenth century, transforming it from the fearful to the beautiful, to be almost eagerly awaited. Many Victorians also glorified the act of dying and the deathbed scene.[126] This culture of sentimentality gave middle-class men and women an opportunity to demonstrate continued gentility even in death. The funeral itself therefore became a powerful form of theater.[127]

Lizida's will has precise instructions for her laying-out and funeral, a detail not seen in earlier wills of her mother or, indeed, any of the other free women of color featured in this research. By the mid-nineteenth century, the corpse itself had also returned to center stage in the drama of death; thus, Lizida left clear instructions for her body's preparation and viewing arrangements and set the scene for maximum dramatic effect.[128] She asked her friends Les Demoiselles Mavioux to prepare and dress her as they had done for her sister Henriette. White curtains were to be hung in the salon and the room where she would be laid out. Her coffin, which would be free of any ornamentation, the inside lined with white cotton, would "be placed on two chairs in the room with four chandeliers and candles around my body." She deliberately staged her laying-out and viewing arrangements, creating a scene very like that depicted in Victorian paintings of the deathbeds of young women. However, these careful preparations were not to be seen by many people, as she only wanted to be viewed by a small number of family and friends, including Estelle and her children, Mr. Lacroix, Loulan, Les Demoiselles Mavioux, and their mother. As for her father and siblings, her final wishes state baldly: "If the rest of my family ask, let them. I know their intention for me. I have already suffered during my lifetime, also Henriette." Her funeral arrangements specified that her hearse would be the simplest one that could be found in New Orleans. She also did not nominate her father or brothers to be pallbearers for her coffin. She asked that Mr. Lacroix perform that service, along with her brother-in-law, Estelle's husband, Louis Bertonneau, and her nephew Arnold. She wished to be buried with her mother and her sister and left money for the opening of the tomb and the inscription.[129]

She also showed her favor for her half sister and her family by leaving most of her money and possessions to them. She did, however, make a bequest to her younger sister Hermina, who received a gold bracelet, along with a bag of money from Lizida's armoire. She left Estelle an evening gown and a collar that had belonged to her sister Henriette. She also bequeathed her a gold bracelet "for the difficulties she will have with my brothers," thus again emphasizing that Estelle would have to stand against the wishes of her family. She left her niece Eugenie Bertonneau a gold bracelet. However, she left the money from her mother's succession, which was probably the bulk of her fortune, to her other niece, Alice Bertonneau, thus demonstrating that she wished to pass on her legacy from her mother to a favored person from the next generation of women. As for her father and brothers, she left two diamond pins, one each to her father and brother Mirtile. She did not mention either of her two other brothers, Telesphore and Laurent, in the will, thus suggesting that they were estranged. Mirtile was younger and therefore perhaps less likely to have been a controlling force in her life, as were the two elder brothers.[130]

Her will supports the idea that there was a rift in the family between herself and the other legitimate children of François Auguste. However, it appears that there was also a subsequent rift between the three remaining brothers: Laurent, Mirtile, and Telesphore. This could have been due to Mirtile's support for Lizida, which may have estranged him from the rest of the family. Or it may have been engendered by the Civil War. Both Mirtile and Telesphore originally signed up with the Confederacy, although Telesphore switched sides and died while serving for the Union, whereas Mirtile did not.[131] While there is no evidence of Laurent joining either side, his subsequent political career made it clear where his support would have lain. Whatever the reason, by the time Mirtile died in 1872 at the age of forty-six, it was obvious that he had lost contact with the remaining members of his family. He died intestate, and as no one came forward to administer his succession, a public administrator was appointed who dealt with the sale of his properties to cover his debts.[132] The Auguste family was definitely a dysfunctional one, split apart by the problematic marriage of Marie Dolores and Auguste.

That they were both desperate to leave the house, if not in life then certainly after their demise, is recorded in Lizida's will. She admitted that her sister had also wanted to leave the house, at least after she died, but that she (Lizida) was afraid to carry out this wish because of the scandal.[133] For her own part, Lizida asked her friend Mr. Lacroix to take her body out of the house after she was dead.[134] So, at this time, while she was prepared to challenge the mores of her society after death by appointing a woman executrix and excluding her family from any of the funeral arrangements, thus making her estrangement from them clear, it appears that neither sister had the will to defy the conventions until one of them died. Perhaps Lizida had found life in the family residence so intolerable without the support of her sister that she finally had to do something. That she chose to return to Paris rather than to remain in New Orleans may indicate that she received social condemnation in her home city.

Increasingly restrictive societal expectations for the behavior of women may have been one of the main reasons why Lizida and Henriette may have found it difficult to challenge the status quo. Although these mores generally appertained to the white American middle classes, wealthy free Black people had often traditionally reflected general cultural mores in their desire to protect their free status. This became even more important during the antebellum period and beyond, as their position in society became eroded. Free Black women were also increasingly vilified, even to the point of being described as "vessels of disorder and filth" to bolster southern pro-slavery ideology and evolving notions of feminine domesticity.[135] Therefore, high-status free women of color may have been forced to emphasize their gentility and high moral standards by displaying even stricter adherence to the behaviors expected of white women. Lizida's will suggests that not doing so risked condemnation from elite free Black society and social exile. And, in a patriarchal society, men could pressure, or indeed force, women to display the behaviors expected for higher-status women in the nineteenth century.

The importance of appearances as a means of maintaining the traditional extra privileges of their community is demonstrated by a judge's assessment of an Afro Creole woman, Josephine Decuir, in an 1872 court case. Decuir won the approbation of Judge Cullom for being "genteel in her manners, modest in her deportment, neat in her appearance and quite fair for one of mixed blood. . . . He concluded that she was never a slave, nor a descendent of a slave."[136] This description of Decuir emphasized her gentility and therefore repudiation of any enslaved past. By displaying the behaviors expected of any high-status woman, these free women of color were demonstrating to the community "a solidarity based on class, public demeanor and appreciation for correct social etiquette."[137] Lizida's mother had already broken these rules by separating from her husband and living in France; therefore, in these increasingly repressive times for middle-class free Black women, Lizida and Henriette were obviously afraid of creating further scandal by any other unorthodox behavior. Thus, they may have been forced by the importance of appearances to live quietly and unhappily in their father's home. Lizida's will made clear how powerful public opinion had become by this time in enforcing the behavior of women. In the mid-Victorian era public facades became increasingly important. Therefore, although "race most clearly affected the depth of a woman's oppression but class, background and the willingness to behave in the prescribed female manner also greatly affected a woman's status among those who wielded power in her community."[138]

Perhaps if Marie Dolores had left Auguste earlier in the marriage and gone to live in France with her two daughters, cutting all ties with her husband, Henriette and Lizida may have felt able to remain there after her death. Thus, her seeming reluctance to take the final step to full independence impacted the lives of her two daughters. But although Lizida felt unable to challenge the status quo while her sister was alive, she eventually removed herself to Paris, out of the reach of societal judgment. Her will had shown signs of an independent spirit in her readiness to defy convention after her death. Also, by her bequests, especially to her eldest niece, who was the daughter of Estelle Auguste, a woman who had already shown her strong and unconstrained character, Lizida gave out the promise of hope for an increased rebellion against convention by the next generation of women in the family. Importantly, she echoed the philosophies of her forebears by providing economic security to her heirs, but also, importantly, for her main beneficiary, she provided financial independence, as her mother had tried to do for her.

REFLECTIONS

One factor that immediately stands out when considering the story of the Macarty and Auguste children is their seeming unwillingness to marry and produce the next generation. Their mothers, like most other women of that era, both had large families. Despite this, Eulalie Mandeville had only six grandchildren, as just two of her children married. Although Marie Dolores had seven children living at the time she died, she only had one granddaughter. None of Marie Dolores's three daughters ever married, although this would have been one way of escaping an unhappy household. Perhaps the sisters feared swapping one form of unhappiness for another. Shifts in views about marriage and family during the mid-nineteenth century may have influenced the decision of the daughters of the Auguste family not to wed. Even before the Civil War, some women had begun to question the benefits of marriage because of the power a husband held over them. They felt that masculine behavior could be a barrier to a happy marriage, especially when it came to excessive drinking and violence. The closeness of the Victorian family may have also been a factor in women choosing not to marry. Some daughters became devoted to other family members in an intense way, making it difficult for them to break free from these emotional bonds.[139] These general trends against matrimony in the more privileged white feminine population may have also become popular within free Black society, thus influencing young women like the Auguste sisters. There is evidence in the handwritten will that Lizida was very close to her mother and her sister Henriette. Also, the sisters probably saw firsthand their father's abuse of their mother, further disinclining them to marry.

That three of Eulalie Mandeville's sons also chose not to marry may have been a result of the turmoil around them. The future may have seemed bleak for free people of color in New Orleans, discouraging any thoughts of reproduction. Since intermarriage with other wealthy free families of color had become popular during the antebellum period, it seems strange that Mandeville's eminently suitable, well-off sons were never pressed into marriage. Neither were Marie Dolores Laveaux's sons very inclined to create large families; two of them married, but only one produced a child. Therefore, if Eulalie Mandeville and Marie Dolores Laveaux had expected to create a dynasty, they would have been disappointed at the lack of marriage partners and children in their respective families.

Indeed, the life histories of the Macarty and the Auguste families demonstrate in many different ways how wealthy Afro Creoles faced changes in society from the end of the antebellum period to the Reconstruction era. Their backgrounds and position in New Orleans society also influenced their decisions in life. Eulalie Mandeville's grandchildren, with their illustrious French pedigrees on both sides, eventually gravitated toward France and entry into French society. Their choices may have been presaged by the ideologies and actions of their grandparents. By educating at least one of their children in France and sending two others to Cuba, Eulalie and Eugène gave their children and their grandchildren a broader perspective on the opportunities outside of New Orleans. Mandeville's possible disinterest in the free Black society, and kinship with her high-society white relatives may have also disinclined her children and grandchildren to feel affiliation with New Orleans's Black community. Although Eugène's and Pierre's wills suggest that they were more supportive than their other siblings, after his brother's death, Pierre seems to have spent more and more time in France, far away from the problems facing his community in New Orleans.

Certainly historians have argued about how far these wealthy aristocratic Afro Creoles with close kinship ties to elite white society identified with other free Black people, or indeed, if they even considered themselves as part of the free Black community.[140] The eventual ambiguous racial designation of Barthélèmy Macarty, as demonstrated by his Cuban will, could suggest that he had a very tenuous link to his interracial background, which was further diluted by the actions of his children.

On the other hand, the Macarty brothers' half sibling Victor Eugène Macarty was a talented musician and composer who could have gone to France to pursue a lucrative career; yet, unlike his colleague Edmond Dédé, he chose to remain in New Orleans, often putting his life in danger to pursue his ideals. Macarty's decision may have also been influenced by his mother's background and lack of contact with his father or his white relatives. His mother's ideals may have been equally shaped by her life in Saint-Domingue, before and after the insurrection. His half brother Pierre Villarceaux, who had grown up in a privileged, secure background, appears to have been more politically conservative than his half brother, showing his support for the Confederacy at the beginning of the war. An article from the *New Orleans Crescent* in 1869 reiterated this conservatism, suggesting that some of the elite Afro Creoles would be as appalled as many white southerners at the thought of equality for the newly freed people, naming those it thought would concur: "We would wager our last dollar that a Macarty, a Joubert, a Rillieux or a Mary would no sooner admit the equality of a Murrell, a François or a Pollard than Wade Hampton or Peyton Randolph would."[141] It is probable that this article was referring to Pierre Villarceaux Macarty rather than Victor Eugène.

Like Victor Eugène Macarty, the Auguste family did not have any strong kinship links with white society, and Marie Dolores's eldest son, Laurent Auguste, entered politics after the Civil War. Although unlike many other political activists, Laurent had no obvious connections to Saint-Domingue, his father, who claimed Irish nationality, more than likely originated from there. Similar to Macarty, Auguste became allied with a political group that was promoting equality for all of New Orleans's Black citizens. Also like the Macartys, the Auguste family may have had links with France, as their mother ended her days there, so they could have considered the option to leave New Orleans. Indeed, eventually, after her sister died, Marie Dolores's daughter took the opportunity to make her own personal bid for freedom from the restrictions on women in New Orleans society. Lizida's rebellion initially amounted to acts of defiance through her will by stipulating the appointment of a feminine relative to oversee her succession and by her bequests to the women rather than the men in her family. However, eventually her rebellious spirit emulated that of her mother in her removing herself from an intolerable situation and seeking a new life abroad. Whereas her forebears had pursued freedom through the acquisition of property, Lizida gained it through leaving behind the strictures of her community. She also helped to empower the next generation by passing on her inheritance from Marie Dolores to her niece. Her younger sister Hermina Auguste also followed in Lizida's footsteps. Although she lived with her father for many years, unlike the two other sisters, this seems to have been a deliberate choice on her part. She retained her money more effectively than her brother Laurent, buying her mother's property from the impecunious Laurent and living with him after her father and Laurent's wife died.[142] After Laurent died in the early 1900s, it seems that Hermina Auguste may have gone to live in California as an independent woman for the remainder of her life, dying in 1921.[143] So, she was the third Auguste woman to leave New Orleans and live somewhere else, away from the strictures of a southern city. In the 1870s, Marie Dolores's only grandchild, Coralie Auguste, came forward and successfully petitioned Laurent and Hermina Auguste for the inheritance from her grandfather, even though she was unknown to the two surviving Auguste family members.[144] Thus, she also emulated the spirit of her grandmother Marie Dolores Laveaux, who all those years ago had used the courts to separate herself from her husband and claim what was rightfully hers.

EPILOGUE

The book has looked at the lives of five free women of color in New Orleans in order to determine how they overcame the challenges posed by their race and gender. They achieved a measure of empowerment and economic security for themselves and their children in a hostile environment. It also demonstrated how the societal and economic changes in New Orleans during the antebellum period, especially with the influx of immigrants from Saint-Domingue and Cuba, and other parts of America and Europe, impacted the lives of these women, presenting them with new challenges but also providing them with opportunities. This work has revealed that their tenacity and determination helped them to achieve financial security, and in mostly being able to keep the rewards of their labors for themselves and their families, in the face of often-severe opposition. They were successful businesswomen, founders of organizations, and philanthropists in a way that would be lauded as a remarkable achievement for a woman even by today's standards. Their success emanated from their own achievements, aided by support networks that they created in both business and domestic life.

They formed strong alliances with other men and women to enhance their economic and personal stability, and in defense against a society that condemned them. These feminine associations could cross racial and class lines, in a negation of the view that all free women of color and white women were adversaries. The women understood how these bonds strengthened their position by providing increased support and protection. Thus, eventually, philanthropists like Henriette Delille and Marie Couvent could extend this provision to help disadvantaged members of the Black community, both enslaved and free. Their influence, especially in the areas of business, charitable, and religious enterprises, impacted their community positively.

The work has also emphasized that free businesswomen of color operated not only in New Orleans but also in the Atlantic World through their business activities in a way that has not been previously acknowledged. This more international outlook may have been engendered by the changes happening in New Orleans, which not only gave them increased business opportunities but also brought about an influx of immigrants from the New and Old Worlds. By the antebellum era, the city was becoming a prosperous port, creating various opportunities for increased trade with other parts of the United States, the Caribbean, and Europe. Cécille Bonille met and had a domestic partnership with one of these newcomers to New Orleans, breaking with the tradition of her family, who had only had relationships with French- or Spanish-descended men. Although Samuel Hart may have attempted to conceal his Jewish origins, it appears that Bonille's children were proud of his ancestry. Her daughter Antoinette named one of her children Joseph Rosendahl Darsse, using Hart's true surname. Eulalie Mandeville relied on the support of her Saint-Domingue–born friend. She also took advantage of the craze for all things French that suffused fashionable New Orleanians. By her importation of goods from Paris, she further ensured the success of her business venture.

The huge influx of people from Cuba and Saint-Domingue also affected the lives of the women in this study, and indeed the free Black community. All the women had friends, family members, and business associates from Saint-Domingue. Juliette Gaudin, the cofounder of the

Sisters of the Holy Family, had Saint-Dominguan origins. She was extremely well educated, like many in Saint-Domingue, and emulated her schoolmaster father by founding her own girls' school in New Orleans. Marie Couvent, who spent most of her adult life in Saint-Domingue, also bequeathed land for the foundation of a school for orphans. Marie Dolores Laveaux married François Auguste, who, although claiming to come from Ireland, more likely came from Saint-Domingue. Like Victor Eugène Macarty and many of the other leading political activists from Saint-Dominguan backgrounds, his son, Laurent, would eventually become heavily involved in politics. That the lives of such a small cohort of free women of color were touched by immigrants from Saint-Domingue is a measure of their influence on the free Black population of New Orleans.

The mass arrival of people from other countries and New Orleans's status as a busy port city may have also turned people's minds to the possibilities of living in another country. It may have engendered an idea of ease of mobility and reinvention of identity in a place where one's origins and status were unknown. This may in turn have influenced free people of color to send their children abroad, not just for their education but for relocation in places that were seen as providing increased opportunities and equality. Thus, the Macartys sent their children to Cuba and France, perhaps in the hope they could eventually eschew their biracial origins.

Indeed, the fluid nature of identity and nationality has been a theme throughout this book. Although they came from diverse backgrounds, many of these women probably considered themselves as Creole; they were all identified as free women of color in legal documents and often specifically characterized as "quadroons." Beyond these classifications, background and status also played a major role in how these women were viewed by society and, for that matter, whether they were deemed to be Black or white. Their identities became even more fluid if they achieved economic success. Thus, in the censuses they could be enumerated as Black, white, or mulatto. The male immigrants they married or with whom they had relationships also had identities that shifted according to expediency. Their immigrant children and grandchildren also took the opportunity to change nationality or origins.

Economic success also provided these women further opportunities to network with other women within the free Black and white communities. Even Marie Couvent, who was by all accounts the most disadvantaged of the five women, enhanced her wealth in New Orleans, in part through the networks that she created. Unlike the other women of this study, Couvent was illiterate, yet she became a reasonably wealthy woman. After being forced to emigrate to New Orleans, she formed supportive networks, first with the white Saint-Dominguans who accompanied her to New Orleans and then, through her marriage, with the free Black and enslaved community of the city.

Conversely, for those who had seemingly more advantages than Couvent, high status and connections with white men did not guarantee continued economic security. Maria Josefa Diaz and her daughter Cécille Bonille were examples of those elite free women of color who suffered from lack of funds and had large debts at the end of their lives. Thus, it could be argued that the women in this study who formed close-knit and supportive networks with other women rather than solely relying on white partners, friends, or husbands were ultimately the most successful in obtaining increased stability, financial success, and possibly even contentment, although that is hard to quantify.

This book also examined how the women's varying backgrounds affected their outlook on life. For example, the well-educated and elite free woman of color Henriette Delille admitted only Afro Creole women from her own background into her religious order and its school. This may have been an attempt to promote an image of religious women who were acceptable to the white community, or it may have been simply that Delille did not want her order of nuns to become servants to the priests. Education was obviously very important to her, as it had been for her mother. Delille had a vision for the order that included the provision of a girls' school, and she needed women who were well educated. Eulalie Mandeville's illustrious heritage on her father's side may have influenced her ambitions for her family. She ensured that two of her sons had close ties with France and Cuba rather than with the free Black population of New Orleans. Her background also impacted the way she viewed slaveholding, perhaps viewing enslaved people only in terms of investment. While Mandeville's view of enslaved people may have been engendered by her upbringing and custom, for many free Black women, choosing to become an enslaver generally meant increased income and better conditions for the family. It may therefore have been a form of defense, distancing these women from the enslaved community and thereby protecting their precarious free status.

Slaveholding by free people of color has always represented a challenge to historians, and therefore this research has also examined the complicated relationships between enslaved and free Black people, and the way in which some of the enslaved were favored by their enslavers over others. This was often the case for those who purchased friends and family. However, these associations between free women of color and the enslaved could also result in them forming new kinship networks. This is exemplified by Marie Couvent, who, when she arrived in New Orleans, appeared to rely on her enslavers for support. By her purchase of enslaved people, she entered the free Black community of New Orleans, resulting in marriage to one of her enslaved men and the engendering of close, almost familial relationships with some of the others. This may have ultimately led to her desire to provide a charitable organization for the community. Indeed, this research has shown that some of these women and their children began to change the way they distributed their wealth, especially after their demise. In the beginning it was all about providing for the next generation, but by the end of the antebellum period, they became more concerned with the future of the free Black community.

Indeed, research has shown how some of the women may have exerted a soft influence, either on their children or, in the case of the nuns, on their students. This book has described how marriage rather than plaçage became more popular in the antebellum period. Although there were many reasons for this change, as educators of young Black women, the Sisters of the Holy Family may have also had an influence. In her work about Delille, Sister Detiege suggested that Delille had induced her niece Antoinette to marry, thus breaking the custom of plaçage that had prevailed for generations in her family. Although there is no supporting evidence except what has been reported by oral tradition, it seems plausible that they could have had an effect on the practices of their students. They also made sure that they received a good education, thus maximizing their choices and opportunities.

During her lifetime Delille gained the respect of the nuns, the students' parents, and, importantly, the white church officials. Eulalie Mandeville was another woman who commanded respect. Her court case shows that she had gained the esteem and approbation of white businessmen for her skills and professionalism, alongside other free Black businesswomen. They had come a long way from being universally derided in the colonial period. Her case also makes clear that free women of color could win in court, even against powerful white families. Henriette Delille also demonstrated that a free woman of color could run a successful organization, and women like Marie Dolores Laveaux made it clear that they would no longer put up with an abusive marriage in silence. Marie Couvent's bequest paved the way for philanthropic gestures from other wealthy members of the free Black population, leading to an upsurge in the building of charitable institutions.

These women's influence on their families was also explored in more detail in the final chapter through an examination of the Macarty and Auguste children from the end of the antebellum period through to Reconstruction. The research suggests that Marie Dolores Laveaux's sons, with their links to the free community through successive marriages and through business links, may have been influenced to ally themselves more strongly with New Orleans's Black community. Members of Eulalie Mandeville's family, on the other hand, sought their fortunes elsewhere. Historians have concentrated on the economic aspects of the legacy these women wished to leave their children, but further investigation beyond the scope of this project may show how gaining increased status for their children, either through immigration to Caribbean or European countries or by passing for white, may have been an equally important legacy that these mothers gifted their descendants.

It is also significant that the only children of Eulalie Mandeville to marry and produce offspring were those who left New Orleans to settle abroad. Thus, only once they were away from the racial hierarchies that still pervaded the United States, did the children of these women feel free to produce the next generation. The free Black population of New Orleans went down drastically at the end of the antebellum period and Reconstruction. This was undoubtedly due to people leaving the city, but it would be interesting to research further whether this reluctance to marry was a general trend among New Orleans's young Black people.

It is difficult to determine what hopes and fears these mothers and educators had for future generations, although their actions very often influenced their descendants' life choices. Delille and Couvent, although childless, founded institutions, one of which, the Sisters of the Holy Family, still exists today. They operated schools for free Black girls from their inception onward. This continued until the inauguration of Saint Mary's Academy in 1867, which ironically was built on the site of one of the ballrooms where the quadroon balls were held. From the beginning, under the guidance of Henriette Delille, the sisters provided a good education for young Black girls. During the civil rights era and continuing until the twenty-first century, they also taught leadership skills and fostered increased self-esteem in young Black women. Student Maci Broaden, seventeen, who was present at the school's 150-year anniversary celebration in 2017, summed up the positive influence of the sisters: "I'm not the same person who came in," she said. "Being at St. Mary's has made me realize that I do matter in the world. And I feel comfortable in my own skin, being myself."[1] Thus, not only did these free women of color contribute to the economic, social, and political life of New Orleans in the antebellum period, but their influence on the next generation also had a beneficial effect, which in the case of the Sisters of the Holy family continues right up until the present day. Therefore, in these uncertain times, it is even more important that the achievements of all five women should be known and recognized by succeeding generations of young women.

Notes

INTRODUCTION

1. See J. M. Johnson, *Wicked Flesh;* Guillory, "Some Enchanted Evening"; Gould, *Chained to the Rock of Adversity;* Fuentes, *Dispossessed Lives;* and Censer, *The Reconstruction of White Womanhood.*

2. Mahmood, *Politics of Piety*, 20.

3. Frederickson, *Gendered Resistance*, 42.

4. J. M. Johnson, *Wicked Flesh*, 194

5. See Milweski, *Litigating Across the Color Line;* and Aslakson, *Making Race in the Courtroom.*

6. W. Johnson, *Soul by Soul*, 139, 150.

7. Thompson, *Exiles at Home*, 8.

8. See Charles E. O'Neill, foreword to Desdunes, *Our People*, x.

1. FAITH, FAMILY, AND ENTERPRISE

1. See Midlo-Hall, *Africans in Colonial Louisiana;* Spear, *Race, Sex and Social Order;* and Hangar, *Bounded Lives: Bounded Places.*

2. Dawdy, *Building the Devil's Empire*, 12.

3. Midlo-Hall, *Africans in Colonial Louisiana*, 4.

4. Ibid.

5. Dawdy, *Building the Devil's Empire*, 169.

6. Midlo-Hall, *Africans in Colonial Louisiana*, 4.

7. Clark and Gould, "The Feminine Face," 41.

8. Ibid., 221.

9. Louisiana Code Noir, 1724.

10. Nelson, "People of Color in Louisiana," 6.

11. Louisiana Code Noir, 1724.

12. Spear, *Race, Sex and Social Order*, 6.

13. 1724 Louisiana Code Noir, Article L.

14. Spear, *Race, Sex and Social Order*, 85.

15. Ibid.

16. Midlo-Hall, *Africans in Colonial Louisiana*, 6.

17. Midlo-Hall, *Slavery and African Ethnicities in the America*, 166.

18. Hangar, "Conflicting Loyalties," 2.

19. Dawdy, *Building the Devil's Empire*, 243–44.

20. Taylor, *Louisiana*, 27.

21. Spear, *Race, Sex and Social Order*, 75.

22. Ibid., 109–10.

23. Long, *A New Orleans Voodou Princess*, 51.

24. Kotlikoff and Robert, "The Manumission of Slaves," 178.

25. Spear, *Race, Sex and Social Order*, 109.

26. Hangar, *Bounded Lives*, 21–34.

27. See Jane E. Dabel's analysis of the occupations of Black women in "My Ma Went to Work Every Mornin'."

28. Spear, *Race, Sex and Social Order*, 142, 154.

29. Fandrich, *The Mysterious Voodoo Queen*, 125.

30. Spear, *Race, Sex and Social Order*, 114.

31. Ibid., 75, 83.

32. Foner, "Free People of Color," 415–16.

33. Schafer, *Becoming Free, Remaining Free*, xv.

34. Taylor, *Louisiana*, 27.

35. Foner, "Free People of Color," 415–16.

36. Foner, *History of Black Americans*, 38.

37. Koger, *Black Slaveowners*, 2–3.

38. Ibid., xiii.

39. Lachance, "The Limits of Privilege," 65–84.

40. M. P. Johnson and Roark, *No Chariot Let Down*, 91.

41. Ibid., 40.

42. Fuentes, *Dispossessed Lives*, 68.

43. Taylor, *Louisiana*, 27.

44. *New Orleans City Guide*, 4.

45. Tulane University Library: Census of New Orleans, 1805, submitted by Matthew Flannery to the City Council of New Orleans, 11 May 1805.

46. Hébrard and Scott, *Freedom Papers*, 3, 21.

47. Foner, *History of Black Americans*, 188.

48. Spear, *Race, Sex, Race and Social Order*, 179.

49. Schafer, *Becoming Free, Remaining Free*, 5.

50. Ibid., 4.

51. Ibid., 6, 7, 12, 130.

52. They were identified by the initials "f.m.c." (free man of color) or "f.w.c." (free woman of color) (see Spear, *Race, Sex and Social Order*, 214).

53. See Clark, *The Strange History of the American Quadroon*.

54. Bennett, *Religion and the Rise of Jim Crow*, 137.

55. 1724 Louisiana Code Noir, Articles II, III.

56. See Clark and Gould, "The Feminine Face," 412.

57. Bennett, *Religion and the Rise of Jim Crow*, 137.

58. Ibid.

59. Ibid., 143.

60. Latrobe, *Impressions*, 6.

61. Morrow, *Persons of Color*, 20.

62. See Clark and Gould, "The Feminine Face," 412.

63. See Long, *A New Orleans Voodou Princess*, 6–8.

64. Clark, *The Strange History of the American Quadroon*, 82.

65. Don Esteban Miró, Deliberations of the Cabildo, 1 June 1786, vol. 3, no. 1, pp. 106–7.

66. Martin, "Plaçage and the Louisiana Gens de Couleur," 57–70.

67. Clark, *The Strange History of the American Quadroon*, 66.

68. See Myers, *Forging Freedom;* Martin, "Plaçage and the Louisiana Gens de Couleur"; Clark, *The Strange History of the American Quadroon;* Aslakson, "The 'Quadroon-Plaçage' Myth"; Wilson, "Plaçage and the Performance of Whiteness"; and Fuentes, *Dispossessed Lives*.

69. Myers, *Forging Freedom*, 7.

70. Frederickson, *Gendered Resistance*, 4.

71. Clark, *The Strange History of the American Quadroon*, 170.

72. Sullivan, *Rambles and Scrambles*, 233.

73. See Bancroft, *Slave-Trading*.

74. Northup, *Twelve Years a Slave*, 5.

75. Clark, *The Strange History of the American Quadroon*, 170.

76. Ibid.

77. Potter, *A Hairdresser's Experience*, 190.

78. Olmsted, *The Cotton Kingdom*, 597.

79. Potter, *A Hairdresser's Experience*, 190.

80. Martineau, *Retrospect of Western Travel*, vol. 1, 255.

81. Tregle, *Louisiana in the Age of Jackson*, 35.

82. See Guillory, "Some Enchanted Evening," 45.

83. Hangar, *Bounded Lives, Bounded Places*, 21–34.

84. Sometimes called the Battalion of Free Men of Color, they fought the British in the Battle of New Orleans 1812 (*The Battle of New Orleans Exhibition*, Louisiana State Exhibit Museum).

85. Aslakson, *Making Race*, 126, 131, 133, 143.

86. *Moniteur Louisiane*, 20 November 1805.

87. Clark, *The Strange History of the American Quadroon*, 70.

88. Asbury, *The French Quarter*, 132–34.

89. Sullivan, *Rambles and Scrambles*, 233.

90. Williams, "Can Quadroon Balls Represent Acquiescence or Resistance?," 116.

91. Sally Miller contended that she was born white and was therefore unlawfully enslaved (see Sally Miller v. Louis Belmonti and John Miller, Supreme Court of Louisiana, 16 July 1845, docket no. 5623, Supreme Court of Louisiana Collection, Earl K. Long Library, University of New Orleans).

92. Octoroons were considered to be only one-eighth African.

93. Clark, *The Strange History of the American Quadroon*, 133–34.

94. S. Brown, *The Negro in American Fiction*, 38.

95. See Child, *The Quadroon;* and Braddon, *The Octoroon or, The Lily of Louisiana.*

96. Raimon, *The Tragic Mulatta Revisited*, 74.

97. Clark, *The Strange History of the American Quadroon*, 133–34.

98. Ibid., 86–88.

99. Louisiana Civil Code, 1808.

100. Clark, *The Strange History of the American Quadroon*, 86, 88.

101. Ibid., 88.

102. According to Sister Detiege, Delille may have persuaded her niece Antoinette Hart to marry rather than become a plaçée (see Detiege, *Henriette Delille*).

103. Jerah Johnson, "Congo Square," 121–22.

104. Schweninger, "Black-Owned Businesses, 26.

105. Jerah Johnson, "Congo Square," 121–22.

106. Schweninger, "Black-Owned Businesses," 27.

107. Montigny, *Memoires Historiques*, 120.

108. Thompson, *Exiles at Home*, 30–31.

109. Schweninger, "Prosperous Blacks," 36.

110. Hogan and Davis, *Natchez*, 23.

111. Ibid.

112. Schweninger, "Prosperous Blacks," 36.

113. Ibid.

114. C. A. Smith, *Market Women*, 24.

115. Rogers-Jones, *They Were Her Property*, 99.

116. Olwell, "Loose, Idle & Disorderly Slave Women," 97–110.

117. Gould, *Coastal Encounters*, 158.

118. Dabel, "My Ma Went to Work Every Mornin'," 217, 223.

119. Ibid., 225.

120. See Fett, "Working Cures."

121. Cable, *The Grandissimes*, 12–13.

122. See Long, *A New Orleans Voodou Princess.*

123. Chakrabarti, *Forging Freedom*, 15–16.

124. M. P. Johnson and Roark, *Black Masters*, 101–2.

2. "WELL-EDUCATED AND REFINED WOMEN"

1. Ochs, *Desegregating the Altar*, 208.

2. Henriette's birth date is approximate because no documented evidence of the date of her birth has ever been found. It has been speculated that her birth may have been mistakenly recorded in the book for white baptisms.

3. *Times-Democrat*, 1891, Newspapers.com.

4. These houses consisted of four rooms with doors opening on the outside. They were built of "bousillage," a combination of clay or plaster and Spanish moss, or of soft brick covered with stucco. They had overhanging gable roofs covered with shingles, slate, or half-round earthenware tiles. Reports from the Louisiana Writers' Project gave an indication of how people lived in these Creole cottages. Most of the domestic activity took place in the backyard. The ever-present danger of fire meant that cooking was generally done in a detached kitchen. Daily trips to the market were essential as there was no means of refrigerating food. A vegetable garden and henhouse were very often also located in the backyard. In the winter, the houses were heated by small coal- or woodburning fireplaces.

5. See Clark and Gould, "The Feminine Face."

6. Civil District Court, New Orleans Parish: Succession of Charles Decoudreaux, vol. 82, pp. 598, 631.

7. J. C. Smith, *Notable Black American Women*, 5.

8. Archives of the Sisters of the Holy Family: Succession of Marie Joseph Dias, 1848.

9. Hobbs, *A Chosen Exile*, 63.

10. Rothman, *Notorious in the Neighborhood*, 205.

11. Sister Mary Bernard Deggs was a nun with the Sisters of the Holy Family. She was tasked with writing the history of the order while she was already ill from tuberculosis. This may have affected her memory and her thought processes. It also appears that French was her first language, and thus she was translating from French into English. Sister Deggs was born in 1846 and joined the order in 1873, so it is very likely that knew the founders (see Sister Mary Deggs, Journal, in *No Cross, No Crown*).

12. J. C. Smith, *Notable Black American Women*.

13. Archives, Oeuvres Pontifical Missionaire, Lyon, France: Duberg to Blanc, New Orleans, 27 June 1824.

14. Archives of the Archdiocese of New Orleans: St. Louis Cathedral Baptisms of Slaves and Free People of Color, Mar. 1825–Dec. 1826, and St. Louis Cathedral Baptisms of Slaves and Free People of Color, Sept. 1827–June 1829.

15. J. C. Smith, *Notable Black American Women*, 5.

16. *Catholic News Service*, 29 March 2004.

17. Samuel Hart was buried in the now-demolished Gates of Mercy Cemetery, the first Jewish cemetery in New Orleans (https://www.jewishgen.org/databases/cemetery/jowbr.php?rec=J_LA_0002682).

18. The reference may be to William R. Bell (1814–1874), New Orleans undertaker and livery owner. John Slidell (1793–1871) was a noted Louisiana lawyer, politician, and businessman.

19. Notarial Archives: Vol: 10a, Acts No: 16, Aug.–Oct. 1832; de Armas, Notary, No: 406.

20. Archives of the Archdiocese of New Orleans: St. Louis Cathedral Baptisms of Slaves and Free People of Color, Mar. 1825–Dec. 1826, and St. Louis Cathedral Baptisms of Slaves and Free People of Color, Sept. 1827–June 1829.

21. Davis, *Henriette Delille*, 40

22. Archives of the Sisters of the Holy Family: "The Rules and Regulations for the Congregation of the Sisters of the Presentation of the Blessed Virgin Mary Under the Invocation of Mary the Virgin of the Holy Presentation. Founded in New Orleans 21 November 1836."

23. Schafer, *Becoming Free*, 6.

24. Rousselon arrived in New Orleans in 1837, where he became chaplain to the Ursuline Convent and school and the Saint-Claude Street School, as well as vicar general of the diocese (see Davis, *Henriette Delille*, 46–47).

25. Although this was the reported date for inauguration of the Sisters of the Holy Family, it appears that Henriette Delille and Juliette Gaudin were the only ones living together in the 1850 census, suggesting that the other sisters joined them after this. Josephine Charles reputedly had to look after her brother, who was very ill, until she could join the others in the house (see Davis, *Henriette Delille*, 50).

26. Archives of the Sisters of the Holy Family: Succession of Marie Joseph Dias, 1848.

27. Davis, *Henriette Delille*, 63.

28. Sister Mary Deggs, Journal, in *No Cross, No Crown*, 10.

29. J. C. Smith, *Notable Black American Women*, 63.

30. Fessenden, "The Sisters of the Holy Family," 190.

31. "Description of Mother Juliette, Nun and Free Woman of Color in New Orleans in the Early Nineteenth Century" (Louisiana Works Progress Administration, 1939), 2.

32. Sister Mary Deggs, Journal, in *No Cross, No Crown*, 11.

33. Ibid., 42.

34. See ibid. for information about white sponsors.

35. Ibid., 11.

36. Ochs, *Desegregating the Altar*, 204.

37. Hart, "A History of the Congregation," 206.

38. Batchen, "Dreams of an Ordinary Life," 91.

39. Morrow, *Persons of Color*, 119.

40. Hart, "A History of the Congregation," 42.

41. Desdunes, *Our People*, 97.

42. Detiege, *Henriette Delille*, 27.

43. Hobbs, *A Chosen Exile*, 34.

44. Notarial Archives: Octave de Armas, No. 161 5/23/1851 Testament de Henriette Delille.

45. Davis, *Henriette Delille*, 61.

46. Archives of the Archdiocese of New Orleans, Register of Saint Louis Cemeteries, 1857–1863.

47. Hart, *Violets in the King's Garden*, 76.

48. Archives of the Sisters of the Holy Family: Receipt from Undertaker P. Casenave.

49. Sister Mary Deggs, Journal, in *No Cross, No Crown*, 12–13.

50. Detiege, *Henriette Delille*, 26–27.

51. Although she was closely associated with the sisters, she was not included in any official lists. She was also not buried in the Holy Family tomb, probably due to the racial strictures of the time (see Sister Mary Deggs, Journal, in *No Cross, No Crown*).

52. Borgia Hart writes that the sisters were perturbed when white friends took the body away. A fire broke out in the house where she was laid out and the body had to be retrieved. It was then taken back to the convent (see Hart, *Violet's in the King's Garden*, 17).

53. Sister Mary Deggs, Journal, in *No Cross, No Crown*, 92.

54. Davis, *Henriette Delille*, 62–63.

55. See 1850 census, which says West Indies; 1860 and 1870 censuses record Cuba; and cemetery records say Haiti.

56. See entry in the City Directory 1830, where Philippe Gaudin is described as a teacher.

57. Hébrard and Scott, *Freedom Papers*, 74.

58. Sister Mary Deggs, Journal, in *No Cross, No Crown*, 17.

59. Sister Mary Deggs, Journal, in *No Cross, No Crown*, 4–5, 6, 14–17.

60. Succession of François Charles, 8 December 1841, Notarial Office, New Orleans.

61. Sister Mary Deggs, Journal, in *No Cross, No Crown*, 102.

62. Fessenden, "The Sisters of the Holy Family," 188.

63. *Times-Picayune*, 21 May 1885: Obituary of Mother Josephine Charles; see also slave dealer James Blakeney's description of the enslaved Mildred Ann Jackson, which ran along the same lines: "Her color was that of a quadroon, very good figure, she is rather tall and slim" (see W. Johnson, *Soul by Soul*, 155).

3. THE PLACÉE AND THE WIFE

1. She wrote in her will that he was living in Cuba (New Orleans Public Library, City Archives: Louisiana Orleans Parish Estate Files 1804–1866. Will Books 1837–1842).

2. White men typically referred to their white children by marriage as legitimate and

their duly acknowledged children of color as their natural children. By the time of her death, it seems that Juan Bonille had predeceased her, as he was called "the late Bonille" in her death certificate (New Orleans Public Library, City Archives: Louisiana Orleans Parish Estate Files 1804–1846: Death Certificate of Cecille Bonille, 1841).

3. See Glymph, *Out of the House of Bondage,* for examples of sexual violence.

4. Gould, "Henriette Delille," 271, 85.

5. Ibid.

6. Davis, *Henriette Delille,* 98.

7. Gould, "Henriette Delille," 271, 85.

8. Ibid.

9. Historic New Orleans Collection: See Collins C. Diboll Vieux Carré Survey, Notarial Records: Vol. 4, 577, Pierre Pedesclaux, sale of 532–534 Burgundy Street from Antione Argot to Marie Joseph Diaz fwc, Vol. 4, Michel de Armas, Aug 3rd, 1810, sale of property from Marie Joseph Dias fwc to Angel Benito de Ariza.

10. Historic New Orleans Collection: See Collins C. Diboll Vieux Carré Survey; Notarial Records 1822, Notary Michel de Armas, Registration of an Act in which Henriette Laveau is described as "a free quarteroon."

11. Castellanos, *New Orleans As It Was,* 61.

12. Ibid.

13. New Orleans Public Library, City Archives: Louisiana Orleans Parish Estate Files 1804–146: Succession of Cécille Bonille, 1842: Bill from the Maison D'Education.

14. Ripley, *Social Life in Old New Orleans,* 30.

15. Potter, *A Hairdresser's Experience,* 188.

16. Olmsted, *The Cotton Kingdom,* 236.

17. Detiege, *Henriette Delille,* 15.

18. Although Sam and Cécille had four children, her birth was the only one found in the archdiocese records. Her father's name was recorded as "Sem, Polish" and her mother's as "Cécile Bonny" (Archives of the Archdiocese of New Orleans: Saint Louis Cathedral, Births of Free Colored People, vol. 16, p. 190).

19. See *The Courage to Love,* Television History Film, Ontario, 2000.

20. Aslakson, "The Quadroon-Plaçage Myth," 717–18.

21. At the time of his death in 1832, Hart was described as being around sixty years old (New Orleans Public Library, City Archives: Louisiana Parish Files 1804–1836, Samuel Hart Record of Death 1832).

22. Clark, *The Strange History of the American Quadroon,* 69.

23. John McDonogh made his fortune in real estate and was at one time director of the Louisiana State Bank. At his death he left his fortune to be used for the education of boys and girls in Baltimore and New Orleans. Thirty-six schools were built in total (see Long, *A New Orleans Voodou Princess*).

24. Detiege, *Henriette Delille,* 15.

25. See Samuel Hart's death certificate will and succession as detailed in note 26 below and in subsequent pages.

26. New Orleans Public Library, City Archives: Louisiana Parish Files 1804–1836; Will of Samuel Hart 1832.

27. Detiege, *Henriette Delille*, 15.

28. Glymph, *Out of the House of Bondage*, 29.

29. Notarial Archives: Acts. No. 16, Aug.–Oct. 1832 De Armas notary. No. 406.

30. New Orleans Public Library, City Archives: Louisiana Parish Files 1804–1836; Will of Samuel Hart 1832.

31. Ibid.

32. The disease first appeared in India in 1817. A medical text published in 1858, *A Treatise on the Practice of Medicine*, by George B. Wood, M.D., described how it spread through most of Asia and the Middle East throughout the 1820s. By 1830, cases had been reported in Moscow, and the following year the epidemic had reached Warsaw, Berlin, and Hamburg. In early 1832, the disease was reported to be in London and then Paris. By early June 1832, the epidemic had crossed the Atlantic, with Canadian cases reported. The disease spread along two distinct pathways into the United States, with reports in the Mississippi Valley in the summer of 1832, and the first case documented in New York City on 24 June 1832. When the epidemic struck the city, as many as one hundred thousand people, nearly half the city's population, fled to the countryside. The movement of the disease across continents and countries was tracked closely, yet how it was transmitted was barely understood.

33. Rosenburg, *The Cholera Years*, 1, 13, 25, 37.

34. New Orleans Public Library, City Archives: Louisiana Wills and Probate Records 1756–1964: Succession of Samuel Hart 1832; Petition of Antoinette Knoll, 2.

35. New Orleans Public Library, City Archives: "Louisiana, U.S., Statewide Death Index 1819–1964": Record of Death 1832.

36. New Orleans Public Library, City Archives: Louisiana Wills and Probate Records 1756–1964: Succession of Samuel Hart 1832; Bill from the undertakers.

37. For Hart's burial place, see https://www.jewishgen.org/databases/cemetery/jowbr.php?rec=J_LA_0002682.

38. New Orleans Public Library, City Archives: Louisiana US Wills and Probate Records 1756–1964: Succession of Samuel Hart 1832.

39. Ibid.

40. John Slidell was a lawyer turned businessman who moved to New Orleans in 1819 to practice law after his business failed. He rose to prominence as a Louisiana politician in the decades before the Civil War (www.knowsouthernhistory.net).

41. Detiege, *Henriette Delille*, 22.

42. He was a rising star of the Democratic Party, noted for his oratory (see Nicolas Theodore Macarty v. Eulalie Mandeville [Supreme Court of Louisiana Historical Archives at the Earl K. Long Library University of New Orleans] 106 U.S. 61 [1846–1861]).

43. December 1833, The Executors v Boni F.W.C, in *Reports of Cases Argued and Determined in the Supreme Court State of Louisiana, Eastern District New Orleans*, ed. Merrit M. Robinson.

44. Ibid.

45. Notarial Archives: Acts of Felix Grima, 1834.

46. Antoinette Darsse v Henry Leaumont & another, Executors of Cecilia Bonilla, in *Reports of Cases Argued and Determined in the Supreme Court State of Louisiana*, vol. 4, ed. Merrit Robinson.

47. Ibid.

48. Historic New Orleans Collection: See City Directories of New Orleans, 1835–36.

49. Gaskell, *Life of Charlotte Brontë*, 353–54.

50. New Orleans Public Library, City Archives: Louisiana Will Books 1837–1842: Last Will and Testament, Bonille, femme de couleur libre, March 29, 1841 (translated from French by author).

51. "Louisiana, U.S., Statewide Death Index, 1819–1964," online database, Ancestry .com, 2002.

52. New Orleans Public Library, City Archives: Louisiana Orleans Parish Estate Files, 1804–1846: Cecilia Bonille, 1841, Court of Probates.

53. New Orleans Public Library, City Archives: Louisiana Parish Estate Files 1804–1846: Succession of Cecilia Bonille, folder 3, Mademoiselle Cecilia Bonille, Bellone Magasin, Savoir, 1836–1840.

54. Ripley, *Social Life in Old New Orleans*, 58.

55. Ibid., 61.

56. Stewart, "Fashioning Frenchness," 32.

57. Myers, *Forging Freedom*, 67.

58. New Orleans Public Library, City Archives: Louisiana Parish Estate Files 1804–1846: Succession of Cecilia Bonille; Petition of Henry Leaumont and William Bell.

59. New Orleans Public Library, City Archives: Louisiana Parish Estate Files 1804–1846: Succession of Cecilia Bonille. Amelia must have subsequently died in about 1843 because her name does not appear in the later succession records.

60. Detiege, *Henriette Delille*, 15.

61. New Orleans Public Library, City Archives: Louisiana Parish Estate Files 1804–1846: Succession of Cecilia Bonille; Petition of Jean Delille, tutor (guardian) of the minors.

62. Antoinette Darsse v Henry Leaumont & another, in *Reports of Cases Argued and Determined in the Supreme Court of Louisiana*, ed. Merrit M. Robinson, vol. 5, 29 May–30 September 1843, New Orleans 1845.

63. New Orleans Public Library, City Archives: Louisiana Parish Estate Files 1804–1846: Succession of Cecilia Bonille; Petition of Jean Delille.

64. Long, *A New Orleans Voudou Princess*, 25.

65. Archives of the Archdiocese of New Orleans: See St. Louis Cathedral Marriages, Free People of Color (1801–1804), pt 1.

66. New Orleans Public Library, City Archives: Louisiana Parish Estate Files 1804–1846: Laveau Mde Charles neé Marie Françoise Dupart Fwc, Estate of 1824.

67. Crary, *Reminiscences of the Old South*, 11.

68. She was at the time in a plaçage relationship with a white Frenchman, Henri D'Arcantel. After her short relationship with Charles Laveaux, she went back to him (see Long, *A New Orleans Voudou Princess*, 65).

69. New Orleans Public Library, City Archives: Louisiana Parish Estate Files 1804–1846: Laveau, Mde. Charles, neé Marie Françoise Dupart, Fwc, Estate of 1824.

70. Inventory of the Estate of Marie Françoise Fanchon Dupart, Wife of Charles Laveaux Fmc, 27 July 1824, typed translation LWP folder 495. Information courtesy of Carolyn Morrow Long.

71. Archives of the Archdiocese of New Orleans: Baptisms of Free Colored People, vol. 13, p. 132.

72. Ibid.

73. Charles Laveaux owned two properties on Dauphine Street, 923–929 and 914–918, from 1804 to 1827. See Historic New Orleans Collection, Vieux Carré Digital Survey.

74. Archives of the Archdiocese of New Orleans: Marriage of Francisco Augusto and Maria Labeau, Slaves and Free People of Color Marriages, vol. 1, p. 58, act 244.

75. Historic New Orleans Collection: In the city directories from 1822 to 1838, his occupation is listed as victualler and butcher.

76. Marriage contract between F. Auguste and Marie Laveaux, Acts of Narcisse Broutin, vol. 37, pp. 367–68, Notarial Archives Research Center; typed translation LWP folder 202.

77. Notarial Archives: On 5 October 1818, Marie Dolores Laveaux, accompanied by her father, signed a marriage contract with François Auguste before the notary Narcisse Broutin (courtesy of Carolyn Morrow Long).

78. Sundberg, "Women and Property in Early Louisiana," 634.

79. Marriage contract between F. Auguste and Marie Laveaux, Acts of Narcisse Broutin, vol. 37, pp. 367–68, Notarial Archives Research Center; typed translation LWP folder 202.

80. In the baptismal record, the father is identified as Francisco Augusto, natural de Irlanda (Baptism of Francsico Detrèn, SLC Baptisms, 22 October 1817, vol. 5, act 911, p. 180).

81. *The Bee*, 1 December 1873: Obituary of François Auguste.

82. "United States Census, 1850," online database, FamilySearch.org, https://familysearch.org/ark/61903/1:1:MCJC-CL1: 12 April 2016, Francois Auguste, New Orleans, ward 4 (1st municipality), Orleans, Louisiana, United States: citing family 896, NARA microfilm publication M432 (National Archives and Records Administration, n.d.).

83. Creté, *Daily Life in Louisiana*, 106.

84. Venturatos, "New Orleans," 1.

85. He gave her a plot of land on Love Street (see Long, *A New Orleans Voudou Princess*, 65).

86. Archives of the Archdiocese of New Orleans: Baptism of Lorenzo Auguste

(born 19 June 1819), Saint Louis Cathedral Baptisms, 18 November 1824, vol. 18, act 861, p. 170 verso; godparents Laurent Charles Laveaux and Marie Madelaine Herveau, wife of Joseph Cabaret (courtesy of Carolyn Morrow Long).

87. Archives of the Archdiocese of New Orleans: See Marriage of Francisco Augusto and Maria Labeau, Slaves and Free People of Color Marriages, vol. 1, act 244, p. 58.

88. Walvin, *An African's Life*, 165.

89. McMahon, *The Global Dimensions of Irish Identity*, 81.

90. New Orleans, Passenger List Quarterly Abstracts, 1820–1875, online database, ancestry.com, 2011.

91. See Historic New Orleans Collection, Vieux Carré Survey: Citation of Owners: François Auguste.

92. *Louisiana Courier*, 24 November 1819; also cited in Dillon, "Voodoo/Marie the Great," p. 4a, LWP folder 319 (courtesy of Carolyn Morrow Long).

93. Schafer, *Becoming Free, Remaining Free*, 35.

94. Marie Henriette Auguste, 1820; Eveline Auguste, 1821; Francisca Auguste, 1823; Joseph Jean Auguste, 1824.

95. "Louisiana, Orleans Parish Estate Files, 1804–1846," database with images, FamilySearch, https://familysearch.org/ark:/61903/1:1:JJC1-N38: 4 December 2014, Marie Françoise Dupart, 1824; citing probate place Orleans Parish, Louisiana, Probate Court, New Orleans City Archives.

96. New Orleans Public Library, City Archives: Marie Laveau wife of François Auguste vs Charles Laveau, Suit no. 387; Laurent Laveau vs Charles Laveau, Suit 392, Court of Probates, microfilm (courtesy of Carolyn Morrow Long).

97. New Orleans Public Library, City Archives: Marie Laveaux Fwc, wife of François Auguste vs François Auguste, Parish Court, Aug.–Oct. 1828, docket no. 5041, microfilm (courtesy of Carolyn Morrow Long).

98. Sundberg, "The Law of Property under Louisiana Civil Law," 38.

99. Wallace, "A Primer on Divorce in Louisiana," 619.

100. Sundberg "Women and Property in Early Louisiana," 32.

101. Sundberg, "The Law of Property under Louisiana Civil Law," 634–36.

102. New Orleans Public Library, City Archives: Marie Laveaux Fwc wife of François Auguste v François Auguste, Parish Court Aug.–Oct. 1828, docket no. 5041 (courtesy of Carolyn Morrow Long).

103. Griswold, "Divorce and the Legal Redefinition of Victorian Manhood," 96–111.

104. Baggett, *Intimate Partner Violence in New Orleans*, 5.

105. New Orleans Public Library, City Archives: Marie Laveaux Fwc, wife of François Auguste v François Auguste, Parish Court Aug.–Oct. 1828, docket no. 5041, microfilm (courtesy of Carolyn Morrow Long).

106. Baggett, *Intimate Partner Violence in New Orleans*, 39.

107. Ibid.

108. New Orleans Public Library, City Archives: Marie Laveaux Fwc, wife of

François Auguste v François Auguste, Parish Court Aug.–Oct. 1828, docket no. 5041, microfilm (courtesy of Carolyn Morrow Long).

109. Ibid.

110. Riley, *Divorce*, 28

111. New Orleans Public Library, City Archives: Marie Laveaux Fwc, wife of François Auguste v François Auguste, Parish Court Aug.–Oct. 1828, docket no. 5041, microfilm (courtesy of Carolyn Morrow Long).

112. Ibid.

113. Grossberg, *Governing the Hearth*, 235.

114. See Furness, *Fanny Kemble*.

115. Riley, *Divorce*, 52.

116. New Orleans Public Library, City Archives, Marie Laveaux Fwc, wife of François Auguste v François Auguste, Parish Court Aug.–Oct. 1828, docket no. 5041, microfilm (courtesy of Carolyn Morrow Long).

117. For further details, see the discussion of Lizida Auguste's life in chapter 5.

118. Basch, *Framing American Divorce*, 61, 63.

119. Notarial Archives: First Will of Marie (Dolores) Charles Laveaux, 19 January 1829, Acts of Louis T Caire, vol. 6, p. 55, act 66.

120. François; Louise Augustine and Marie Hermina.

121. New Orleans Public Library, City Archives: Louisiana Parish Will Books 1837–1842: Marie Laveaux, 25 March 1839.

122. New Orleans Public Library, City Archives, Louisiana Parish Files 1804–1836: Succession of Marie Laveaux, 1841; Petition of François Auguste.

123. Archives of the Archdiocese of New Orleans: St. Louis Cemetery Records: Interment Book, St. Louis Cemetery No. 1, 1839.

124. "New Orleans, Passenger List Quarterly Abstracts, 1820–1875," online database, Ancestry.com, 2011. Lizida may have been a pet name derived from her second name, Elizabeth; see also Louisiana State Archives, Baton Rouge: Orleans Death Indices 1804–1876, vol. 14, p. 265.

125. The ships were both called *Lafayette* coming from Havre.

126. New Orleans Public Library, City Archives: Louisiana Orleans Parish Will Books 1857–1860: Lizida Auguste, Probate Date: 6 April 1858 (translated from French by author).

127. New Orleans Public Library, City Archives: Louisiana Wills and Probate Records 1756–1984: Marie Laveau, New Orleans, 1841.

128. Ibid.

4. TWO OF NEW ORLEANS'S BIG BUSINESSWOMEN

1. Little is known of Eulalie Mandeville's mother. Her name, Jean Marie Dutiel, appears only once in the document of Mandeville's illicit marriage to Eugène Macarty.

2. King, *Creole Families of New Orleans*, 18–19.

3. *Macarty v Mandeville:* Testimony of Bernard Marigny, 137.

4. Dictionary of Louisiana Biography–M–Louisiana Historical Association, lahistory.org.

5. *Macarty V Mandeville:* Testimony of J. Enould Livaudais, 164.

6. Testimony of Bernard Marigny, 136.

7. Ibid., 137.

8. *Mandeville v Macarty:* Testimony of Bernard Marigny, 137.

9. Arthur, *Old New Orleans*, 22.

10. Archdiocese Records, Baptisms Free People of Color, vol. 6, p. 182; ibid., vol. 8, p. 219.

11. Calas are dumplings composed primarily of cooked rice, yeast, sugar, eggs, and flour; the resulting batter is deep-fried. It is traditionally a breakfast dish, served with coffee or cafe au lait, and has a mention in most Creole cuisine cookbooks (see Cable, *Historical Sketchbook*, 13).

12. Latrobe, *The Journal of Latrobe*, 202.

13. Ibid., 203.

14. Hangar, "Desiring Total Tranquility and Not Getting It," 549.

15. Olwell, "Loose, Idle & Disorderly Slave Women," 97–110.

16. Gould, *Coastal Encounters*, 158.

17. Hangar, "Avenues to Freedom," 140–41.

18. *Macarty v Mandeville:* Testimony of Bernard Marigny, 137.

19. Cohen's New Orleans and Southern Directory (1853).

20. *Macarty v Mandeville:* Testimony of L. Sejour, 79–80.

21. *Macarty v Mandeville:* Testimony of Bernard Marigny, 137; Testimony of Joseph Blache, 163.

22. Historic New Orleans Collection: New Orleans Census 1830.

23. *Macarty v Mandeville:* Testimony of Widow Chavenet, 243.

24. *Macarty v Mandeville:* Testimony of Casimir Lacoste, 152; Testimony of Terence Le Blanc, 100.

25. Cocuzza, "The Dress of the Free Colored Women in New Orleans," 17, 37.

26. Reynolds, "Slaves to Fashion Not Society," 92.

27. Cocuzza, "The Dress of the Free Colored Women in New Orleans," 17, 37.

28. Ripley, *Social Life in New Orleans*, 110.

29. Cocuzza, "The Dress of the Free Colored Women in New Orleans," 17, 37.

30. Ripley, *Social Life in New Orleans*, 68.

31. In eighteenth-century France, "Monsieur," "Sieur," "Mademoiselle," and "Madame" were titles given only to respectable members of society in documents. In colonial and antebellum Louisiana, they were mainly given to white people and even then only to those of some social standing (see Ulentin, "Shades of Grey," 57).

32. Reynolds, "Slaves to Fashion Not Society," 10.

33. Mitchell, *Raising Freedom's Children*, 121.

34. *Macarty v Mandeville:* Brief for the Defendant 1848, 103.

35. Thompson, *Exiles at Home*, 79.

36. Barthélèmy's youngest grandchild, Marceline Vedey, was born in Santiago de Cuba in 1859, suggesting that the family moved to France after that date.

37. *Macarty v Mandeville:* Testimony of L. Sejour, 161.

38. The Couvent School for free colored children refers to the school that opened in 1848. It was founded by Marie Couvent, formerly enslaved, who emigrated from Haiti to New Orleans around 1806 (see Mary Niall Mitchell, *Raising Freedom's Children*).

39. Ibid., 15.

40. *Macarty v Mandeville:* Testimony of Victor Romerage, 159.

41. *Macarty v Mandeville:* Testimony of Duncan Kennedy, 104.

42. *Macarty v Mandeville:* Testimony of L. Sejour, 161.

43. *Macarty v Mandeville:* Testimony of Michael V. Durel, 240.

44. New Orleans Public Library, City Archives: Louisiana, Wills and Probate Records, 1756–1984: Free Black women were unable to legally wed their white partners, thus by law their children could inherit no more than one-tenth of the father's estate, and even that tenth was subject to loss if legitimate heirs sued to acquire it. See also P. W. Johnson, "Eulalie de Mandeville."

45. Long, *Madame Lalaurie*, 11.

46. Historic New Orleans Collection: See New Orleans census of 1850. Héloise Croy is listed as being born in Santo Domingo.

47. See *Macarty v Mandeville.*

48. Preservation Hall was established in 1961 to preserve, perpetuate, and protect traditional New Orleans jazz. Operating as a music venue, a touring band (the Preservation Hall Jazz Band), a record label, and a nonprofit organization, Preservation Hall continues its mission today as a cornerstone of New Orleans music and culture.

49. Historic New Orleans Collection: See Collins C. Diboll Vieux Carré Survey: Eulalie Mandeville: Citation of owners.

50. See Collins Diboll Vieux Carré Digital Survey online for information about Agathe Fauchon's properties (http://www.hnoc.org/vcs/property_info.php?lot=18808).

51. See Marler, *The Merchant's Capital.*

52. *Macarty v Mandeville:* Testimony of Michel V. Durel, 240.

53. Sister Mary Deggs, Journal, in *No Cross: No Crown*, 12.

54. White, *Ar'n't I a Woman?*, 199–200.

55. *Mandeville v Macarty:* Testimony of Marie Louise Panis. Panis bought and sold several properties in the French Quarter of New Orleans beginning in 1795, when she was twenty-six years old. At age sixty-two, she exchanged her properties on Royal Street and in St. Bernard Parish, on the site of the Battle of New Orleans, with Bernard Marigny, for a plantation he owned in St. John the Baptist Parish valued at about $75,000. By the time she died in 1852 at the age of eighty-four, the value of her plantation, the en-

slaved people, and the buildings on the property would have been worth over $1 million in 2020 dollars. See also note of New Orleans Genealogical Research Society talk given by Emory Vebre, 16 April 2001.

56. *Mandeville v Macarty:* Testimony of Marie Louise Panis.

57. *Macarty v Mandeville:* Testimony of Sophie Macarty, 235.

58. Her will of 1855 describes her as Sophie Mousante alias Sophie Macarty ("Louisiana, U.S., Wills and Probate Records, 1756–1984," online database, Ancestry.com, 2015).

59. She had two children by him: Augustine Modeste Casimir Lacoste (1793) and Josephine Lacoste Foucher (1800). She also had children by Barthélèmy Lafon, an architect, engineer, and town planner, and Pierre Lafon. She was the mother of Thomy Lafon, a renowned free colored philanthropist (see Louisiana Historical Association's online dictionary of biography: http://www.lahistory.org/site29.ph).

60. *Macarty v Mandeville:* Testimony of Sophie Macarty, 235; Testimony of Modeste Foucher, 235.

61. Ibid.

62. *Macarty v Mandeville:* Testimony of L. Sejour, 162.

63. *Macarty v Mandeville:* Testimony of E. Forrest, 112.

64. *Macarty v Mandeville:* Testimony of Martin Duralde, 78.

65. New Orleans Public Library, City Archives: Louisiana Parish Files 1804–1846: Heno, District Court 1821.

66. Jones-Rogers, *They Were Her Property*, xiii.

67. *Macarty v Mandeville:* Testimony of Widow Chavenet, 243.

68. See King, *New Orleans: The Place and the People.*

69. *Macarty v Mandeville:* Testimony of Widow Chavenet, 243.

70. Ibid., 244

71. See Wilson, "Plaçage and the Performance of Whiteness."

72. *Macarty v Mandeville:* Testimony of Bernard Marigny, 1.

73. Thompson, *Exiles at Home*, 196–97.

74. *Macarty v Mandeville:* Testimony of Victor Visinier, 20.

75. Although she used a number of different names with different spellings throughout her lifetime, to avoid confusion I will refer to her as Marie Couvent throughout this chapter.

76. New Orleans Public Library, City Archives: New Orleans Will Parish Books 1805–1820, Marie Couvent, 1832.

77. See Lovejoy, "The Children of Slavery," 197–217.

78. Ibid.

79. Notarial Archives: Acts of Broutin 1812, 27, 119.

80. Neidenbach, "Mes Dernieres Volantés," 4.

81. Ibid.

82. Scott and Hébrard, *Freedom Papers*, 151.

83. Cable, *Historical Sketchbook*, 30.

84. See Tregle, "Early New Orleans Society," 20–36.

85. Spear, *Race, Sex and Social Order*, 190–91.

86. Neidenbach, "Refugee from Saint-Domingue," 841.

87. Ibid.

88. Notarial Archives: Acts of Broutin, 1812, 27, 199.

89. As a universal legatee he would receive any property or assets that remained after her debts were paid.

90. Neidenbach, "Refugee from Saint-Domingue," 843.

91. Julienne dite Lyonais was born in Santiago de Cuba in 1806. Antoine Besset and Marie Moreau's marriage in 1823 legitimized her birth (see *Sacramental Records of the Roman Catholic Church of the Diocese of New Orleans*, vol. 16, ed. Charles E. Nolan, 1823–25).

92. Glymph, *Out of the House of Bondage*, 29.

93. Notarial Archives: Acts of Broutin, 1812, vol. 27, p. 199.

94. Neidenbach, "Refugee from Saint-Domingue," 843.

95. Appiah and Gates, *Africana: The Encyclopaedia of the African American Experience*, 251.

96. Neidenbach, "Mes Dernieres Volantés," 5.

97. Archives of the Archdiocese of New Orleans: Saint Louis Cathedral Marriages, Free People of Color, pt. 1, 1812–1819.

98. Enslaved women in Saint-Domingue often used various nicknames (see Hébrard and Scott, *Freedom Papers*, 31).

99. Neidenbach, "Refugee from Saint-Domingue," 84.

100. Hébrard and Scott, *Freedom Papers*, 74.

101. Notarial Archives: Vente d 'Esclave par Mde Wheaton a Marie Jn Sirnir, Acts of N. Broutin, 14 February 1811, vol. 25, p. 46.

102. Jennifer M. Spear found that while only one-fourth of manumissions of slaves under thirty years old were granted through baptism before 1807, the proportion rose to one-half after the law went into effect in September 1807. Even baptisms recorded as late as 1832 declared that the enslaved child was baptized as free (see *Race, Sex & Social Order*, 113, 194, 189, 196).

103. Hébrard and Scott, *Freedom Papers*, 3.

104. Neidenbach, "The Life and Legacy of Marie Couvent," 306.

105. New Orleans Public Library, City Archives: Louisiana U.S., Wills and Probate Records, 1756–1984, for Madame Bernard Couvent, Inventories of Estates, 1837.

106. Ibid.

107. Neidenbach, "The Life and Legacy of Marie Couvent," 306.

108. Notarial Archives: Acts of Broutin, 1806, vol. 13, p. 59.

109. Notarial Archives: Vente de terrain par Dame Marie de los Santos Dias a Marie Justine Simir, Testament, 1812; the 1822 City Directory listed a woman named Leonora Remy at "28 Barrack bel. Conde," which is the same address provided for Bernard Couvent.

110. Notarial Archives: Vente d'esclaves par Mouro & C. e à Marie Justine, Esther,

March 20, 1810; M. Ant. E. Duverney, Vente d'esclaves à Marie Justine Sirnir, femme Bernard Couvent, 20 October 1823.

111. Notarial Archives: Séraphine Negress Esclave, 4 November 1832; [Emancipation of Séraphine by Justine Sirnar] (widow of Bernard Couvent), 5 October 1831, Acts of C. Pollock, vol. 36, p. 394.

112. Neidenbach, "The Life and Legacy of Marie Couvent," 306.

113. New Orleans Public Library, City Archives: Probate Court Suit, No. 1322, 15 December 1839; Archives of the Archdiocese of New Orleans: Saint Louis Cathedral, Funerals of Slaves and Free People of Color, vol. 9, pt. 2: 1831–1832, No. 2055.

114. New Orleans Public Library, City Archives: New Orleans Parish Will Books 1833–1837: Marie Couvent, 11 November 1832 (translated from French by author).

115. *The Bee*, 21 September 1837.

116. Neidenbach, "The Life and Legacy of Marie Couvent," 306.

117. Ibid.

118. Bernard Couvent had a son with an enslaved woman named Helena in 1792. The couple named the child Bernard and had him baptized as free in 1797. Bernard Couvent fils was also a carpenter and had several children with his longtime partner (Archives of the Archdiocese of New Orleans: Rosette Jacques, 9 April 1797, no. 452, p. 354, St. Louis Cathedral, New Orleans, Baptism, 1792–1798).

119. Archives of the Archdiocese of New Orleans: Bernard, negre lib de cette ville, 17 May 1814, no. 184, p. 25, in St. Louis Cathedral Baptisms of Slaves and Free People of Color, vol. 14, pt. 1, 1814–1815.

120. The Dolliole family in New Orleans were well-known builders and architects, responsible for building many of the houses and cottages of the French Quarter (see Neidenbach, "The Life and Legacy of Marie Couvent").

121. New Orleans Public Library, City Archives: New Orleans Parish Will Books 1833–1837.

122. Neidenbach, "The Life and Legacy of Marie Couvent," 213, 282.

123. King, *Blue Coat or Powdered Wig*, 39.

124. New Orleans Public Library, City Archives: New Orleans Parish Will Books 1833–1837.

125. Desdunes, *Our People*, 102.

126. However, eventually many of Desdunes's friends and contemporaries became involved with the foundation of the Couvent School.

127. Neidenbach, "The Life and Legacy of Marie Couvent," 357.

128. See Hébrard and Scott, *Freedom Papers*, 19, for discussion about the importance of documents for people of color.

129. Neidenbach, "The Life and Legacy of Marie Couvent," 329.

130. New Orleans Public Library, City Archives: New Orleans Parish Will Books 1833–1837.

131. Desdunes, *Our People and Our History*, 102.

132. Christian, "The Negro in Louisiana."

133. Baudier, *The Catholic Church in Louisiana*, 3, 4.

134. Neidenbach, "The Life and Legacy of Marie Couvent," 408.

135. Ibid.

136. Desdunes, *Our People*, 102.

137. Ibid., 104.

138. Mitchell, *Raising Freedom's Children*, 17–18.

139. Desdunes, *Our People*, 103.

140. See Blassingame, *Black New Orleans*, 60; and Mitchell, *Raising Freedom's Children*, 18.

141. Devore, "Race Relations & Community Development," 237.

5. RESILIENCE AND TRANSITION

1. Schweninger, "Antebellum Free Persons of Color," 354.

2. Ibid.

3. Nystrom, "In My Father's House," 298.

4. Ibid., 288.

5. Schweninger, "Antebellum Free Persons of Color," 352.

6. Vandal, "Black Utopia in Early Reconstruction New Orleans," 438.

7. See Rankin, "The Origins of Black Leadership"; and Roudané, "The Color of Freedom."

8. McKee, *The Exile's Song*, 163.

9. *Gazette and Sentinel*, 27 April 1861.

10. *New Orleans Daily Picayune*, 29 November 1861; 3 January 1862.

11. Schweninger, "Antebellum Free People of Color," 346.

12. Hollandsworth, *The Louisiana Native Guards*, 105.

13. New Orleans Public Library, City Archives: Louisiana Wills and Probate Records 1756–1984: Pierre Villarceaux Macarty, 30 August 1878.

14. McKee, *The Exile's Song*, 63.

15. Schafer, *Becoming Free, Remaining Free*, 156.

16. Many free men of color, including immigrants from the Saint-Domingue revolution, formed an African American battalion. For the first time, African American soldiers earned the same wages as their white counterparts (*The Battle of New Orleans Exhibition*, Louisiana State Exhibit Museum).

17. Hébrard and Scott, *Freedom Papers*, 36.

18. Terry L. Jones, "The Free Men of Color Go to War," *New York Times*, 19 October 2012.

19. Schweninger, "Antebellum Free People of Color," 351.

20. See Holden, *Futile Valor*.

21. Louisiana Confederate Soldiers Index 1861–1865.

22. U.S Civil War Soldier Records and Profiles 1861–1865.

23. See Thompson, *Exiles at Home.*

24. New Orleans Public Library, City Archives: Succession of Eulalie Mandeville, 1848.

25. Ibid.

26. See Thompson, *Exiles at Home,* 192.

27. Nystrom, "In My Father's House," 298.

28. King, *Creole Families of New Orleans,* 363.

29. Thompson, *Exiles at Home,* 192.

30. Notarial Archives: Phillipe Lacoste Notary Public, Acts 115–218 for mention of mortgage lending by Eugène Macarty Jr.

31. Cable, *The Grandissimes,* 268.

32. Bollini, "*The Grandissimes* and Political Transition," 171.

33. Campbell, "The Negro in Cable's *The Grandissimes,*" 167.

34. Tulane University, Amistad Research Center: "List of Negroes in New Orleans possessing $2000 or more in property," compiled from the 1850 census by John W. Blassingame, John W. Blassingame Papers.

35. *The Bee* obituaries, 13 December 1854.

36. See Collins C. Diboll Vieux Carré Digital Survey: see online for information about Theodule Macarty's properties: https://www.hnoc.org/vcs/property_info.php?lot=23057.

37. New Orleans Public Library, City Archives: Louisiana Wills and Probate Records 1855–1857.

38. Singleton, "Slavery and Spatial Dialects," 99.

39. Hodes, *The Sea Captain's Wife,* 221.

40. Singleton, "Slavery and Spatial Dialects," 100.

41. National Archives, Washington, DC: "Work Projects Administration Transcript of Passenger Lists of Vessels Arriving at New Orleans, Louisiana, 1813–1849."

42. Singleton, "Slavery and Spatial Dialects," 100.

43. Succession Records, 1846–1880; Index, 1846–1880; Author: Louisiana. District Court (Orleans Parish); Probate Place: Louisiana.

44. Louisiana State Archives, Baton Rouge: Orleans Death Indices 1804–1876.

45. See New Orleans Public Library, City Archives: Louisiana Wills and Probate Records 1756–1984: Pierre Villarceaux Macarty, 30 August 1878.

46. New Orleans Public Library, City Archives: Louisiana Wills and Probate Records 1855–1857, 24–12–1855.

47. Scott, *Degrees of Freedom,* 96.

48. New Orleans Public Library, City Archives: Louisiana Wills and Probate Records 1756–1984 1865–1867, 21–06–1866. Piastres had the same value as dollars.

49. Ibid.

50. Thompson, *Exiles at Home,* 232.

51. Rankin, "The Origins of Black Leadership," 299.

52. Schweninger, "Antebellum Free People of Color," 356.

53. New Orleans Public Library, City Archives: Louisiana Wills and Probate Records 1756–1984: Pierre Villarceaux Macarty, 30 August 1878.

54. Thompson, *Exiles at Home*, 221.

55. Hébrard and Scott, *Freedom Papers*, 84.

56. Salenius, "Troubling the White Supremacy," 153.

57. Ibid.

58. Blassingame, *Black New Orleans*, table 1.

59. Thompson, *Exiles at Home*, 221.

60. Library of Congress: *House Reports*, 19th Cong., 2nd sess., no. 15. p. 12.

61. In 1845, a volume of eighty-five poems, *Les Cenelles: Choix de Poesies Indigines*, was published by a group of seventeen New Orleanians, all of whom were free men of color. The poets of *Les Cenelles* were men of culture and learning (a number of them educated in France) (see McKee, *A Family Long Free*, 37).

62. Thompson, *Exiles at Home*, 221.

63. Ibid., 152.

64. New Orleans Public Library, City Archives: Louisiana Wills and Probate Records 1756–1984: Pierre Villarceaux Macarty, 30 August 1878.

65. McKee, *The Exile's Song*, 158.

66. National Archives, Washington, DC: "Passenger Lists of Vessels Arriving at New York, New York, 1820–1897"; Microfilm Serial or NAID: M237; RG Title: Records of the U.S. Customs Service; RG: 36.

67. New Orleans Public Library, City Archives: Louisiana Wills and Probate Records 1756–1984: Pierre Villarceaux Macarty, 30 August 1878.

68. National Archives, Washington, DC: "Passenger Lists of Vessels Arriving at New York, New York, 1820–1897"; Microfilm Serial or NAID: M237; RG Title: Records of the U.S. Customs Service; RG: 36.

69. Notarial Archives: 18 June 1879, 1227 Dauphine Street, Succession: From Pierre Villarceaux Macarty to Isadore Albin Albert Macarty. Notary: A Villeré, COB, vol. 109, p. 872, 19 May 1890. Succession: From Isabel Rigaud to Isadore Albin Albert Macarty, Notary: A Villeré, COB, vol. 132, p. 529.

70. National Archives, Washington, DC: "Passenger Lists of Vessels Arriving at New Orleans, Louisiana, 1820–1902."

71. New Orleans Public Library, City Archives: Louisiana Wills 1889–1890: Isabelle Chery Rigaud, case no. 29064.

72. See "Paris, France & Vicinity Marriage Banns, 1860–1902," online database, Ancestry.com, 2008.

73. The 1850 census gives his age as twenty-eight.

74. Notarial Archives: Sale of a Slave, John Woolfork to Heloise Croy, William Boswell, Notary, New Orleans, 12 June 1827, vol. 3, p. 389, NARC; Release, Payment of Heloise Croy to Estate of Antoine Abat, Carlile Pollock, Notary, New Orleans, 1 May 1832, vol. 38A, 273, NARC; Vente d'esclave, Heloise Croy to Madame Honorine Saint

Clair, Carlile Pollock, Notary, New Orleans, 27 April 1832, vol. 40, p. 291, NARC; Vente d'esclave, Héloïse Croix to Charles Becquet, Louis T. Caire, Notary, New Orleans, 15 January 1839, act 25, vol. 69, p. 56.

75. Dessens, *From Saint-Domingue to New Orleans*, 147.

76. Tulane University, Howard-Tilton Memorial Library: Victor Eugène Macarty, *Fleurs des Salons: Two Favorite Polkas* (Wehrman, 1854), box 34, folder 2, William Ransome Hogan Jazz Archive.

77. *The Tribune*, 20 June 1865.

78. Horne, "From Art to Activism," 507.

79. *The Tribune*, 8 July 1869.

80. Summers, "Black and White in New Orleans," 25.

81. Ibid., 29.

82. Thompson, *Exiles at Home*, 77.

83. Ibid., 29, 31.

84. Roudanez and Roudanez, "The Color of Freedom," 10.

85. Nystrom, *New Orleans After the Civil War*, 159.

86. *New Orleans Bulletin*, 15 September 1875.

87. Ibid., 20 November 1875.

88. *Weekly Louisianan*, 17 September 1875.

89. *New Orleans Republican*, 17 September 1875.

90. New Orleans Public Library. City Archives: Inventory 21 September 1877: Succession of Elizabeth Lucie Lee, Case 39759, Orleans Second District Court.

91. Historic New Orleans Collection: See Victor Eugène Macarty's household with Elizabeth, 1870 census, Ward 6, Orleans Parish; and Eugène Macarty's household with Rosalie, 1870 census, Ward 6, Orleans Parish.

92. Historic New Orleans Collection: 1880 census, Baton Rouge.

93. Thompson, *Exiles at Home*, 67.

94. New Orleans Public Library, City Archives: Corilla Marie Macarty, emancipation, 7 September 1877, case number 39756, Second District Court. The 1880 census of New Orleans records Corilla's age as twenty, putting her birth date sometime in 1860.

95. Horne, "From Art to Activism," 524.

96. *Weekly Louisianan* obituaries, 2 July 1881.

97. *The Tribune*, 8 July 1869.

98. New Orleans Public Library, City Archives: See Louisiana, Orleans Parish Estate Files, Louisiana, Probate Court (Orleans Parish); Probate Place: Orleans, Louisiana, Louisiana, Wills and Probate Records, 1756–1984: Succession of Marie Laveau, 1841.

99. New Orleans Public Library, City Archives: See Louisiana Parish Marriages 1837–1957; United States Freedman's Bureau, roll 47, Register of Claimants, Oct. 1872–May 1878.

100. New Orleans Public Library, City Archives: Louisiana Orleans Parish, Second District Court Case files, 1873, docket no. 3601: Succession of François Auguste.

101. New Orleans Public Library, City Archives: Freedman's Bank Records 1865–1874, 1 July 1868.

102. New Orleans Public Library, City Archives: Louisiana Successions 1846–1880: Mrytile (*sic*) Auguste, 1872.

103. Rankin, "The Origins of Black Leadership," 428.

104. Historic New Orleans Collection: For Auguste's occupation, see City Directories of 1861, 1864, 1866, and 1867.

105. Nystrom, *New Orleans After the Civil War*, 172.

106. *New Orleans Crusader*, 3 March 1867.

107. Hoping to strike down segregation laws, the Citizens' Committee of New Orleans (Comité des Citoyens) recruited Plessy to deliberately violate Louisiana's 1890 separate-car law. To pose a clear test, the Citizens' Committee gave notice of Plessy's intent to the railroad, which opposed the law because it required adding more cars to its trains.

108. Nystrom, *New Orleans After the Civil War*, 172.

109. *New Orleans Daily Democrat*, 6 September 1877.

110. Ibid.

111. Ibid., 18 September 1877.

112. Ibid., 2 October 1877.

113. Historic New Orleans Collection: See New Orleans Census 1900.

114. "Louisiana Parish Marriages, 1837–1957," database with images, FamilySearch, https://familysearch.org/ark:/61903/1:1:QKJ8-2T2D: 4 April 2020, Laurent Auguste and Lucie Masters, 20 April 1858; citing Orleans, Louisiana, United States, various parish courthouses, Louisiana; FHL microfilm 1,734,768.

115. New Orleans Historical Collection: Collins C. Diboll Vieux Carré Survey: Laurent Auguste; Citation of Owners.

116. Ibid. See also the census of 1900.

117. "Louisiana, U.S., Statewide Death Index, 1819–1964," online database, Ancestry.com: Lucie Masters, 2 February 1895.

118. Censer, *The Reconstruction of White Womanhood*, 54.

119. "U.S., Statewide Death Index, 1819–1964," 4 March 1903, online database, Ancestry.com, 2002.

120. See 1856 Orleans Parish Clerk of the Civil Court; New Orleans, Louisiana, Laresche, Paul E., 1845–1871, vols. 1–35.

121. Succession Records 1846–1880; Index 1846–1880; Louisiana District Court (Orleans Parish).

122. Henriette died in 1853. She may have been a victim that summer of the worst yellow fever epidemic to ever have hit the city (Louisiana State Archives, Baton Rouge: Orleans Death Indices 1804–1876, vol. 14, p. 236).

123. New Orleans Public Library, City Archives: Louisiana Orleans Parish Will Books 1857–1860: Lizida Auguste, Probate Date: 6 April 1858 (translated from French by author).

124. Ibid.

125. See "The Treasury Inquiry, Examination of the Witnesses," *New Orleans Daily Democrat*, 18 September 1877.

126. Jalland, *Death in the Victorian Family*, 8.

127. Halttunen, *Confidence Men and Painted Women*, 124, 169.

128. Ibid., 169.

129. New Orleans Public Library, City Archives: Louisiana Orleans Parish Will Books; Louisiana Will Book.

130. Ibid.

131. National Park Service, "U.S., Civil War Soldiers, 1861–1865," online database, Ancestry.com, 2007.

132. Succession Records, 1846–1880; Index, 1846–1880; Author: Louisiana. District Court (Orleans Parish); Probate Place: Louisiana.

133. New Orleans Public Library, City Archives: Louisiana Orleans Parish Will Books 1857–1860, Lizida Auguste, Probate Date: 6 April 1858.

134. Ibid.

135. Glymph, *Out of the House of Bondage*, 65.

136. Josephine Decuir vs. Joseph Benson of the Gov Allen Steamship, 1872, Superior District Court. She was denied access to the "lady's cabin" reserved for whites but which by custom had always been available for "ladies of color," probably only of Decuir's class. She had paid the extra money for the ticket, and therefore the judge allowed that by law she should have been allowed access.

137. Thompson, *Exiles at Home*, 264.

138. Schweninger, "Prosperous Blacks," 57.

139. Censer, *The Reconstruction of Southern Womanhood*, 31, 33–34, 36.

140. See Nystrom, *New Orleans After the Civil War*.

141. *New Orleans Crescent*, 14 January 1869.

142. Year: 1900; Census Place: New Orleans Ward 6, Orleans, Louisiana; Roll: 572; Page: 10; Enumeration District: 0057.

143. "California, U.S., Death Index, 1905–1939," online database, Ancestry.com, 2013.

144. Succession Records, 1846–1880; Index, 1846–1880; Author: Louisiana. District Court (Orleans Parish); Probate Place: Louisiana.

EPILOGUE

1. Quoted in nola.com, 10 March 2017.

Bibliography

PRIMARY SOURCES

Archives and Manuscripts

Archdiocese of New Orleans Original Sacramental Records

Interment Book, St. Louis Cemetery No. 1. 1839

Register of Saint Louis Cemeteries, 1857–1863

St. Louis Cathedral Baptisms of Slaves and Free People of Color, vol. 14, pt. 1: 1814–1815

St. Louis Cathedral, Funerals of Slaves and Free People of Color, vol. 9, pt. 2: 1831–1832, No. 2055

St. Louis Cathedral Marriages, Free People of Color, 1801–1804, pt. 1

St. Louis Cathedral, New Orleans, Baptism, 1792–1798

The Historic New Orleans Collection

City Directories (1822–1875)

Cohen's New Orleans and Southern Directory (1853)

The Collins C. Diboll Vieux Carré Digital Survey

Louisiana Civil Code (1825)

Williams Research Center

New Orleans Notarial Archives (Acts of Named Notaries)

Andres Almonester y Roxas

Michel de Armas

Octave de Armas

William Boswell

Narcissus Broutin

Louis T Caire

Félix Grima

Phillipe Lacoste

Pierre Pedesclaux

Carlile Pollock A. Villeré

New Orleans Public Library

City Archives
Exhibitions

The Sisters of the Holy Family Archival Records (New Orleans)

Receipt for Henriette Delille's funeral from Undertaker P. Casenave (1861)
The Rules and Regulations for the Congregation of the Sisters of the Presentation of the Blessed Virgin Mary Under the Invocation of Mary the Virgin of the Holy Presentation (1863)
Succession of Marie Joseph Dias (1848)

Tulane University

Amistad Research Center, Tilton Memorial Hall
John W. Blassingame Papers, Census of New Orleans, 1805, submitted by Matthew Flannery to the City Council of New Orleans, 11 May 1805
Tulane University Digital Library

University of New Orleans

Historical Archives of the Supreme Court of Louisiana, Earl K. Long Library
The Ethel & Herman L. Midlo Center for New Orleans Studies

The Ursuline Convent (New Orleans)

Ledgers (1827)

Published Primary Sources

Bernhard, Carl Duke of Saxe-Weimar Eisenach. *Travels Through North America During the Years 1825 & 1826*. Lea & Cary, 1828.

Cable, George Washington. *Historical Sketchbook and Guide to New Orleans and Environs*. William H. Coleman, 1885.

Deggs, Sister Mary. Journal. In *No Cross, No Crown: Black Nuns in Nineteenth-Century New Orleans*, edited by Virginia Meacham Gould and Charles E. Nolan. Indiana University Press, 2001.

Deliberations of the Cabildo, 1 June 1786, vol. 3, no. 1 (1784–87).

Desdunes, Rodolphe Lucien. *Our People and Our History: Fifty Creole Portraits*. Translated and edited by Sister Dorothea Olga McCants. Louisiana State University Press, 1973.

Gayarré, Charles. *History of Louisiana: The French Domination*. Vol. 1. William. J. Widdleton, 1866.

Hogan, William, and Davis Edwin, eds. *Natchez: The Ante-Bellum Diary of a Free Negro*. Louisiana State University Press, 1951.

King, Grace. *Creole Families of New Orleans*. Macmillan, 1912.

———. *New Orleans: The Place and the People*. Macmillan, 1895.

Latrobe, Benjamin Henry. *Impressions Respecting New Orleans Diary and Sketches, 1818–1820*. Edited by Samuel Wilson Jr. Columbia University Press, 1951.

———. *The Journal of Latrobe. Being the Notes and Sketches of an Architect, Naturalist and Traveler in the US from 1796–1820*. D. Appleton, 1905.

Library of Congress. House Reports, 19th Cong., 2nd sess., no. 15. p. 12.

Louisiana Code Noir, 1808, 1724, Article vi, Article L, Articles XXII and XXII.

Martineau, Harriet. *Retrospect of Western Travel*. Vol. 1. Harper Bros., 1838.

Montigny, Jean François-Benjamin Dumont de. *Memoires Historiques sur la Louisiane*. 2 vols. Claude Jean Baptiste Bauche, 1753. Translated as *History of Louisiana* by Benjamin F. French. 5 vols. Daniels & Smith, 1846–53.

Northup, Solomon. *Twelve Years a Slave*. Edited by Sue Eakin and Joseph Logsdon. Louisiana State University Press, 1968.

Olmsted, Frederick Law. *The Cotton Kingdom: A Traveller's Observations on Cotton and Slavery in the American Slaves States, 1853–1861*. Vol. 2. Mason Brothers, 1861.

———. *A Journey in the Seaboard Slave States*. Dix & Edwards; and Sampson Low, 1856.

"The Original Diary of the Oblate Sisters of Providence." Translation. Vols. 1 and 2, box 47, vol. 1, p. 61. Archives of the Oblate Sisters of Providence.

Potter, Eliza. *A Hairdresser's Experience in High Life*. Cincinnati, 1859.

Reports of Cases Argued and Determined in the Supreme Court State of Louisiana, Eastern District New Orleans. Vols. 4, 5, and 6. Edited by Merrit M. Robinson. E. Johns & Company, 1845.

Ripley, Eliza. *Social Life in Old New Orleans: Being Recollections of My Girlhood*. D. Appleton, 1912.

Sacramental Records of the Roman Catholic Church of the Archdiocese of New Orleans. 10 vols. Edited by Earl C. Woods and Charles Nolan. Archdiocese of New Orleans, 1987–95.

Stoddard, Major Amos. *Sketches, Historical & Descriptive of Louisiana*. AMS, 1812.

Sullivan, Edward. *Rambles and Scrambles in North and South America*. Richard Bentley, 1852.

Tasistro, Louis Fitzgerald. *Random Shots and Southern Breezes*. Vol. 1. Harper Brothers, 1842.

Newspapers

L'Abeille (The Bee)
Baltimore Sun
The Bulletin
Catholic News Service
Daily Crescent
Daily Picayune
Gazette and Sentinel
Moniteur Louisiane
New Orleans Crescent
New Orleans Crusader
New Orleans Daily Democrat
New Orleans Republican
New York Times
Times-Democrat
Times-Picayune
The Tribune
The Union
Weekly Louisianan

Sources Consulted Online

"California, U.S., Death Index, 1905–1939." Online database. Ancestry.com. 2013.

"California, Death Index, 1905–1939." FamilySearch.org.

Collins C. Diboll Vieux Carré Digital Survey. https//www.hnoc.org/vcs/.

Jewish Cemetery Records of New Orleans. https://www.jewishgen.org/databases.

Knowsouthernhistory.net.

"Louisiana, Civil War Service Records of Confederate Soldiers, 1861–1865." FamilySearch.org.

"Louisiana, New Orleans, Quarterly Abstracts of Passenger Lists of Vessels Arriving at New Orleans, 1820–1875." FamilySearch.org.

"Louisiana, Orleans Parish Estate Files,1804–1846." Online database with images. FamilySearch.org.

"Louisiana Parish Marriages, 1837–1957." Online database with images. FamilySearch.org.

"Louisiana, U.S., Compiled Census and Census Substitutes Index, 1791–1890." Online database. Ancestry.com. 1999.

"Louisiana, U.S., Confederate Soldiers Index, 1861–1865." Online database. Ancestry.com. 1997.

"Louisiana, U.S., Statewide Death Index, 1819–1964." Online database. Ancestry.com. 2002.

Louisiana Historical Association's online dictionary of biography. http://www.lahistory.org.

"New Orleans, Passenger List Quarterly Abstracts, 1820–1875." Online database. Ancestry.com. 2011.

"Paris, France & Vicinity Marriage Banns, 1860–1902." Online database.

Ancestry.com. 2008. "Actes de mariage, Paris, France, 1860–1918." Family Search.org.
United States Census, 1850. Online database. Familysearch.org: Orleans, Louisiana, United States; citing family 896, NARA microfilm publication M432, National Archives and Records Administration. 12 April 2016.
"United States Civil War Soldiers Index, 1861–1865." Online database. Family Search.org citing multiple microfilm publications, National Archives and Records Administration. 14 June 2016.
"United States, Freedman's Bank Records, 1865–1874." FamilySearch.org.
"U.S., Freedman's Bank Records, 1865–1874." Online database. Ancestry.com.
"U.S., Freedmen's Bureau Records of Field Offices, 1863–1878." Online database. Ancestry.com. 2017.

SECONDARY SOURCES

Ahlstrom, Courtney Lee. "A Space in Between: Material Enclosures for the Women of New Orleans, 1850–1870." PhD diss., Corcoran College of Art & Design, Department of History of Decorative Arts, 2012.
Appiah, Kwami Anthony, and Henry Louis Gates, eds. *Africana: The Encyclopaedia of the African American Experience*. Oxford University Press, 2006.
Arthur, Stanley Clisby. *Old New Orleans*. Harmanson, 1936
Asbury, Herbert. *The French Quarter*. New York, 1936.
Aslakson, Kenneth. "Making Race: The Role of Free Blacks in the Development of New Orleans' Three Caste System 1791–1812." PhD thesis, University of Texas at Austin, 2007.
———. *Making Race in the Courtroom: The Legal Construction of Three Races in Early New Orleans*. New York University Press, 2014.
———. "Quadroon-Plaçage: Myth of Antebellum New Orleans: Anglo-American (Mis)interpretations of a French-Caribbean Phenomenon." *Journal of Social History* 45, no. 3 (Spring 2012): 709–34
Baggett, Ashley. *Intimate Partner Violence in New Orleans: Gender, Race and Reform 1840–1900*. University Press of Mississippi, 2017.
Bancroft, Frederick. *Slave-Trading in the Old South*. J. H. Furst, 1931.
Basch, Norma. *Framing American Divorce from the Revolutionary Generation to the Victorian*. University of California Press, 1999.
Batchen, Geoffrey. "Dreams of an Ordinary Life: Cartes-de-visites and the Bourgeois Imagination." In *Image and Imagination*, edited by M. Langford, 63–74. McGill-Queen's University Press, 2005.

Baudier, Roger. *The Catholic Church in Louisiana*. A. W. Hyatt Stationery, 1939.

Bennett, James B. *Religion and the Rise of Jim Crow in New Orleans*. Princeton University Press, 2005.

Blassingame, John W. *Black New Orleans 1860–1880*. University of Chicago Press, 1973.

Bollini, Christopher. "*The Grandissimes* and Political Transition: The Threat of Genealogical Violence as the Bringer of Change." *Mississippi Quarterly* 69, no. 2 (Spring 2016): 167–84.

Braddon, Mary Elizabeth. *The Octoroon or, The Lily of Louisiana*. De Witt, 1861.

Broadman, Kay. "The Ideology of Domesticity: The Regulation of the Household Economy in Victorian Women's Magazines." *Victorian Periodicals Review* 33, no. 2 (Summer 2000):150–64.

Brown, Dale Patrick. *Literary Cincinnati: The Missing Chapter*. Ohio University Press, 2011.

Brown, Sterling. *The Negro in American Fiction*. Reprint, Arno, 1969.

Cable, George Washington. *The Grandissimes*. Hill and Wang, 1879.

Campbell, Michael L. "The Negro in Cable's *The Grandissimes*." *Mississippi Quarterly* 27, no. 2 (Spring 1974): 165–78.

Carnes, Mark C., and Griffen Clyde, eds. *Meanings of Manhood: Constructions of Masculinity in Victorian America*. University of Chicago Press, 1990.

Censer, Jane Turner. *The Reconstruction of White Womanhood*. Louisiana State University Press, 2003.

Child, Lydia Maria. *The Quadroons*. Liberty Bell, 1842.

Christian, Marcus B. "The Negro in Louisiana." Unpublished document, 1938. University of New Orleans, Marcus Christian Collection.

Clark, Emily. *The Strange History of the American Quadroon: Free Women of Color in the Revolutionary Atlantic World*. University of North Carolina Press, 2013.

Clark, Emily, and Virginia Meacham Gould. "The Feminine Face of Afro-Catholicism in New Orleans, 1727–1852." *William and Mary Quarterly*, 3rd ser., vol. 59, no. 2 (April 2002): 409–48

Clinton, Catherine, and Michele Gillespie, eds. *The Devil's Lane: Sex and Race in the Early South*. Oxford University Press, 1997.

Cocuzza, Dominic. "The Dress of the Free Colored Women in New Orleans." Master's thesis, State University of New York, Fashion Institute of Technology, 2001.

Copeland, M. Shawn. *The Subversive Power of Love: The Vision of Henriette Delille*. Paulist, 2007.

Dabel, Jane E. "My Ma Went to Work Every Mornin': Color, Gender & Occupation in New Orleans 1840–1860." *Journal of Louisiana Historical Association* 41, no. 2 (Spring 2000): 217–29.

Davis, Cyprien. *Henriette Delille: Servant of Slaves: Witness to the Poor.* Archdiocese of New Orleans, 2004.

Dawdy, Shannon Lee. *Building the Devil's Empire: French Colonial New Orleans.* University of Chicago Press, 2008.

Dessens, Nathalie. *From Saint-Domingue to New Orleans: Migration and Influences.* University Press of Florida, 2007.

Detiege, Sister Audrey Marie. *Henriette Delille: Free Woman of Color: Foundress of the Sisters of the Holy Family.* Sisters of the Holy Family, 1976.

Devore, Donald E. "Race Relations & Community Development: The Education of Blacks in New Orleans 1862–1960." PhD diss., Louisiana State University and Mechanical & Agricultural College, 1989.

Dominguez, Virginia R. *White by Definition: Social Classification in Creole Louisiana.* Rutgers University Press, 1986.

Elfenbein, Anna Shannon. *Women on the Color Line: Evolving Stereotypes and the Writings of George Washington Cable, Grace King, Kate Chopin.* University Press of Virginia, 1989.

Fandrich, Ina Johanna. *The Mysterious Voodoo Queen, Marie Laveau: A Study of Powerful Female Leadership in Nineteenth-Century New Orleans.* Louisiana State University Press, 2012.

Farrelly, Maura Jane. "American Slavery, American Freedom, American Catholicism." *Early American Studies* 10, no.1 (Winter 2002): 69–100.

Fessenden, Tracy. "The Sisters of the Holy Family and the Veil of Race, Religious and American Culture." *Journal of Interpretation* 10, no. 2 (Summer 2000): 187–244.

Fett, Sharla M. *Working Cures: Healing, Health and Power on Southern Slave Plantations.* University of North Carolina Press, 2002.

Foner, Laura. "Free People of Color in Louisiana and St. Domingue: A Comparative Portrait of Two Three-Caste Slave Societies." *Journal of Social History* 3, no. 4 (1970): 406–30.

Foner, Philip S. *History of Black Americans from the Emergence of the Cotton Kingdom to the Eve of the Compromise of 1850.* Greenwood, 1983.

Frederickson, Mary E. *Gendered Resistance, Women, Slavery, and the Legacy of Margaret Garner.* University of Illinois Press, 2013.

Fuentes, Marissa J. *Dispossessed Lives, Enslaved Women, Violence, and the Archive.* University of Pennsylvania Press, 2016.

Furness, J. C. *Fanny Kemble: Leading Lady of the Nineteenth Century Stage.* Dial, 1982.

Gardner, Bettye J. "Ante-Bellum Black Education in Baltimore." *Maryland Historical Magazine* 71, no. 3 (1976): 360–66.

Gaspar, David Barry, and Darlene Hine Clark, eds. *Black Women and Slavery in the Americas: More Than Chattel.* Indiana University Press, 1996.

Gehman, Mary. *Women and New Orleans.* Margaret Media, 2000.

Glymph, Thavolia. *Out of the House of Bondage: The Transformation of the Plantation Household.* Cambridge University Press, 2008.

Gould, Virginia Meacham, ed. *Chained to the Rock of Adversity: To Be Free, Black and Female in the Old South.* University of Georgia Press, 1998.

———. *Coastal Encounters: The Transformation of the Gulf South in the Eighteenth Century.* University of Nebraska Press, 2007.

———. "Henriette Delille, Free Women of Color, and Catholicism in Antebellum New Orleans, 1727–1852." In *Beyond Bondage: Free Women of Color in the Americas,* edited by David Barry Gaspar and Darleen Clark Hine. University of Illinois Press, 2004.

Griswold, Robert L. "Divorce and the Legal Redefinition of Victorian Manhood." In *Meanings of Manhood: Constructions of Masculinity in Victorian America,* edited by Mark C. Carnes and Clyde Griffen. University of Chicago Press, 1990.

Grossberg, Michael. *Governing the Hearth.* University of North Carolina Press, 1985.

Guillory, Monique. "Some Enchanted Evening on the Auction Block: The Cultural Legacy of New Orleans' Quadroon Balls." PhD diss., New York University, 1999.

Hall, Gwendolyn Midlo. *Africans in Colonial Louisiana: The Development of Afro Creole Culture in the Eighteenth Century.* Louisiana State University Press, 1992.

———. *Slavery and African Ethnicities in the Americas: Restoring the Links.* University of North Carolina Press, 2005.

Halttunen, Karen. *Confidence Men and Painted Women: A Study of Middle-Class Culture in America 1830–1870.* Yale University Press, 1983.

Hangar, Kimberley S. "Avenues to Freedom Open to New Orleans' Black Population 1769–1779." *Louisiana History: The Journal of Louisiana Historical Association* 31, no. 3 (Summer 1990): 237–64.

———. *Bounded Lives, Bounded Places: Free Black Society in Colonial New Orleans 1769–1803.* Duke University Press, 1997.

———. "Conflicting Loyalties: The French Revolution and Free People of Color Spanish New Orleans." *Louisiana History: The Journal of Louisiana Historical Association* 34, no. 1 (Winter 1990): 5–33.

———. "Coping in a Complex World: Free Black Women in Colonial New Orleans." In *The Devil's Lane: Sex and Race in the Early South,* edited by Catherine Clinton and Michele Gillespie. Oxford University Press, 1997.

———. "Desiring Total Tranquility and Not Getting It: Conflict Involving

Free Black Women in Spanish New Orleans." *The Americas* 54, no. 4 (April 1998): 541–56.

Hart, Sister Mary Francis Borgia. "A History of the Congregation of the Sisters of the Holy Family of New Orleans." Bachelor's thesis, Xavier College, New Orleans, 1931.

———. *Violets in the King's Garden: A History of the Sisters of the Holy Family in New Orleans*. Sisters of the Holy Family, 1976.

Hobbs, Allyson. *A Chosen Exile: A History of Racial Passing in American Life*. Harvard University Press, 2014.

Hodes, Martha. *The Sea Captain's Wife: A True Story of Love, Race and War in the Nineteenth Century*. Norton, 2006.

Holden, Randall G. *Futile Valor*. MCG, 1998.

Hollandsworth, James G. *The Louisiana Native Guards: The Black Military Experience During the Civil War*. University of Louisiana Press, 1995.

Horne, William I. "Victor Eugène Macarty: From Art to Activism in Reconstruction-era New Orleans." *Atlantic Review* 73, no. 2 (Spring 2008): 496–525

Hunter, Tera W. *Bound in Wedlock: Slave and Free Black Marriage in the Nineteenth Century*. Harvard University Press, 2017.

Jalland, Pat. *Death in the Victorian Family*. Oxford University Press, 1996.

Johnson, Jerah. "New Orleans' Congo Square: An Urban Setting for Early Afro-American Culture Formation." *Louisiana History: The Journal of the Louisiana Historical Society* 32, no. 2 (Spring 1919): 117–57.

Johnson, Jessica Marie. *Wicked Flesh, Black Women, Intimacy and Freedom in the Atlantic World*. University of Pennsylvania Press, 2020.

Johnson, Michael P., and James L. Roark. *Black Masters: A Free Family of Color in the Old South*. Norton, 1984

———, eds. *No Chariot Let Down: Charleston's Free People of Color on the Eve of the Civil War*. Norton, 1984.

Johnson, Penny Ward. "Eulalie de Mandeville: An Ethnohistorical Investigation Challenging Notions of Plaçage in New Orleans as Revealed Through the Lived Experiences of a Free Woman of Color." Master's thesis, University of New Orleans, 2010.

Johnson, Walter. *Soul by Soul: Life Inside the Antebellum Slave Market*. Harvard University Press, 2001.

King, Grace. *Monsieur Motte*. Landor, 1888.

King, Stewart. *Blue Coat or Powdered Wig: Free People of Color in Pre-Revolutionary Saint-Domingue*. University of Georgia Press, 2007.

Klein, Sybil, ed. *Creole: The History and Legacy of Louisiana's Free People of Color*. Louisiana State University Press, 2000.

Koger, Larry. *Black Slaveowners: Free Black Slave Masters in South Carolina: 1790–1860*. University of South Carolina Press, 1995.

Kotlikoff, Laurence J., and Anton J. Robert. "The Manumission of Slaves in New Orleans 1827–1846." *Southern Studies* 19, no. 2 (1980): 173–81.

Lachance, Paul. "The Limits of Privilege: Where Free Persons of Color Stood in the Hierarchy of Wealth in Antebellum New Orleans." In *Against the Odds: Free Blacks in the Slave Societies of the Americas,* edited by Jane Landers. Frank Cass, 1996.

———. "Were Saint-Domingue Refugees a Distinctive Cultural Group in Antebellum New Orleans? Evidence from Patterns and Strategies of Property Holding." *Revista/Review Interamericana* 29, no. 1 (1999): 171–92.

Long, Carolyn Morrow. *Madame Lalaurie Mistress of the Haunted House*. University Press of Florida, 2012.

———. *A New Orleans Voodou Princess: The Legend and Reality of Marie Laveau*. University Press of Florida, 2006.

Longstreet, Stephen. *Sportin' House: A History of New Orleans' Sinners and the Birth of Jazz*. Sherbourne, 1965.

Lovato, Frank Joseph. "Households and Neighborhoods Among Free People of Color in New Orleans, View from the Census 1850–1860." Master's thesis, University of New Orleans, 2010.

Mahmood, Saba. *Politics of Piety: The Islamist Revival and the Feminist Subject*. Princeton University Press, 2005.

Marler, Scott P. *The Merchant's Capital: New Orleans & the Political Economy of the Nineteenth-Century South*. Cambridge University Press, 2013.

Martin, Joan M. "Plaçage and the Louisiana Gens de Couleur." In *Creole: The History and Legacy of Louisiana's Free People of Color,* edited by Sybil Klein. Louisiana State University Press, 2000.

McKee, Sally. *The Exile's Song. Edmond Dédé and the Unfinished Revolutions of the Atlantic World*. Yale University Press, 2017.

———. *A Family Long Free*. Yale University Press, 2017.

McMahon, Clan T. *The Global Dimensions of Irish Identity: Race, Nation and the Popular Press*. University of North Carolina Press, 2015.

Milweski, Melissa. *Litigating Across the Color Line: Cases Between Black and White from the End of Slavery to Civil Rights*. Oxford University Press, 2017.

Mitchell, Mary Niall. *Raising Freedom's Children*. New York University Press, 2008.

Montgomery, William L. "The Oblate Sisters of Providence." *US Catholic Historian* 24, no. 2 (Spring 2002): 41–55.

Morrow, Diane Batts. *Persons of Color and Religious at the Same Time: The Oblate Sisters of Providence 1828–1860*. University of North Carolina Press, 2002.

Myers, Amrita Chakrabarti. *Forging Freedom: Black Women in the Pursuit of Liberty in Antebellum Charleston*. University of North Carolina Press, 2011.
Neidenbach, Elizabeth C. "The Life and Legacy of Marie Couvent: Social Networks, Property Ownership and the Making of a Free People of Color. Master's thesis, College of William & Mary, Arts & Sciences, 2015.
———. "Mes Dernieres Volantés: Testaments to the Life of Marie Couvent, a Former Slave in New Orleans." *Transatlantica: Revue d'Études Américaines* (2012): 1–13.
———. "Refugee from Saint-Domingue Living in this City." *Journal of Urban History* 42, no. 5 (2016): 841–62.
Nelson-Dunbar, Alice. *The Goodness of Saint Rocque and Other Stories*. Dodd, Mead, 1899.
New Orleans City Guide. Written and compiled by the Federal Writers Project of the Works Progress Administration for the City of New Orleans. Houghton Mifflin, 1938.
Nystrom, Justin. "In My Father's House: Relationships and Identity in an Interracial New Orleans Creole Family 1845–1875." *Journal of the Louisiana Historical Association* 49, no. 3 (Summer 2008): 287–313.
———. *New Orleans After the Civil War: Race, Politics, and a New Birth of Freedom*. University of Georgia Press, 2010.
Oakes, James. *The Ruling Race: A History of American Slaveholders*. Norton, 1982.
Ochs, Stephen J. *Desegregating the Altar: The Josephites and the Struggle for Black Priests*. Louisiana State University Press, 1990.
Olivarious, Kathryn. "Immunity, Capital, and Power in Antebellum New Orleans." *American Historical Association* 124, no. 2 (April 2019): 425–55.
Olwell, Robert. "Loose, Idle & Disorderly Slave Women in the Eighteenth-Century Charleston Market Place." In *Black Women and Slavery in the Americas: More Than Chattel*, edited by David Barry Gaspar and Darlene Hine Clark. Indiana University Press, 1996.
Penn, Roslyn Terborg. "Through an African Feminist Theoretical Lens: Viewing Caribbean Women's History Cross-Culturally." In *Engendering History: Caribbean Women in Historical Perspective*, edited by Verene Shepherd, Bridget Brereton, and Barbara Bailey. St. Martin's, 1995.
Posey, Thaddeus J. "An Unwanted Commitment: The Spirituality of the Early Oblate Sisters of Providence, 1829–1890." PhD diss., Saint Louis University, 1993.
Raimon, Allegra Eve. *The Tragic Mulatta Revisited in the Nineteenth-Century Anti-Slavery Fiction*. Rutgers University Press, 2004.
Rankin, David. "The Origins of Black Leadership in New Orleans During the Reconstruction." *Journal of Southern History* 40, no. 3 (August 1974).

Reilly, Timothy F. "Heterodox New Orleans and the Protestant South, 1800–1861." *Louisiana Studies* (Fall 1973): 533–51.

Reynolds, Virginia "Slaves to Fashion Not Society: Elizabeth Keckley & Washington D.C.'s African American Dressmakers 1860–1870." *Washington History* 26, no. 2 (Fall 2014): 4–17.

Riley, Glenda. *Divorce: An American Tradition*. Oxford University Press, 1991.

Rogers-Jones, Stephanie E. *They Were Her Property: White Women as Slave Owners in the American South*. Yale University Press, 2019.

Rosenburg, Charles. *The Cholera Years: The United States in 1832, 1849 and 1866*. University of Chicago Press, 1962.

Rothman, Joshua D. *Notorious in the Neighborhood: Sex and Families Across the Color Line in Virginia*. University of North Carolina Press, 2003.

Roudané, Mark Charles. "The Color of Freedom: Louis Charles Roudenez, New Orleans and the Transnational Origins of the African American Freedom Movement." *South Atlantic Review* 73, no. 2 (Spring 2008): 1–6.

Salenius, Sirpa. "Troubling the White Supremacy Black Inferiority Paradigm: Frederick Douglas and William Wells Brown in Europe." *Transatlantic Studies*, 14 June 2016: 152–63.

Schafer, Judith Kelleher. *Becoming Free, Remaining Free: Manumission and Enslavement in New Orleans, 1846–1862*. Louisiana State University Press, 2003.

Schweninger, Loren. Antebellum Free Persons of Color in Postbellum Louisiana," *Louisiana History* 30 (Fall 1989): 345–64.

———. "Black-Owned Businesses in the South, 1790–1880." *Business History Review* 63, no. 1 (Spring 1989): 22–60.

———. "Prosperous Blacks in the South 1790–1880." *American Historical Review* 95 (February 1990): 31–56.

Scott, Rebecca J. *Degrees of Freedom: Louisiana and Cuba After Slavery*. Harvard University Press, 2005.

Scott, Rebecca, and Jean Hébrard. *Freedom Papers: An Atlantic Odyssey in the Age of Emancipation*. Harvard University Press, 2012.

Singleton, Theresa A. "Slavery and Spatial Dialects on Cuban Coffee Plantations." *World Archaeology* 33, no. 1 (June 2001): 98–114.

Smith, Cheryl A. *Market Women: Black Women Entrepreneurs, Past, Present and Future*. Praeger, 2005.

Smith, Jessie Carney, ed. *Notable Black American Women*. Gale Research, 1992.

Spear, Jennifer M. *Race, Sex and Social Order in Early New Orleans*. John Hopkins University Press, 2009.

Sterkx, H. E. *The Free Negro in Ante-Bellum Louisiana*. Fairleigh Dickinson University Press, 1972.

Stewart, Whitney Nell. "Fashioning Frenchness: Gens de Couleur Libres and the

Cultural Struggle for Power in Antebellum New Orleans." *Journal of Social History* 51, no. 3 (Spring 2018): 526–56.
Summers, Dale A. "Black and White in New Orleans: A Study in Urban Race Relations 1865–1900. *Journal of Southern History* 40, no. 1 (February 1974): 19–42.
Sundberg, Sara Jane Brooks. "Women and Property in Early Louisiana: Legal Systems at Odds." *Journal of the Early Republic* 32, no. 4 (Winter 2012): 633–55.
———. "Women and the Law of Property Under Louisiana Civil Law 1782–1835." PhD diss., University of Wisconsin, 2001
Taylor, Joe Gray. *Louisiana: A Bicentennial History.* Louisiana State Museum, 1976.
Thompson, Shirley E. *Exiles at Home: The Struggle to Become American in Creole New Orleans.* Harvard University Press, 2009.
Tregle, Joseph. "Early New Orleans Society: A Reappraisal." *Journal of Southern History* 18, no. 1 (February 1952): 20–36.
———. *Louisiana in the Age of Jackson.* Louisiana State University Press, 1999.
Turpin, Joanne. *Women in Church History: 20 Stories for 20 Centuries.* Saint Anthony Messenger Press, 1990.
Ulentin, Anne. "Free Women of Color and Slaveholding in New Orleans 1810–1830." Master's thesis, Louisiana State University, 2007.
Vandal, Gilles. "Black Utopia in Early Reconstruction New Orleans: The People's Bakery as a Case Study." *Journal of Louisiana History Association* 9, no. 3 (Summer 1968): 437–52.
Venturatos, Kathryn. "New Orleans: The Changing Concept of the Family and Its Effect on Louisiana Succession Law." *Louisiana Law Review* 63 (Summer 2003): 1161–81.
Voltz, Nöel Mellick. "Black Female Agency and Sexual Exploitation: Quadroon Balls and Plaçage Relationships." PhD diss., Ohio State University, 2008.
Wallace, Monica Hoff. "A Primer on Divorce in Louisiana." *Loyola Law Review* 69, no. 1 (Fall 2022): 133–58.
Walvin, James. *An African's Life: The Life and Times of Olaudah Equiano, 1745–1797.* Continuum International, 1998.
White, Deborah Gray *Ar'n't I a Woman? Female Slaves in the Plantation South.* Norton, 1985.
Williams, Diana. "Can Quadroon Balls Represent Acquiescence or Resistance?" In *Resistance, Women, Slavery and the Legacy of Margaret Garner,* edited by Mary E. Frederickson and Dolores M. Winters. University of Illinois Press, 2013.
Wilson, Carol. "Plaçage and the Performance of Whiteness: The Trial of Eulalie

Mandeville, Free Colored Woman, of Antebellum New Orleans." *American Nineteenth Century History* 15, no. 2 (2014): 187–209.

Winters, Liza Ze. "More Desultory and Unconnected Than Any Other: Geography, Desire and Freedom in Eliza Potter's 'A Hairdresser's Experience in High Life.'" *American Quarterly* 61, no. 3 (September 2009): 455–75.

Woodson, Carter G. "Free Negro Owners of Slaves in the United States in 1830." *Journal of Negro History* 9 (January 1924): 41–85.

Film

The Courage to Love. Television History Film. Ontario, 2000.

Index